AN UNLIKELY LEADER
The life and times of Captain John Hunter

Robert Barnes

SYDNEY UNIVERSITY PRESS

Published 2009 by Sydney University Press

SYDNEY UNIVERSITY PRESS
University of Sydney Library
www.sup.usyd.edu.au

© Robert Barnes 2009
© Sydney University Press 2009

Reproduction and Communication for other purposes
Except as permitted under the Act, no part of this edition may be reproduced, stored in a retrieval system, or communicated in any form or by any means without prior written permission. All requests for reproduction or communication should be made to Sydney University Press at the address below:

Sydney University Press
Fisher Library F03
University of Sydney NSW 2006 AUSTRALIA
Email: info@sup.usyd.edu.au

National Library of Australia Cataloguing-in-Publication entry

Author: Barnes, Robert, (Robert Winstanley), 1942-
Title: An unlikely leader : the life and times of Captain John Hunter / Robert Barnes.
ISBN: 9781920899196 (pbk.)
Notes: Bibliography.
Subjects: Hunter, John, 1737-1821
Governors--New South Wales--Biography.
First Fleet, 1787-1788--Biography.
New South Wales--History--1788-1851.
Dewey Number: 994.402092

Cover image: *The First Fleet*, by John Allcot O.B.E., F.R.A.S. Reproduced with permission of The Allcot Trust.
Cover design by Miguel Yamin, the University Publishing Service
The University of Sydney

Contents

Foreword	v
Acknowledgements	vii
Introduction—an unlikely leader	viii

1	Setting the scene	1
2	Influencing factors	22
3	Promotion deferred	50
4	Commissioned without command	77
5	A veiled alliance	106
6	Whence came the pox?	151
7	The challenge of New South Wales	166
8	A governor under siege	193
9	The mind, the eye and the pen	226
10	Restored and respected	266

Notes	286
Appendix 1: Hunter Family Tree	308
Appendix 2: John Hunter's statement of the loss of the *Sirius*	309
Bibliography	313
Index	323

Foreword

Captain John Hunter is one of the lost leaders of Australia. While his surname is remembered in the dynamic Hunter Valley and in many lesser geographical landmarks, he is not usually given a place in modern lists of the 100 or even 200 most influential Australians of all time. And yet he was the second governor of New South Wales in the second half of the 1790s when that colony spanned all of eastern Australia. Indeed he was the virtual ruler for slightly longer than the first governor, Captain Arthur Phillip, and—as Robert Barnes explains—he had to face obstacles just as formidable.

As a British naval officer, Hunter had much to be proud of. Late in achieving real promotion in the navy, he commanded the main part of the First Fleet when it entered Botany Bay in January 1788, thus concluding one of the more remarkable voyages of colonisation in the world's history.

Later that year he commanded the HMS *Sirius* in what was really a mercy mission: she sailed right around the world to gather supplies. In the first leg of that voyage, past the icebergs drifting near Cape Horn, he effectively opened—somewhat to the surprise of Governor Phillip—a sea route which was vital for Australian commerce in the next 100 or more years. He proved beyond doubt that a sailing ship leaving Australia and bound for Europe should steer towards South America rather than South Africa, thus making use of the strong westerlies.

This is the first full-length biography of Hunter. It describes how various earlier historians were confused about the date and even year of his birth at the Scottish port of Leith; how he first went to sea with his father at the age of eight and was shipwrecked off the coast of Norway; how he advanced slowly in the navy, becoming a lieutenant only at the age of 43; and how Australia at last offered him a stage on which to make his mark.

As an officer in what was then the world's leading navy, Hunter was probably not in the top class of competence—he lost two ships—but his honesty, generosity and 'common touch' were valuable qualities when he presided over the infant Sydney and ruled a population in which six of every ten were convicts.

Robert Barnes is fair towards Hunter and resists the temptation to make him either a giant or a pygmy. He offers a calm assessment of what Hunter achieved and where he failed. He explains at length the grave problems which would have vexed, frustrated or totally thwarted any governor, no matter how experienced. Hunter had to combat officers of the New South Wales Corps who simply snatched economic power, but in any dispute with them he could not confidently expect early or even useful support from the British government which was now immersed in the perilous war against revolutionary France.

One vital chapter of the book tests the accusation that the early British settlers 'waged biological war' on the Aborigines around Sydney. In the end the book hoses down this inflammable topic.

Geoffrey Blainey
Melbourne, March 2009

Acknowledgements

The seed for this book was sown in the 1970s while researching for a thesis on David Collins, Lt. Governor of Van Diemen's Land 1804–10. I noticed that very little had been written on John Hunter and my then supervisor, Prof. Russell Ward at the University of New England suggested I keep this in mind for the future. I then began collecting references to Hunter over the next 25 years.

The book may not have seen the light of day however, without the guidance and encouragement of my PhD supervisor, Assoc. Prof. Don Garden at the University of Melbourne.

The staff at the La Trobe Library, Melbourne, the State Library of New South Wales, the National Maritime Museum, Greenwich, the British Library and the Public Records Office at Kew were always helpful and courteous.

I am most grateful for the kind permission of Prof. John White at the ANU, Canberra, to reproduce the portrait of Captain William Kent in his possession. I should also acknowledge the patient advice and assistance of Susan Murray-Smith at Sydney University Press who guided me through the labyrinth of the publication process.

Special thanks goes to Lucille Andel and Alison Boldys for their input and stenographical assistance.

While all these contributions are greatly appreciated, any errors or faults are solely my responsibility.

Robert Barnes

Introduction—an unlikely leader

This book is about a shadowy figure in early Australian colonial history, John Hunter, the second governor of New South Wales. Not in any sinister sense, but rather because Hunter is largely unknown as a person. Very little has been written about him, and almost nothing of any substance. Even historians cast him as a bland performer, a supporting player who rarely appears as part of the main theme in early colonial times.

He is mainly remembered by those who have read or studied our first 20 years of European settlement, as one who lost the *Sirius* at Norfolk Island and who, as governor, was out-smarted by John Macarthur and the New South Wales Corps. Beyond this, one is usually regarded with blank looks and furrowed brows. The aim of this book is to bring John Hunter out of the shadows and into the light in order to cast him as a person deserving of more recognition and to discover what drove and motivated him, what influenced his character, actions, achievements and failures.

Hunter is styled an unlikely leader because after 20 years of naval service as a technically proficient non-commissioned officer and unused to strategic leadership, he was suddenly promoted to lieutenant, then commander and finally post captain in the short space of six years. Within a further nine years, he was the governor of a remote and complex colony, with limited leadership experience (especially over non-naval people), probably due more to the influence of his patron than to any proven leadership qualities.

He did, in fact, lack the experience needed to benignly rule the complicated system he inherited in Sydney, while his innate courtesy, trustfulness and kindness were exploited by his enemies to their advantage. His appointment as governor could well have been met with some surprise by those peers who knew him; certainly he was not Arthur Phillip's preference.

The following pages are a portrayal of the life and times of John Hunter (1737–1821), his decades of naval service, the negative and then positive influences that patronage had upon him, his fluctuating fortunes, his term as second governor of New South Wales and his later years spent in active retirement. It examines the peaks and troughs of his record as a seaman and the factors which caused his governorship to falter, but demonstrates that Hunter did in fact leave some legacies both as a maritime technician and during his term as governor.

The major events which shaped his career included:

- being the second governor of New South Wales between 1795 and 1800
- serving as a serving naval officer for 50 years from 1754 to 1804.

Hunter's principal maritime milestones included:

- the near wrecking of HMS *Carysfort* in 1770
- appointed second captain of HMS *Sirius* in 1787 to take the First Fleet to Botany Bay. This became a key turning point in his career as he was then associated with New South Wales in a variety of capacities (governor, critic, advisor and commentator) for the next 30 years
- the two near-losses of HMS *Sirius* under this command

Figure 1–2. Scale models of the *Sirius* and *Supply*. Formerly on display at the Powerhouse Museum (Museum of Applied Arts and Sciences), Sydney.

- the loss of the *Sirius* at Norfolk Island in 1790
- the recall from the New South Wales governorship in 1800 under something of a cloud and the subsequent reinstatement of his reputation
- the loss of HMS *Venerable* in 1804
- the ultimate promotion to rear admiral in 1807 and vice admiral in 1810.

Any biography of substance on John Hunter needs to address questions such as: how competent was Hunter as a seaman, navigator, leader, politician, diplomat, governor, communicator and journalist? What sort of a person was he and what early influences shaped his character and attitudes? What were his strengths and failings? Were his achievements solely based on experience, judgement and abilities or were there some external factors or patrons assisting him? Was he merely in the right place at the right time? Did he create the opportunities that came his way or did he just take advantage of any openings before him? What were his relations with his peers, colleagues, superiors and those under his command? How was he regarded by them—was he respected, liked or feared? Were there any hindrances or impediments that checked or retarded his promotional prospects? How important was patronage to Hunter's career? What about his private life? What do his letters and journal reveal of him? In short, was his competence sufficient to warrant the appointments and authority conferred upon him or was he promoted beyond his capabilities? Did he deserve the rank of Captain and then Governor and did he execute these roles satisfactorily?

In addition, it is intended to fill out the picture with an insight into the world in which John Hunter lived, both at sea and on land. For example, to fully appreciate the man, it is necessary to have some awareness of life in an 18th-century warship and the political and social pressures which applied in English society at that time. The difficulties that Hunter faced were considerable and the ways in which he met these challenges can be better grasped with some understanding of how the world worked in those days.

It is difficult now to envisage just how harsh, unjust and unremitting life could be 200 years ago—the long separation from families, poor quality food and health care facilities, and the shortened life expectancy which then applied. Communications were drawn out, with transport then taking weeks or months in contrast to modern times of hours or days.

Hunter endured his share of setbacks, but ultimately became a respected retired Admiral. This book traces the see-saw of his ups and downs and hopefully will assist the reader to better appreciate Hunter's life and to more fully understand the world in which he lived.

1
Setting the scene

At the end of the 18th century, Sydney was a small town, not only hemmed in by the trees and the water, but at the other end of the earth to the country most would call home, even if home was cold, unjust, harsh and rigidly socially structured. It was six to eight months' sailing away from families and friends as well as the familiar fields, woods, crops, villages, customs, seasons, cities and lifestyles. The seasons were back to front, with Christmas occurring in the middle of summer, instead of a chilly, snowy winter. The flowers, animals, trees and weather patterns were strange and different in New South Wales and the enforced confinement and isolation from the rest of the world encouraged minds and personalities to see small matters in exaggerated light, while petty personal differences became magnified and protracted. This brought out the best and worst in many of those in Sydney during its formative years and made it a difficult place to govern.

Of all the characters on the Sydney stage during the period between 1788 and 1810, most of the principal players have had biographies written, or have been analysed as part of their inter-play with others on that rather small, isolated and somewhat incestuous platform called New South Wales during the first 20 years of its development.

Some of the players were natural leaders and achievers, while others simply became big fish in a little pond, who would probably not have achieved similar status or wealth back in the United Kingdom. It was also a segregated town, for although the convicts and the free population had to rub shoulders because of its constricted area, they had little to do with each other socially or culturally. For most, there was no release or escape from the suffocation of Sydney life and its population; no means of getting away from the pressures of the town, with most being dependent on others, including those controlling government stores, for provisions and other necessities of life. The smarter, more cunning and more ruthless of the players recognised the opportunities to advance themselves and profit from the prevailing system and conditions, while others less sharp and determined became victims of the same set of circumstances. The former are the subject of biographies while the latter are generally nameless or, at best, mentioned as asides. The senior officers were generally men of some ability (but not always so) who were selected in London for their particular role or task. Some perhaps deserved their biographies, although it is unlikely that John Macarthur, David Collins or Samuel Marsden would have earned one had they simply followed a normal service or civilian career, rather than accepting a post in the far-flung antipodes. Most of these biographies were not written until approximately 150 years or more after their subjects had passed across the stage. Very few were written prior to the Second World War while almost none were produced in the 19th century.

Biographical hurdles

Of the first five governors of New South Wales—Phillip, Hunter, King, Bligh and Macquarie—there are considerable writings on Phillip, Bligh and Macquarie, however there are no detailed biographical assessments of substance of the second and third governors, John Hunter and Philip Gidley King. Hunter features in most general Australian history books as a bit player rather than occupying any pivotal role and is generally dismissed as a kindly old man, much out of his depth as governor and completely out-manoeuvred by John Macarthur in their battle to control the economy of New South Wales between 1795 and 1800. Hunter is portrayed as being overshadowed by the vision and leadership of Phillip before him and the colour of Bligh and high profile of Macquarie after him. He was treated by writers more as a pedestrian person who oversaw a somewhat disreputable and less exciting period in Australia's early history.

These histories all adopted the same line; that while Hunter as governor may not have received adequate support from the Colonial Office in London, the three-year interregnum period from 1792 to 1795 after Phillip left allowed some members of the New South Wales Corps to divert the colony's economic system to their own advantage and profit, to the point where it was so entrenched that Hunter was unable to remove or correct it. Hunter himself did not possess the capacity or strength of character to assume dominance over Macarthur and his Corps followers. In other words, the task was beyond him. Scant reference is made to his lesser role as Captain of the *Sirius,* and reports of its destruction at Norfolk Island are uncritical and bland.

Hunter is similarly treated (or dismissed) by the biographers of others present at Port Jackson during his two terms there. Malcolm Ellis tended vigorously to defend Macarthur against any criticism, which required him to denigrate Macarthur's opponents, including Hunter[1], whereas Duffy leaned towards a more balanced view of Macarthur, including an acceptance of his faults and deficiencies, thereby being more reasoned in his description of Macarthur's adversaries, Hunter included.[2] Further, Hunter is always incidental to the main character and is not heavily portrayed or assessed. The biographers of Phillip, Flinders, Marsden, Collins and Wentworth also depicted Hunter as an 'extra' and only superficially referred to his role, actions or motivations. This is perhaps to be expected, as those biographies are centred upon another person, so it is therefore difficult to gain any meaningful insight into John Hunter by reference to these works. Even the few articles on Hunter in the Royal Australian Historical Society's *Journal* since its inception in 1901 are more descriptive than analytical. He is then, a figure that most people know of, but little about.

The entries on Hunter in reference books such as the *Dictionary of National Biography,* the *Australian Dictionary of Biography,* the *Dictionary of Australian History,* the *National Dictionary of Biography,* the *Dictionary of Australian Biography,* and the *Australian Encyclopaedia,* do provide a more detailed narrative of Hunter's career but make little attempt to ascribe reasons, motivations, influences or causes relating to his decisions and actions and pay scant regard to his character, strengths and weaknesses and influencing factors. Being general overviews, they occasionally make basic errors regarding relatively accessible data such as year of birth, but they do at least provide a resume of the subject's career path, although precious little about his private life. It must be conceded, however, that when a contributor is allocated only a couple of thousand words to encapsulate a person's life story, cuts, omissions and concessions of this nature must, of necessity, be made.

On balance then, there have been few attempts to draw a more substantial portrayal of John Hunter; in fact they can be counted on the fingers of two hands if the dictionary references mentioned above are included. In the 1893 Introduction to Volume III of *Historical Records of New South Wales,* there is a 17-page article on Hunter by the editor, F.M. Bladen. However, this deals mainly with Hunter's term as governor, and conveys very little insight into his life before and after New South Wales. Six years later, Bladen wrote a more general article on Hunter for the (then) Australian Historical Society in 1901, its first year of existence. This contribution extends for only seven pages and contains a number of errors (University of Edinburgh instead of

Aberdeen, and omits birth date, for instance) but does briefly dwell on Hunter's movements before 1787, although it contains little of what happened after 1800. He described Hunter as 'being too weak for the position' and 'at 60, an old man' who for too long had been in subordinate positions.[3]

In 1914, Frederick Watson wrote the introduction for Volume 1, Part 2 of *Historical Records of Australia* covering Hunter's term as governor. This 16-page dissertation also concentrates on the period 1795–1800 with limited discussion on his earlier or later days. Watson is kind to Hunter, perhaps one-sidedly so, describing him as 'honest and straight forward', a man whose 'judgement was sound, his conclusions rational and his suggested reforms far sighted', but he lacked sufficient vigour to overcome the obstacles before him.[4] Little more of consequence on Hunter appeared for the next 50 years, when in 1962 Manning Clark did at least make some effort to assess Hunter's character and actions in New South Wales—'Events in New South Wales simply did not correspond with Hunter's view of the world'[5] and 'Hunter was horrified' at the treatment by some settlers of the Aborigines.[6] Six years later, in 1968, there appeared the first publication solely devoted to Hunter, a small booklet of 30 pages written by James Auchmuty as part of the 'Great Australians' series for younger readers. There is, understandably, little analysis in the narrative and Auchmuty relied on only three references—the *Australian Dictionary of Biography*, the *Australian Encyclopaedia* and *Hunter's Journal*, edited by John Bach, which was published in the same year. Again Hunter was gently treated, being described as 'a man of honour and of human sympathy' who 'was eminently likeable'.[7] Bach's introduction to *Hunter's Journal* is somewhat light in background information on Hunter and skims fairly quickly and superficially over his career. He summarises Hunter by noting that 'whatever John Hunter's faults as a diplomat and judge of character, neither his honesty nor his loyalty has ever been questioned'.[8]

In 1975 the first of two fuller narratives on the life of John Hunter appeared in print, neither of which, however, could be described as analytical biographies. B.R. Blaze wrote *Great Scot—A Re-assessment of the life and achievements of John Hunter* as a limited edition, printed for private circulation. *Great Scot* is a hagiography, or a work written in praise of the subject, rebutting and refuting any criticism of Hunter, and there is little new material and considerable extraneous commentary to make up the 150 pages.

In 2001, Arthur Hoyle published *The Life of John Hunter,* a book of 170 pages which is also short on biographical balance and analysis and spends much time in outlining moderately relevant background issues at length, such as the Napoleonic Wars and conditions in the Royal Navy. It is seemingly aimed at school readers, which is not surprising given that Hoyle was a school teacher himself.

How much did Bladen, Watson, Clark, Blaze and Hoyle deliberately or inadvertently omit when writing about Hunter? How much of what they wrote could be construed as slanted? Even autobiographies require the biases and vested interests of the author to be taken into account—notwithstanding he or she knowing 'everything' about the subject. Are any sins of omission committed to present a more favourable picture? Only the author knows how much.

In Hunter's case, there are substantial gaps in the material available on him, and very little real analytical detail. The field is therefore relatively clear of biased obstacles and preconceptions to develop a comprehensive and disinterested evaluation of Hunter the person and to draw some conclusions not always favourable to him or to the culture and systems in which he operated and which influenced him and his career path.

The art of writing biographies has changed considerably over the past 150 years. Victorian biographies could be described as inspirational or uplifting, emphasizing the heroic and ignoring the shortcomings, so that 'boys own' heroes such as Clive of India, Wellington, Lord Kitchener, George Washington, Gordon of Khartoum or Cecil Rhodes were described as role models for future generations, designed to instil a feeling of pride in their achievements and the Empire. They were the archetypical hagiographies. Over the past 40 years on the other hand, there has been a tendency to be more revealing of the subject, a warts-and-all approach so that all sides of a persona are exposed, which allows a freer interpretation of motivations, driving forces and reasons behind decisions taken. This change can be explained as an extension of a more open and critical press and a relaxation of standards in writing and the cinema. This changing trend is reflected in Australian biography over the past 70 years. M. Barnard Eldershaw's *Phillip of Australia* published in 1938 is of the narrative, inspirational mode, whereas Alan Frost's 1987 *Arthur Phillip, His Voyaging* is more incisive and of the later genre of biography. Similarly, Malcolm Ellis' two landmark accounts of Lachlan Macquarie in 1947 and John Macarthur in 1955 are mostly defensive and supportive, which can be contrasted with more recent treatments, John Ritchie's *Lachlan Macquarie* in 1988 and Michael Duffy's *Man of Honour: John Macarthur*, published in 2003.[9] Both latter works present a more even-handed picture of these two early colonists and are more likely to concede negatives.

In this context, while it is necessary to understand John Hunter as fully as possible and what made and drove him, in order to appreciate what sort of leader and governor he was and why, it is not possible to present *all* the material on him, however it is absolutely essential to try for what is truthfully representative.

While a biographer may aspire to write like the genius of Boswell with seemingly total command over vast tracts of resource material, it is difficult to avoid distortions flowing from excessive information where, as one commentator put it, 'the writer may produce a warehouse instead of a portrait'.[10] The balance of biography then would appear to require a combination of a comprehensive picture of the subject (short of overload) combined with an illumination or hint of the age or background in which the person lived, as part of a portrait that includes the shadows and backdrop as well as the colour of the subject's life.

Any biography of substance must of necessity, delve into the psychological composition of the subject to understand their make-up; for example, the recognition that every human being has basic needs for love and self-esteem from others; that everyone has to struggle with some degree of hatred and self-centredness, the contribution of good or bad luck and the influences of parents or early environmental experiences. It is important to empathise in order to gain an appreciation of the inner experience of the other person. By placing oneself in the subject's shoes, the biographer is better enabled to understand why the subject acted or decided as he or she did. In order to better comprehend John Hunter, instead of asking, 'What would I have done in that situation?' the question can be improved by being armed with an insight into Hunter's own experiences and then becomes, 'If I was John Hunter, knowing something of his background of life experiences to date, how might I feel under these given set of circumstances at this point in time?' Furthermore, simply taking a series of literary snapshots does not properly convey the movement, development and growth between life stages and reduces the opportunity to differentiate between the person's various milestones. The exuberance of youth makes way for the maturing of the young adult with high hopes and expectations, which leads to a later realisation of the realities of life followed by a mellowing in old age as life's goals become a reflection rather than an aspiration. Did John Hunter ever have a mid-life crisis; did he despair of ever receiving a commission; were his two courts martial for the loss of the ships under his command regarded by Hunter as problems to bear or challenges to beat? Did he as governor intend to merely foil or thwart his enemies or did he work to destroy them, i.e., was Hunter vindictive?

How important in a biography is the recognition of the subconscious? Can any slip of the pen be detected which reveals some inner thoughts or fears? Does the tone of Hunter's letters reveal anything? Can we read anything between the lines? Is there any message or feeling consciously concealed but actually revealed? Empathising is a useful biographical tool but due diligence is required to minimise translocating the biographer's prejudices into the biography. The writer needs to sanitise or disinfect himself as far as possible before entering the empathy chamber, recognising that, as with sterilizing medical instruments, the process is not always completely perfect.

A balanced, middle-of-the road approach to this issue appears to be the safe option to pursue, because 'psychological factors by themselves are not fully determinative of the subject's personality, and other factors—sociological, cultural and historical—also matter.'[11] This re-affirms the need for a background canopy, but the challenge is to strike the correct balance between life and times. Too little 'times' detracts from the context in which the subject is placed, while too much creates the perception of padding and submerges the subject under excessive extraneous detail to the point where there is more emphasis on the scenery than the principal on the stage.

As Hunter did not marry or have direct issue, there was no funnelling of his memorabilia down through a direct family line and any private papers of Hunter's have dissipated. This is not to imply that there are no extant letters from Hunter. There are originals of private correspondence written by him to friends when he was governor (as opposed to his official despatches) now kept at the British Library as well as ships' logs he wrote, held in the Maritime Museum at Greenwich and the Public Record Office at Kew Gardens, which also holds Royal Navy records of courts martial and official correspondence. In addition, some letters to and from Joseph Banks are included in Banks' Papers, while official letters from his term as governor and beyond are held in London, much of which is accessible through the Historical Records of Australia and Historical Records of New South Wales series.

John Hunter casts a shadowy figure over the history of early colonial Australia, hovering in the wings behind Governor Arthur Phillip and later Captain John Macarthur, making occasional cameo appearances when he lost the *Sirius* and in clashes with the New South Wales Corps, before retreating back into the penumbra of Australian history. His skills and achievements go largely unrecognised by most, as do his defects.

Some Australians may associate him with the Hunter Valley and Hunter River in New South Wales and perhaps the John Hunter Hospital in Newcastle, but few could recite anything more about him. Others may recall he was an early governor of New South Wales, but would have precious little knowledge beyond that. This situation is as much a by-product of the change of emphasis on Australian history at secondary school level as it is on the relative impact of Hunter's contribution and visibility to early colonial history vis-a-vis Phillip, Macarthur, Macquarie, Flinders, Bass and Bligh. Hunter, however, did cram much into his 83 years.

Early days

John Hunter (middle and lower classes rarely had a middle name in 18th-century Britain) was born in Leith, near Edinburgh, on 29 August 1737—or was he? A number of reputable biographical dictionaries and entries on Hunter quote September 1738 as his birth year, but interestingly, none quote a day. For example, the entry for Hunter in the *Dictionary of National Biography* states he 'was born in Leith in September 1738'[12], and the *Dictionary of Australian History* also quotes September 1738.[13] The first edition of Manning Clark's *A*

History of Australia Volume 1 contains two errors in the one sentence: 'Born at Leith, Scotland, in 1738, he was ten years older than Governor Phillip.'[14] Firstly, Hunter's birth year is incorrect, which is then compounded by the inference that Phillip was born ten years later in 1748. In fact, Phillip was born on 11 October 1738, which makes him one year younger than Hunter. These mistakes were obviously detected and corrected in subsequent editions. The common source for these erroneous claims is to be found in an account of Hunter's life to 1800 entitled 'Biographical Memoirs of Captain John Hunter', published in the *Naval Chronicle* in 1801, in which it is recorded, 'The subject of this Memoir was born in Leith, in September 1738.'[15]

Hunter was not alone however, in having his birth details inaccurately described. Following the death of Lt. Governor David Collins on 24 March 1810, a large monument to him was erected in 1838 in a park off Davey Street, Hobart. The inscription not only implies that he was born in 1754, whereas the correct date was 3 March 1756, it also states he was a lieutenant colonel, whereas he was promoted to full colonel in 1808, and misquotes the day of his death as 28 March 1810, whereas this was the day his large funeral took place in Hobart.[16] The monument was erected only 28 years after his death, so the three errors are the more surprising, given that many people who knew Collins and were present at his funeral were still alive. In view of the laxity of public records in the 1700s and before, it is not surprising that discrepancies did occur. However, in Hunter's case, the details of his birth were clearly recorded and more careful researchers such as Bladen[17] and Watson[18] noted it accordingly.

John Hunter was in fact born on 29 August 1737, the third son and fifth child of William Hunter, Shipmaster and Helen Drummond, his wife (see Appendix 1). He was baptised in the Parish Church at South Leith on 1 September 1737, and the respective church entry relates:

> Hunter William Hunter, Shipsmaster in Leith & Helen Drummond his G[ood]wife had a son named John, Born 29 August & Baptized 1 September 1737, with Archibald Cameron, Landwaiter there & William Hunter, Taylor, Burgess of Edgh. Esqr.[19]

The William Hunter listed as a witness in this baptismal entry was John Hunter's grandfather, who was appointed one of his guardians or godparents. This William Hunter was a tailor and later Burgess of Edinburgh. The Testamentary papers for the Edinburgh Commissary Court show that William Hunter, Tailor and Burgess of Edinburgh died in 1756 leaving his son William Hunter, a Shipsmaster in Leith his nearest kin, his executor and lawful heir.[20] Both Hunter's father and Hunter's eldest brother carried the same name as the Edinburgh tailor.

Hunter's father, William Hunter, is described as a 'Mercht' on the baptismal records of his first three children. It is not clear whether this means he was in the merchant service, was working for a merchandising house or was carrying on business in his own right as a merchant. Whatever the case, by the time of John Hunter's birth in 1737 the family had moved from the Edinburgh Parish to the South Leith Parish and on the baptismal registers of the younger children William Hunter is shown as being a 'shipsmaster'. John Hunter's mother was the only daughter of John Drummond whose brother George Drummond was several times Provost (or Mayor) of Edinburgh.[21] The marriage certificate of William Hunter and Helen Drummond has not been located, but there were at least ten children of the marriage[22], not seven as claimed by Blaze.[23]

While Hunter's parents were disposed towards steering him towards a career in the church, Hunter expressed an interest in going to sea and so in the following year, 1746, perhaps in order to quash or confirm his inclinations, Hunter's father took the boy on a short trading voyage to Scandinavia. The vessel was wrecked off the coast of Norway and

Hunter, his father and the crew were rescued and cared for by the inhabitants of a small nearby fishing village.

After his return to Scotland, he was sent to the small town of Lynn (now King's Lynn) in Norfolk to live with his uncle, to continue his schooling. It is not clear exactly why this took place but it is possible that Hunter's father would not have been sufficiently wealthy to educate all his children properly. In view of Hunter's intelligence and his father's desire to keep him away from the sea, the move to Lynn under the care of his better-off uncle would enhance his education and distract him from following in his father's footsteps. The wreck of the vessel off the coast of Norway would surely have caused some financial loss to William Hunter and his family. His livelihood as a shipping merchant would have been affected, as well as any associated losses as a shareholder in the ship. Another major factor which would have added weight to the decision to send John Hunter to his uncle was the death of his mother in 1748 at age 35, when Hunter was just ten years old, with four younger siblings also requiring care and attention.

Hunter had already displayed musical and artistic talents, and while in Lynn, he decided that he wanted to become a musician, however, his uncle would not permit John to leave school, but agreed to him following his musical interests as an extra-curricular activity. Towards the end of 1752 or early in 1753, when Hunter was 15, his interest in joining the church was rekindled, but soon dissipated and by the following year, 1754, Hunter had convinced his family that a naval career was his true vocation. Once again, his uncle, Robert Hunter, used his Lynn connections and in May of that year, the 16-year-old signed on as a captain's servant to Captain Thomas Knackson on the sloop *Grampus*, stationed at Lynn. Physically, he can be presumed to have been slight and nimble in his youth, being described as a 'small delicate boy'[24] when rescued from his father's ship aged eight. Hunter's seafaring career extended over the next 50 years, the only breaks of any length being the three years between the Treaty of Versailles in 1783 and his appointment to the *Sirius* in 1786, the five years he spent as governor of New South Wales from 1795 to 1800 and the three-year period between his return to England in 1801 and assuming command of HMS *Venerable* in 1804. This represents a total of 11 years, the other 39 spent on almost continuous service at sea; a reflection of his diligence, ability, perseverance, good health and luck.

Figure 3. Hunter's portrait 1792. From Hunter's *Journal*. Courtesy of the Royal Australian Historical Society.

Physical characteristics

There are four extant portraits of John Hunter, none of which portray him before being made post captain in 1786, probably due partly to lack of available funds, possibly because he was not in England long enough to sit for the painter and because of the lack of suitable lodgings to store or to display the finished product. The first was painted by R. Dighton and engraved by D. Orme and appeared in Hunter's journal printed in January 1793. It is assumed that the portrait was commissioned in the previous year after Hunter returned to England in the *Waaksamheyd* in April 1792, when he was 55. Although he had been a post captain for six years, he is not shown wearing any epaulettes. The use of epaulettes originated in Europe but was not authorised in the British navy until 1795, after which admirals and post captains with over three years' seniority wore two. Junior captains wore one on their right shoulder and commanders one on their left. Lieutenants at that time wore none. This changed in 1812 when they were permitted to wear one on their right shoulder while commanders could wear two, with captains and admirals increasingly embellished to denote their rank. Hunter's later portraits reflect these innovations.

The second portrait appears beside the opening page of his memoir of 1801, with the caption 'Eng. by Ridley from an Original Picture'. More likely this portrait was commissioned upon his return from New South Wales in May that year, rather than being painted in Sydney and brought back with him. He was wearing his two epaulettes as a post captain and was 64 years of age. The portrait is slightly disjointed, with the top of his left-hand coat lapel being different from the right, and somewhat stylised, but does show Hunter as a fit and healthy person at that time. The third painting depicts Hunter in an admiral's uniform and could well have been completed soon after he was promoted to rear admiral in 1807, when he was 70, but the painting is undated and the artist unknown. It currently resides in the Rex Nan Kivell collection at the National Library of Australia. The last portrait was painted by W.M. Bennett in 1813 (when Hunter was 76), three years after he was promoted to vice admiral. It is housed at the Dixson Galleries in the State Library of New South Wales, Sydney.

Figure 4. 1801 portrait from his memoir in the *Naval Chronicle*. Dixson Library, State Library of NSW.

From these portraits, it can be observed that Hunter had a strong face with a firm and somewhat pronounced lower jaw. His lips were thin and his nose and nostrils prominent. He had strong eyebrows, blue eyes and a receding hairline, but appeared to retain most of his hair in his advanced years. None of the pictures seems to have him wearing a wig and his hair would appear to have been a light brown colour, turning white in old age. He could not be described as handsome in the classical sense, nor could his face be portrayed as hard. Rather, he had a determined or even craggy visage, which belied the softer side of Hunter's character.

There is no evidence of his height, weight or other physical characteristics, but it can be safely presumed that he was physically in very good shape. His time as a topman in his early seafaring days would confirm the description of him then as 'light, active and zealous'[25], so he was probably lean, nimble and of average height and weight, perhaps five feet eight or ten inches (Cook was tall at six feet), with a strong constitution. His years as a sailor, midshipman and master required a strong physical capacity and Hunter would have climbed the rigging to the tops of many ships' masts in his 30s and 40s. There is a reference to him making drawings from the masthead in 1771 when he was 34[26], and his exertions on the quarterdeck in rough weather would have maintained his physical edge.

He was rarely ill and there is only one reference to any serious ailment, but his body carried signs of wounds incurred from an active and sometimes hazardous sea life. On one occasion Hunter's leg was 'caught in the bite of the cable, and brought the anchor up, but the bone was not broke; and he was still able to walk' and 'in cutting the main mast away, his right hand was lamed in such a manner as to deprive him of its use for some time.' Later

> Mr Hunter's great exertions occasioned the rupture of a blood vessel in his lungs, which discharged so great a quantity of blood as to induce the surgeon to think he could not live more

Figure 5. 1808 portrait in the Rex Nan Kivell Collection, National Library of Australia.

> than two days, however, naturally of a good constitution, he surmounted all these misfortunes.[27]

When Hunter was 40, he received a severe contusion on his shoulder that kept him lame for some time.

When the *Sirius* was wrecked in March 1791 at Norfolk Island (Hunter was 52), a flying-fox device was rigged between the hull and a large tall tree on the shore to rescue the crew and haul provisions ashore. This necessitated crew members being pulled on a grating through heavy surf, which midshipman Southwell recorded

> frequently broke down over our heads, keeping them a considerable time under water, some of them coming on shore half-drowned and a good deal bruised. Captain Hunter was a good deal hurt, and with repeated seas knock'd off the grating, in so much that all the lookers on fear'd greatly for his letting go, but he got on shore safe, and his hurts by no means dangerous.[28]

It would have been a harrowing and exhausting experience and reflected well on Hunter's fitness. Similarly, when the *Venerable* was breaking up in 1804 the crew, including Hunter who was 67, had to climb down ropes hanging over the stern into lifeboats which were being tossed about in a raging surf. That his physical abilities were quite outstanding is confirmed by him walking long distances by current standards; for example, when at Sydney in 1789 after returning from Cape Town, his journal records him walking from Sydney Cove to Botany Bay and back, as well as twice from Manly to Pittwater and return through uncleared country. As governor, he walked from Parramatta to the cow pastures behind present-day Camden, a distance of around 34 miles, or 55 kilometres, to check on a cattle herd.

Hunter's longevity is also worthy of note. He lived for 83 years in an era when the average life expectancy in mid-18th century England was 36.6 years for men and women, and slightly lower in London.[29] This was only 18 months longer than the average life expectancy in London in the 1660s, 100 years earlier.[30] The current life span in Great Britain is 74.6 years for men and 79.7 for women.[31] Hunter's 83 years were more than double the contemporary average, but not unique. The composer Joseph Haydn was 77 when he died in 1809, and King George III died in 1820 aged 82.

Figure 6. Vice Admiral John Hunter, aged 76 (1813). Portrait held in the Dixson Gallery, State Library of New South Wales.

Sir Joseph Banks was 77 when he died in 1820. Hunter's father lived for 73 years, his elder brother William 79, and younger brother James and younger sister Janet also lived longer than normal lives. Not only was Hunter physically active he was also genetically predisposed to a long life, notwithstanding the poor diet he received during his decades at sea, his exposure to diseases and the indifferent medical services then available.

2
Influencing factors

Environment

Leith was a small fishing town and the trading doorway to Edinburgh. To appreciate its environment and character in the mid-1700s as well as that of south-eastern Scotland, and its impact on a young boy, it will be useful to draw a brief backdrop of events which shaped Leith and its inhabitants by the 1740s, i.e. during Hunter's developmental years.

In the 1600s, the Scottish economy was, at best, stagnant. Scotland's trade was small, with virtually non-existent manufacturing. Its agriculture was primitive, communications were poor, roads were few and in sub-standard condition, its society was culturally backwards and politically archaic. Even the most patriotic Scot would have conceded that the country was motionless, directionless and leader-less. Its politics was corrupted and dislocated and its future was bleak. By the end of the 17th century the Scottish nobility realised that their interests were not being served by such stagnation and agreed to exchange political independence (which Scotland did not need) for economic opportunities (which it desperately needed). Accordingly, in 1707, 30 years before Hunter was born, the parliaments of England and Scotland passed Acts of Union, whereby the two Kingdoms were fused into the one Kingdom of Great Britain and the English parliament absorbed the Scottish parliamentary system and its representatives. It was agreed however that the state church should remain Presbyterian in

Scotland and Anglican in England. The English Parliament effectively became the British Parliament.

The economic and social benefits of this union appeared slowly and gradually, as they were starting from a low base. In the first quarter of the 18th century, linen became the country's main manufacturing and export item, while tobacco from the English colonies in North America became a major import through Glasgow, three-quarters of which was then re-exported. By 1760, Paisley silk merchants had opened shops in Paris, while Edinburgh damasks were gaining an enviable reputation. In 1732, damask output was four and a half million yards; by 1748 seven and a third million and by 1800, over 20 million yards. As agricultural techniques advanced, so did the quality of the lint and hemp grown, together with improved spinning skills, which produced more and better linen. Between 1728 and 1738, the manufacture of linen for export more than doubled.

Aberdeenshire developed a stocking industry which became worth over £120,000 per year before the French revolution severely restricted trade to Europe. International trade required shipping, but just prior to the 1707 union, there were fewer than 100 ships flying the cross of St Andrew; by 1760 there were more than 1000 Scottish ships and ten years later this number had increased by another 50 per cent. Hunter's father would have been part of this trade and shipping boom. The Scottish coastal fishing industry also grew in the 1700s, gradually supplanting the traditional Dutch hold on this activity. This would also have impacted favourably on the Leith economy, but the impact was slow to take hold—by 1761, the Dutch still had 152 vessels engaged in fishing off the Scottish coasts, while the Scots had only 17, some of which were based at Leith. As trade and industry developed, so the Scottish banking system became more sophisticated and competitive to support the commercial growth. These changes took decades to establish themselves but would have been more apparent around the southern area bounded by Glasgow, Aberdeen and Edinburgh, with Leith benefiting from the increasing business activity emanating from Edinburgh.

For the universities to respond to the needs of the time, they were compelled to institute three essential reforms: the church domination of teachers had to be discarded; the old system of regenting (where teachers taught a variety of subjects instead of concentrating on their speciality) needed to be abandoned; and thirdly, new subjects had to be introduced and taught by people specifically trained to teach them. These three changes were eventually adopted but it took most of the first half of the century to take effect in the two major universities of Edinburgh and Glasgow and longer at others such as St Andrews and Aberdeen. When Hunter attended Aberdeen University in the early 1750s, it was still struggling under its medieval structure, which could well have been a factor in convincing Hunter that academic studies were not for him.

In the 1740s, the town of Leith, nestled on the shores of the Firth of Forth, provided port facilities for Edinburgh, one and a half miles away on top of the hills overlooking the estuary. They were connected by a winding road, with farms and open spaces on either side, with the journey on foot taking about 90 minutes; a far cry from the broad, bustling, sloping thoroughfare now called Leith Walk, with continuous houses and shops on both sides. The bus trip now takes 15–20 minutes, including stops. Leith was essentially a merchant town based upon trade with Northern Europe and fishing in the North Sea. As a working man's town, Hunter would have quickly been exposed to the associated egalitarian attitudes and lifestyle, mixed with strong religious overtones.

Life would have been industrious and unrelenting, but largely shielded from the politics of the day. In 1745 a rebellion was ignited in Scotland following the landing of the Young Pretender Prince Charles Stuart, or

Bonnie Prince Charlie, to reclaim the country. This caused some concern in Leith but would have had little impact on the eight-year-old Hunter, except perhaps to provide some basic insight into the catholic Jacobite and protestant Hanovarian causes. As a lowlander, Hunter would have been surrounded by the pro-Hanovarian population of Leith and influenced accordingly.

The era and sense of improving prosperity and progress would have had a slow but distinctive impact on the inhabitants of Leith. It may have been the port for Edinburgh, but it still had several restrictions on its rate of development. During Hunter's time there, in the 1740s and 1750s, the harbour of Leith was in essence, a tidal channel with a bar that stretched across its mouth. This affected the movement and passage of ships, especially at low tide and near to the shoreline, and would have compromised the loading and discharging of Hunter's father's merchant ship. To partially alleviate this, a stone pier was built in the 1720s together with a small dock nearby. It was not until 1777 (the year Hunter's father died) that a more substantial pier was constructed. The bar continued to be a problem, being sometimes impassable for days, and it was not until 1817 that engineering works managed to overcome this handicap.

The Leith of Hunter's day was a relatively small but generally prosperous port, with living conditions as good as could be expected for that time. There were schools, reasonable employment prospects for the unskilled and the benefits of a larger city only a 90-minute walk away. Hunter's childhood was therefore spent in an environment of hard work and limited prospects, which would have alerted him to realise that, if he was to make something of his life, he would need to leave Leith and seek his opportunities elsewhere. His father's maritime merchant occupation was uncertain, sometimes hazardous and always unpredictable, which may well have inclined Hunter towards a career of greater security, for example the church or the armed services.

Early influences

Hunter's mother died in 1748 when he was ten years old, after which he was sent to his uncle Robert Hunter, who had served in the Royal Navy and was Purser on HM Sloop *Lizard* on the Bristol station in 1745. He became a successful merchant in King's Lynn on the Norfolk coast near The Wash, about 160 kilometres north of London and 80 kilometres north of Cambridge. It was also some nearly 500 kilometres south of Leith so Hunter would have gone there by coach or by sea, a long journey either way, especially when the weather was inclement. How often Hunter made the trip between Leith and Lynn Regis over the next four or five years is unknown, but it can be presumed he would have been initially accompanied by his father, uncle or family friend. The trip by coach would have taken three or four days with stopovers and by sea perhaps the same duration, depending upon winds and weather. Either way, it would have been a mind-expanding experience for young Hunter, as most teenage boys then would not travel far from home, unless they had formally gone to sea.

The time spent with his uncle was during his early teens, an impressionable age for most young men. His early schooling had been in Edinburgh, rather than Leith, more than likely because of the better standard of schools there and the influence of his mother's family in a city then testing and flexing its cultural, educational and economic capabilities. The reason for Hunter going to live with his uncle was probably that Robert Hunter, now in his early 30s and a relatively successful businessman, could afford to take in and educate his teenage nephew, whereas Hunter's father could have been struggling to raise and educate his children with his limited income and his wife then deceased. John was enrolled at the school attached to St Margaret's Church (now known as King Edward VII School); the master of which was John Daville. The curriculum would have revolved around the classics and divinity as would have been the case at most church schools in England in the mid-18th century.

The major influence upon Hunter at that time was to be the celebrated church organist, pianist, composer and music historian, Dr Charles Burney, who had relocated from London for health reasons in 1751. Born in 1726, Burney was 11 years older than Hunter and made a significant impression upon the teenager, to the extent that he began to show an interest in being educated as a musician. His uncle did not allow him to fulfil this desire, but did permit him to study music in his spare time. This would indicate that Hunter must have had a reasonable musical aptitude for Burney to agree to teach him and he probably retained an interest in music, although there is no indication that Hunter played any musical instrument later in life. As Burney was a close friend of the Hunters', young John would have known Burney's children. One became the famous novelist Fanny Burney and another, James, sailed with Cook as a lieutenant on his second and third voyages. James Burney became a rear admiral in 1821, just before Hunter's death.

It is highly probable that a lifelong friendship existed between Dr Charles Burney and Hunter, especially as Burney was also to become a friend of Joseph Banks. It is also likely that Hunter would have remained acquainted with his son James, particularly in view of their mutual interest in the Pacific Ocean. Charles Burney was

> a keen amateur astronomer, something of a poet, a connoisseur of painting, a man of considerable learning and a genial companion, the friend of Johnson and Garrick, Reynolds, Burke, and of many of the leaders in the politics, science, art and literature of his time.[1]

Such broad interests could well have appealed to John Hunter, which not only would have broadened his education and outlook, but also influenced his attitude towards music and the arts. Burney also wrote a four-volume history of music as well as books on his travels in Europe.

He died in London in 1814, aged 78, and it is probable that he and Hunter spent many hours together in their senior years as Hunter also lived in London. He possibly attended Burney's funeral.

Once Hunter realised that a musical career was not going to be encouraged, an interest in divinity emerged and with his uncle's assistance, he 'was sent to the University of Aberdeen'[2], not Edinburgh University as claimed by Serle in his *Dictionary of Australian Biography*.[3] However, attempts to locate evidence of his enrolment and academic record at the University of Aberdeen have proved fruitless, owing to the inadequacy of the records for that time, but it can be assumed that he did not relish his Greek, Latin, Classics and Theological studies. The Scottish university system of the mid-18th century was in the process of emerging from its medieval cocoon, with some Universities still academically stagnant. The academic year then lasted five months.

To travel to Aberdeen University would have involved the long journey north from Norfolk to Leith and then another 160 kilometre coach ride to Aberdeen. His interest in entering the church could have developed from his early church attendances at Leith and his association with St Margaret's Anglican Church at King's Lynn, plus its security and social respectability. It is also likely that once the initial gloss or appeal wore off, his impressions of life as a clergyman, the reality of church life, plus the poor quality of education at Aberdeen University at that time combined to convince Hunter that, notwithstanding the security and stature of the profession, the lifestyle and hardships were not to his liking.

The other options open to him were an army or marine career but they had limited advancement prospects because commissions were generally bought and Hunter did not have the financial resources to make such a purchase. His memoir stated that 'he expressed to his uncle [perhaps his father was away on a trading voyage and his uncle had navy connections] a wish to embark again on a sea life.'[4] However, he did not choose the merchant service, having concluded that, from his father's experiences, merchant ships or colliers were a risky business and not well paid. Merchant ships were often tied up over winter from December to March, thus losing valuable trading time, and they had to contend with poor loading and unloading facilities. The North Sea had its hazards of storms, sandbanks and racing tides and there were limited social advancement opportunities.

His choice of the Royal Navy was probably the end result of several factors. Hunter already had an affinity with the sea, having grown up in a seaside port with a father whose livelihood involved regular trading voyages, of which Hunter had some experience. His elder brother William had joined the navy, so young John would have heard stories from him and perhaps sought to emulate him. His uncle's house at King's Lynn was also near the sea and a naval station, so the association was maintained during the years he spent there. Another attraction was that naval commissions were not for sale. The principal prerequisites for a successful naval career were generally patronage plus some experience and ability in managing a ship and her crew, which Hunter would have viewed as more attainable and provided a realistic chance to improve himself. Security was reasonably assured, (unless prematurely terminated by death or injury) especially for commissioned officers, even for those on half-pay awaiting their next appointment, while there was a certain prestige attached to naval officers. When these factors were aggregated and weighed, they would have presented an attractive prospect to John Hunter. He would have to prove his technical skills and find a suitable patron, but both were within the realm of reasonable possibility. Hunter was undoubtedly ambitious, security conscious and eager to master the skills of his chosen craft, but the cards were still stacked against him.

Naval officers of the late 18th century mostly came from the titled ranks, the landed gentry or professional classes (around 90 per cent) while only 10 per cent of officers were sons of business or commercial families or the working classes. But over half of those midshipmen from business related families became lieutenants and 50 per cent of those reached the rank of Captain or above. This meant that while the chances may have been loaded against Hunter's promotional opportunities, the door to promotion and success was ajar and some like Hunter, Bligh and Cook managed to slip through. On balance then, a career in the navy was Hunter's preferred option. That decided, it was his uncle's naval contacts that found him a place in 1754 on a naval sloop operating at Lynn Station in Norfolk.

Family

As with any young and impressionable child, Hunter's character would have been materially moulded by his experiences with his family and close friends during his formative and youthful years. As a member of a large family, he would have had to learn to share, to accommodate other people's views and wishes, wear handed-down clothes, wait his turn, know his place in the pecking order and perform his allotted tasks around the house. It can be presumed that Hunter's family was adequately clothed and fed rather than being wealthy, but following the loss of his father's trading ship off the coast of Norway in 1746, family income and living standards may have slipped or been stretched. Hunter's family was from the middle order rather than working class and was described by his grand-niece as being 'a good but impoverished family'.[5]

His father was a merchant whose antecedents were tailors, while his mother's father was somewhat better-off. Her uncle was George Drummond, the Lord Provost (or Lord Mayor) of Edinburgh on six occasions, which provided significant local status and a moderate

Figure 7. St John's Church, Hackney. Photograph courtesy of the author.

income. He was part of a committee that in 1759 drew up a Bill to re-create a Scottish Militia and was one of the city's more influential figures who helped to found the Edinburgh Medical School. He also assisted in reviving Edinburgh's fortunes by promoting musical culture in the form of the Edinburgh Musical Society, which met on Friday evenings at 6.00 pm in St Mary's Chapel to present concerts to the exclusive membership, for which there was a long waiting list to join. He was a man of considerable achievements, and would have had some influence on young John.

Hunter therefore grew up in a family environment where success had to be earned rather than conferred.

Hunter's relationship with his brother William, who also served in the navy for over 40 years and was seven years older, appeared to be especially close, and could well have been a factor in influencing John to go to sea. It would not be the first case of a younger sibling looking up to his elder brother as an example to follow. William's biography was published in a later edition of the *Naval Chronicle*[6] and provides some useful insights and reflections into his younger brother. William was born on 6 May 1730 in Edinburgh and also 'went to sea at the early age of 12 years with my father, in the Brittania merchantman fitted out from Leith belonging to the London trade.'[7] During the next two years, William made several more voyages in her and in the ships *James* and *John*. When William was 12, John was five, so it is likely that it was in one of those ships that Hunter was wrecked with his father three years later, in 1746.

Like John, William appeared to be close to his father, which was probably intensified by the death of their mother. William's memoir makes a number of references to returning to Leith, for example, 'to see my Father and sisters' in 1754[8] (Hunter had just gone to sea in that year) and again in 1763 after the conclusion of the Seven Years' War, 'At the Peace, I returned once more to my worthy father in Scotland, and remained there on half-pay for about five months.'[9] Upon learning of his father's death at the age of 73, William recorded 'This event quite unmanned me! Until I lost my worthy Father, though I sincerely loved him, I had never been sufficiently sensible of what I should feel when he was no more.'[10] While John made no specific reference to his father's death in his own memoir, the fact that he too returned to Leith, when he could, would infer similar family ties.

While John Hunter's memoir makes no reference to his brother, it is possible, by cross-referencing William's comments on ships he served on and when, with those related by John, to deduce that both men's service careers intersected on more than one occasion in the 1760s. John, as a master, could well have observed and noted his older brother's performance as a commissioned officer. For example, John Hunter's memoir refers to him being 'on board the Tweed frigate, commanded by the Hon Captain T. Percival, on the Newfoundland station; on this service he became Master's Mate, and continued during the years 1764 and 1765'[11], but made no mention of his brother. William, who was a lieutenant at this time, recorded that Captain Percival's father, Lord Egmont (familial patronage at work), placed him [Percival] 'in a more active ship, the Tweed, 32 guns, then on the Newfoundland Station. I was removed with the Captain and we sailed to join our ship in September 1764.'[12] This would imply that the two brothers were serving on the same ship for at least some months. John Hunter was appointed to HMS *Launceston* as master's mate from 1766 to 1769 and in 1766 William was also appointed to the *Launceston*. Both memoirs referred to the death of Admiral Durell in 1766, a mutual potential benefactor, which confirms their presence in Halifax at the same time; John—'His hopes [for promotion] were, however, but of short duration, they were clouded by the death of the Admiral, which melancholy event took place three days after his arrival at Halifax'[13]; William—'During our passage the Admiral was taken ill and died the second day after our arrival at Halifax—with him I lost such a friend as I never recovered.'[14] Again, neither brother referred to the other. Without influence, William did not advance any further in the navy, having had an adventurous if unspectacular career, and instead needed to later rely upon the influence of his younger sibling.

> [W]hen the gallant veteran Earl Howe was placed at the head of The Board, my younger Brother Captain John Hunter, of the Royal Navy, late Governor of New South Wales, applied to him, to appoint me Lieutenant of the Royal Hospital of Greenwich
> ...
> His Lordship willingly complied, and I accordingly succeeded to Lieutenant Larcock's Berth on the 15th October, 1787, satisfied and happy.[15]

John was obviously willing to make these representations on behalf of his brother with whom he shared much—a strong family tie, service together in the navy, good health, a long service career (John 50 years and William 44 years) and a long life—John 83 years, while William died on 17 February 1810, aged 79. William's daughter, Penelope, who married her cousin Henry Kent in 1794 and was widowed by 1801, and her only surviving daughter Penelope Percival Kent, were particularly close to John Hunter in his declining years. Hunter recorded in his will that the 'kind and affectionate attentions' to him by Penelope [Kent] 'have been unremitting'. The importance and value that Hunter placed upon his family was undoubtedly influenced by the fact that he did not marry or have a family of his own, so he would have been more reliant upon and genuinely interested in his siblings and their families as a result.

At the commencement of his memoir, there is an engraving of William Hunter from an original picture, when he was in his forties or early fifties. He had a longer and more jovial or even friendly face, small mouth and fuller lips than the portrait of his younger brother in the 1801 edition of the *Chronicle* four years earlier, to the extent that they would not necessarily be taken as brothers at first glance. Both retained their hair into older age and both appeared to have somewhat prominent noses.

The family tie endured into Hunter's senior years and his retirement as a vice admiral, when he regularly journeyed from London to Leith to stay at the house he bought in 1803 in Cassels Place, described as being 'of grey stone, three stories, three windows abreast and has no pretensions of any sort to architectural beauty. It contains 7 or 8 good rooms, besides the kitchen floor and offices.'[16] In 1808 he assigned the house to his sister Mrs Janet Maule, and Hunter stayed with them during his subsequent annual visits there. After Janet Maule's death Hunter made over this house to the daughters of his late sister, indicating how attached Hunter was to his extended family and the influence they in turn had on him. Hunter's grand-niece Mrs

Figure 8. Captain William Kent RN, John Hunter's nephew. Original portrait in the possession of Professor John White, Research School of Chemistry, ANU.

Aitchison 'remembers the Admiral perfectly well; he was always a genial man, with a store of sugared-coated almonds in his pocket for his child friends.'[17]

As a further indication of the strength of the family ties, Hunter arranged for the son of his elder sister Mary, Lt. William Kent (Hunter's nephew), his wife and their only child, a two-year-old daughter named Eliza, to accompany him to Sydney in 1795, with

William Kent commanding the second ship, the by then rather worn-out HMS *Supply*.

The Kent family lived with Hunter at Government House during his five-year term, with Mrs Kent acting as first lady to the bachelor Hunter. William Kent died in 1812, predeceasing his uncle who was appointed by the will as one of Kent's executors. Such was the closeness of Hunter to the Kents that he named Kent Street in Sydney and Flinders named the Kent Group of Islands in Bass Strait in 1798 after William Kent. Hunter and the Kents remained close after returning to London in 1801. When Hunter died in London in 1821, it was decided by the Kent family to bury him in a vault at St John's Church, Lower Clapton Road, Hackney, which contained the remains of distant members of this family.

The infant child mentioned above, Eliza Kent, who accompanied her parents to New South Wales in 1795, married James Charles Grant of Burton Crescent, London. He died in 1818 soon after their marriage and was buried in the Hackney cemetery. In 1819 a niece of J.C. Grant was interred in the same plot. Hunter's was the third burial in the site. The last burial was Hunter's niece, Penelope (Hunter) Kent who died on 21 January 1843.

Hunter's innate tenderness towards children was further illustrated by an incident which took place in June 1789. A party comprising Governor Phillip, Hunter, David Collins, the surgeons John White and George Worgan, plus four others set off from near Manly to walk along the coast to Broken Bay. On the evening of the first day, they stumbled across a terrified girl, weakened from the recent small-pox epidemic, cowering in long, wet grass. Hunter reported, 'She was very much frightened on our approaching her, and shed many tears, with piteous lamentations.'[18] A fire was hastily made, food was provided and

Figure 9. The Grant family vault at St John's, Hackney. Photograph courtesy of the author.

The inscription reads:

> SACRED TO THE MEMORY OF JOHN HUNTER ESQ., Vice Admiral of the Red Squadron of His Majesty's Fleet, and formerly Governor of New South Wales, who departed this life on 13th March 1821, aged 83 years. He was born in Leith, in Scotland, and belonged to the Naval Service of his country sixty-eight years, more than fifty of which he was actively employed in every quarter of the globe.
>
> In conjunction with Governor Phillip he formed the first settlement of New South Wales, and for many years had the chief command of that distant colony, where his mild benevolent disposition endeared him to all classes of society. His name will ever be remembered here with veneration. He will be classed by impartial posterity with those generous benefactors of mankind who diffuse among savage tribes the blessing of civilisation, who recalled the unthinking and profligate from error and vice, and confirmed every precept of wisdom and goodness by the irresistible force of example.

she was covered with warm, dry grass. The next day the girl had moved to a little bark hut nearby and had a two-year-old girl with her whom she was trying to protect from the falling rain. Hunter described her as 'the most miserable spectacle in the human shape I ever beheld: the little infant could not be prevailed on to look up; it lay with its face upon the ground and one hand covering its eyes.'[19] More food and covering were supplied and, following a number of repeated visits, the infant gained sufficient confidence to 'allow us to take hold of its hand'.[20] Hunter devoted two pages of his journal to relate this episode.

John Hunter comes across as a benevolent kind-hearted and caring person, much of which emanated from his strong sense of family, which was engendered by his good fortune in being influenced by his close-knit relations.

Naval influences

As with any young, ambitious youth in his late teens and 20s, Hunter was a keen observer of those around and above him and he identified the characteristics of the ones who succeeded in the service and the flaws of those who failed. As a member of the foc'sle (or forecastle) crew, he would have mixed with a great range of seamen, young and old, hard and soft, experienced and green. Life was tough on 18th-century naval ships and not all would have been able to cope with the weather, the heights, the discipline, the range of punishments, long hours on duty, poor food and the ever-present proximity to others. There was nowhere to hide on a royal navy ship. Scurvy and disease were always a threat. Some sailors were undoubtedly escaping from past transgressions while many were either pressed or enlisted through lack of alternative employment. Others joined up because of a desire to pursue a naval career. A broad mix of men, both heterosexual and homosexual, confined in narrow spaces for months, even years on end, made lasting impressions on all youths, including Hunter.

Amongst the crew there would have been bullies and mentors, leaders and loners, all providing a range of influences for the young and impressionable to follow. Hunter's innate sense of duty and decency saw him through these early months at sea.

On his first ship, the *Grampus*, Hunter befriended one of the midshipmen, a Mr Allen, who taught him all he knew of navigation, and when Hunter wanted to learn advanced mathematics, the midshipman conceded the task was beyond him and could only refer him to books on the subject, which were neither accessible nor affordable by Hunter.

His second captain, William Brown of the *Centaur*, seemingly recognised his talents and promoted him to midshipman in 1756, and would have been one of Hunter's early role models. Hunter also impressed William Hay, the captain of the *Carysfort*, who entrusted him to draw impressions of Spanish fortifications at Havannah and who, with Hunter, successfully oversaw the rescue of the ship from sinking on a reef in the Gulf of Florida. Hunter learnt much on emergency procedures from Hay on that occasion and he put this experience into practise during the later sinking of the *Sirius* and *Venerable*.

During his term on the *Intrepid*, his captain, James Cranson, taught Hunter advanced astronomy and honed his maritime surveying skills. While it was the task of captains of smaller naval vessels to teach and train the midshipmen, it was fortunate that his early superior officers took a special interest in his practical and mathematical education, in part due to Hunter's own interest, enthusiasm and willingness to learn. One motivating factor for Hunter to excel would have been the lack of patronage supporting him, thus requiring him to advance by performance rather than through family connections.

The major influential factor on Hunter's mid-career prospects was undoubtedly Lord Howe, who observed Hunter performing creditably as master and lieutenant as well as in the survey work he undertook in

North America. While Howe was impressed with Hunter in a technical sense, it is unlikely he would have supported him had he not approved of his character, demeanour and attitude. It is also likely that some of Howe rubbed off onto Hunter, who would then have been sufficiently mature and experienced enough to know how to attract the attention of his superior officers and potential patron, and shrewd enough to absorb and apply the lessons of naval politics. With 20 years as a midshipman and master before being commissioned, Hunter had ample time to learn from his captains and officers.

While Hunter's personality was initially moulded by his family and early friends in Leith, Edinburgh and King's Lynn, his outlook, ambitions and behaviour would have been heavily influenced by his naval mentors, his peers and senior officers. As a result, by the time he was appointed post captain in 1786 aged 49, the manner in which he related to people and the impression he made on them (generally favourable) was well entrenched in his personality. He came across as likeable, dependable, reliable, tactful, patient and technically competent. He was physically robust and healthy, probably of average height and weight, not noticeably handsome but perhaps more plain and craggy in appearance. How much of his Scottish accent he retained is unknown, but it would have become increasingly blurred after decades in the Royal Navy and living in the south of England. He attended Anglican services in the navy, New South Wales and elsewhere, so his initial Presbyterian inclinations became blurred in later life, which would imply a strong degree of tolerance, probably instilled in him at an early age by the realisation that for Scotland to advance, it had to work closely with England, a relationship regarded by many Scots with great suspicion.

Enlightenment

The Enlightenment movement of the 18th century would have had some impact on Hunter, but not so much during his childhood in Leith. To consider this requires some understanding of the Enlightenment which swept across Europe, and the extent to which it affected south-east Scotland. During the latter part of the 17th and most of the 18th century, there was a gradual shift in intellectual interests from the constrictions of supernatural religion to the broader understanding of the natural sciences. This change became known as the Enlightenment, as scientists and philosophers and later bankers, businessmen and aristocrats learnt more of the physical universe and, as a result, became 'enlightened'. Carlton Hayes, the American historian, summarised the Enlightenment as possessing four principal objectives:

- Naturalism—the substitution of the natural for the supernatural, i.e. science for theology
- Rationalism—the exalting of the power of human reason to discover the laws of nature
- Optimistic Progress—the belief in bettering and perfecting mankind, using reason and a greater understanding of natural laws
- Humanitarianism—the regard for a person's natural rights and the advances to be made by implementing Enlightenment principles.[21]

This was activated by dissecting religious, political and social issues to discover whether they were in harmony with natural law, promoted ideas of human progress, advanced human rights and provided some benefit to the world.

The 1707 Act of Union traded Scottish political independence for better economic prosperity with England. While Scotland retained its own Kirk, legal and educational systems, the political move to London and the rise of commercial activity saw the emergence of an educated middle class (the new elite) and the gradual modernising of the universities which resulted in the freeing of intellectual thought. The church also went through a modernising process whereby from 1712 clergy were no longer chosen by uneducated, peasant parishioners who were often persuaded to nominate men of mean abilities, low breeding and gross fanaticism. Instead, clergy were selected by the gentry who replaced the fundamentalists with moderates who were better educated with liberal ideas. As a youth, Hunter witnessed some of these changes, which could have propelled him into considering the church as a vocation.

The degree to which the basic principles of the Enlightenment had permeated the coffee houses or meal table discussions in the port of Leith by the 1740s is uncertain. However, while the town would have seen business grow with the rise of the linen trade as well as imports and exports to Edinburgh, it is unlikely that topics relating to naturalism, rationalism, optimistic progress and humanitarianism would have featured very highly in a working man's town struggling to feed its families, including the Hunter family. The cultural advances in Edinburgh, epitomised by new clubs, newspapers, publishers and improvement societies as well as the emergence of writers and philosophers such as David Hume, William Robertson and Adam Smith, would have been initially confined to the intellectual circles of Edinburgh and Glasgow, rather than the ordinary residences of Leith. These changes moreover, both economic and philosophical, spread across the Scottish lowlands well before having any impact on the more remote highlands.

Once Hunter went to sea in 1754, his contact with Leith and any Enlightenment influence it had on him would have diminished. Nevertheless, he was exposed to the broader concepts of the Enlightenment with fellow naval officers and people in the various ports he called at, especially London. His active mind would have welcomed discussions on natural science, while his egalitarian upbringing would have facilitated acceptance of the concepts of natural rights and the amelioration of mankind. His enthusiasm to record, draw and send samples back home of new species of flora and fauna from New South Wales is an indication of his interest in natural history. Hunter may not have been a child of the Enlightenment, but it left some impression on him.

Religion

There is no evidence to suggest that Hunter was devout in a religious sense, notwithstanding his flirtation with the Kirk in his mid-teens. Hunter was brought up a protestant, and while only eight years old during the Jacobite uprising of 1745, he at least learnt of the differences and tensions between the protestant and catholic denominations. Hunter lived in a highly sectarian society, with the Presbyterians of southern Scotland having strong anti-catholic views. He would have been told of the historical implications of Bonnie Prince Charlie's quest to occupy Scotland (which nearly succeeded for a few months) and then claim the crown of England, only to be defeated at Culloden on 16 April 1746, seven months after controlling Edinburgh and surrounding areas, including Leith. He would have seen the occupying Jacobite forces around Leith in late 1745 and would have overheard adults talking about the invaders, but the events would not have had a great impact on him as his father's business activities continued with minimal disruption; family life would not have been seriously compromised by the uprising. However, this could partially explain his reservations about the Irish Catholic convicts during his governorship.

Hunter could probably be regarded as a religious moderate. He would have been exposed to regular Anglican-based divine service on board naval ships and he re-introduced religious observance when he arrived back in Sydney as governor in 1795 and was a regular attendee thereafter. Whether this was to lead by example or from an intrinsic sense of religious devotion is unclear, but most likely a combination of both. Mary Johnson, the wife of the first chaplain to the colony between 1788 and 1800, Richard Johnson, wrote a letter to a family friend in Portsmouth on 21 December 1795:

> Our new Governor arrived here in September; since that time the Lord Day has been better observed we have a tolerable congregation not quite so good as yours—the Governor and his family always attending on sunday morning and wish the other officers would take example by him.[22]

Hunter also attempted to improve the moral tone of the colony by re-issuing decrees requiring convicts to attend church services (it would seem that leading by example was insufficient). This partially raised congregation numbers, but following a further attempt by Hunter to coerce officers and overseers to attend more regularly in 1798, the church was wilfully set on fire and was completely consumed in the space of two hours. Hunter quickly assigned a recently completed storehouse as an interim church and offered a pardon and a £30 reward for information leading to the conviction of the arsonist, but the offer was not taken up. However, convicts were no longer forcibly driven to church. While Hunter was not deeply religious, he did take more than a casual interest in the church; certainly more so than did Phillip, King or Bligh.

Relationships

Hunter's relatively egalitarian upbringing in a working-man's town enabled him to mix easily with the lower classes, while his mother's family connections exposed him to a higher social order in Edinburgh. His exposure to a wider variety of people and outlooks broadened while living with his uncle in Norfolk, particularly through his association with the cultured and musical Charles Burney. His time at Aberdeen University also taught him about the politics of student and academic life, even if this experience helped dissuade him from continuing his studies. The navy reinforced his capacity to relate to people of equal or superior standing, together with developing his capacity for self discipline, obedience to orders and application. Having ascended from the lowest naval rank, Hunter's time as a crew member gave him a keen insight into the minds of those he later commanded, with the result that Hunter was respected by his men and he could relate well to them.

What he was not trained for was to deal with difficult equals or civilians outside his direct naval authority who operated beyond the naval regulations system that Hunter lived with for 40 years. He had not had to cope with people like John Macarthur before in his life; navy rules and procedures were strict and exacting and had to be followed. To undermine a colleague as Macarthur undermined Hunter was a scenario Hunter was unprepared for and thus totally inexperienced. The fact he had not been exposed to such behaviour could be interpreted as lacking broader political skills, so that in this sense, his education, life experiences and external influences left him less than adequately equipped to handle and manage such people and circumstances.

Why did Hunter not marry? In the first place, there is no evidence to suggest that Hunter was homosexual. Did his mother's death when he was ten have any influence? The family would have been dislocated after she died, when Hunter was sent to live with his uncle 500 kilometres away. He had sisters and seemed to mix well enough at his uncle's house and with the Burney family. He would therefore have had positive role-model families to observe the processes and outcomes of satisfactory marriages. He was apparently close to his brothers and sisters and their families, which intensified after he retired and lived in London, travelling to Leith once a year to spend time with those living there as well as maintaining contact with those in London.

While Hunter was not strictly handsome, he was not unattractive either, and probably could have married if he really wished to. However, a likely answer is that, without influence, Hunter had to single-mindedly apply himself to his naval career if he was going to impress enough people to warrant a promotion to commissioned rank. He spent little time ashore between postings, so would have had a limited period in any one place to locate and court a potential bride. Perhaps he did meet possible partners, but either they were not interested in him, or there was not sufficient time to pursue the relationship. His upbringing made it unlikely that he was only interested in women above his station, who would elevate his social standing, financial position or even his career prospects, as his Leith and Scottish upbringing probably precluded any tendency to snobbishness or pretentiousness. Alternatively, Hunter could have been one of those men who were simply not interested in marriage, notwithstanding his affinity with children. Not being married made him more available for the next ship and Hunter busily sought a new assignment almost as soon as he had completed the previous voyage. Many of his appointments took him away for a couple of years or more and it might have been only some weeks or months ashore before he was leaving port again on another ship. Between the ages of 17 and 50, Hunter was in Great Britain for a series of short periods totalling only six years; not a great deal of time to find a wife and be a father and family man. Even when he became a post captain in 1786, he was then away from 1787 to 1792 and 1795 to 1801, thus he was only home for three out of the ensuing 14 years. James Cook was home for only three years out of the 11 from 1768 to 1779, but he was already married with children before he embarked on his long voyages to the Pacific. In all likelihood, Hunter was simply too busy furthering his career to find a bride.

Hunter emerges from his years as a subordinate officer as a thoroughly decent, industrious, competent and respected person. Although not having extensive command experience, he had the background and ability to relate well with those above and below him. His reputation enabled Phillip to be quite satisfied with Hunter's appointment as second captain of the *Sirius*, which he noted to Lord Sydney 'lays me under a very good obligation to Lord Howe, for there are not many officers in the Line of Service so equal to the task.'[23] Soon after arriving at Sydney Cove, Daniel Southwell, one of the *Sirius*' midshipmen wrote to his mother, saying 'He's a man devoid of stiff pride, most accomplish'd in this profession, and to sum up all, is a worthy man', and two years later 'Much also may be expected from Captain Hunter, whose virtue and integrity is as conspicuous as his merit.'[24]

His popularity amongst his equals is also demonstrated by the captains who supported him by recommending his commission; by a captain friend who wrote to the *Naval Chronicle* in 1811 in support of Hunter's design of an unsinkable lifeboat; and the letter of support from Governor Phillip to his court martial over the loss of the *Sirius*. Hunter appeared to work at maintaining friendships by corresponding with them, particularly letters he wrote to people such as Joseph Banks and Samuel Bentham as well as those he undoubtedly wrote to his family but which are not known to have survived. Being single, and from a close family network, he knew the value of friendships and ensured that he preserved them. While Hunter did have difficulties and differences with Major Ross on Norfolk Island, this was more an outcome of the fractious nature of Ross, who managed to alienate most of his peers, including Phillip and Bradley. Phillip actually transferred Ross to Norfolk Island to rid himself of this troublesome individual.

While John Hunter was a product of his environment—industrious, lower-middle-class surroundings, high standards and educated—he seemed to absorb those characteristics which exemplified the principles by which he was brought up to respect and follow. He did not bear grudges against people like Macarthur and King, both of whom deprecated him, and he won the respect of fellow officers for his technical competence.

If these were the positive features which resulted from early influencing factors, what negatives can be detected from these same elements? Perhaps his inability to stand up to and handle troublesome people outside the navy was an indication of his lack of civilian political experience. Hunter may not have played the patronage stakes as shrewdly as he could have, resulting in his delayed commissioning. He could well have been naive in some respects, with his upbringing sheltering him from manipulators and the politics of upper echelon naval ranks. Though well-meaning and honest, he was possibly gullible and not very 'street smart' as a result of his fairly straightforward early life experiences. He did not live in a big city until later in life, so was more used to mixing with smaller intimate communities and the social disciplines required to survive in these tight circles. The consequences flowing from his command inexperience were not a result of any flaw or earlier influences, but rather the by-product of not having sufficient or appropriate patronage early enough—a misfortune rather than a character defect.

John Hunter's early experiences prepared him quite well for his adult life. His elder brother William was also resourceful, friendly and ambitious, but unlike his younger brother, lacked the ultimate patronage to rise above lieutenant. John Hunter was ambitious too;

both brothers were taught the same fundamental lessons of life and how to succeed, but John was more successful in fulfilling his goals.

On balance, John Hunter's early influencing factors collaborated to enable him to make something of his life—there was the drive to succeed combined with ability and personality to implement his will to do well. Those early guide-posts also assisted Hunter to develop competencies of a high quality in a range of fields (but ill-equipped him in others) and to make the most of the openings that became available to him, while acquiring a circle of friends and supporters in the process.

3
Promotion deferred

> His persevering efforts, more useful than brilliant, will command the applause of those best judges of naval merit, his brother Officers.[1]

This quotation from his memoir aptly sums up Hunter's achievements as a sailor—persevering, useful and commanding the respect of his colleagues, i.e. a competent seaman. The phrase 'more useful than brilliant' is a perceptive insight into his abilities (and perhaps damning with faint praise) but all of these attributes could be cancelled out by the lack of recognition from those above who dispensed promotions supported by patronage. The lack of 'interest' by someone influential in the Royal Navy of the 18th century could stall an otherwise competent officer's career for years (as in Hunter's case) or even indefinitely.

In the 18th century, a competent seaman would have been able to perform the various tasks in any sailing ship—whether below deck, on the deck or aloft. For officers, this would also involve navigation, working the ship according to the weather, wind and sea conditions, signalling, attending to the log and monitoring the general seaworthiness of the ship. To this should be added the ability to anticipate changes in weather conditions and their consequences and to be prepared for any likelihoods which may affect the safety or efficiency of the ship. Without engines or propellers, sailing ships took much longer to react to sudden changes or incidents and were restricted in their manoeuvrability in relation to the direction of the wind. For instance, square-rigged ships could not sail directly into the wind but were compelled to tack, or zigzag, to make forward progress, which could have implications in a bay, narrow passage or channel. So seamanship included anticipating events or options and having contingency plans in place; just as the word 'airmanship' today includes 'being ahead of the aircraft' in order to anticipate weather or terrain changes and being able to make the necessary adjustments in time as a consequence. Hunter did not always demonstrate this particular requirement of competent seamanship.

How good was John Hunter's seamanship as a seaman, midshipman, master, lieutenant and captain? There is no doubt that Hunter was an exceptionally skilled and proficient seaman in a technical sense. He also became an excellent navigator, draughtsman, sketcher and manager of ships during his 50-year career. The ships he served on up to the *Sirius* are listed below.

Their logs disclose nothing relating to Hunter's performance during his time on them and it seems that there are no revealing diaries of others who served with him; the exception is a reference to Hunter when the *Carysfort* was nearly lost in 1770 and the part he played in its recovery, which will be discussed later.

The only contemporary material on Hunter's early naval activities is to be found in an 18-page contribution to the *Naval Chronicle* of 1801 entitled 'Biographical Memoirs of Captain John Hunter, late Governor of New South Wales'. Hunter arrived at Spithead on the *Buffalo*, still smarting at his recall as Governor of New South Wales, on 24 May 1801, seven months before the sixth volume of the *Naval Chronicle* was published in December of that year.

Period	Ship	Rank
1754–55	HMS *Grampus*	Captain's Servant
1755–57	HMS *Centaur*	Seaman/Midshipman
1757–57	HMS *Union*	Midshipman
1757–60	HMS *Neptune*	"
1760–60	HMS *Royal Anne*	"
1760–60	HMS *Princess Amelia*	"
1760–63	HMS *Royal George*	"
1763–66	HMS *Tweed*	Master's Mate
1766–69	HMS *Launceston*	Master
1769–72	HMS *Carysfort*	"
1772–74	HMS *Intrepid*	"
1775–75	HMS *Kent*	"
1775–76	HMS *Foudroyant*	"
1776–79	HMS *Eagle*	"
1779–80	HMS *Berwick*	Lieutenant
1780–80	HMS *Union*	"
1780–81	HMS *Berwick*	"
1782–82	HMS *Victory*	"
1782–82	HMS *Spitfire*	Master and Commander
1782–83	HMS *Marquis de Seignelay*	"
1786–90	HMS *Sirius*	Second Captain

Table 1. Ships on which Hunter served, 1754–90.

The author of the contribution is not stated, but it must have either been written by Hunter himself in the third person or written by someone else using extensive and detailed input by Hunter (which is more likely, judging by the prose), as only he would have possessed all the specific facts outlined in the memoir. Hunter may have drafted it, or at least planned it, during the six months' voyage back to England as part of his determination to vindicate and rehabilitate himself and his government, following his removal by the Duke of Portland (William Henry Cavendish Bentinck, 1738–1809 and briefly Prime Minister from 1807 to 1809) the previous year.

Equally, he could have prepared it or assisted in its compilation after his arrival as he had some months to oversee or orchestrate its preparation. It is possible, but unlikely, that the memoir was published spontaneously at the instigation of a third party with some influence, especially as Hunter's reputation was under a cloud at the time and Portland had refused to see him on his return to London. While it is virtually inconceivable that it would have been written in the detail that it was without input from Hunter himself, there is one glaring inaccuracy on the first page where, once again, Hunter's birth date was incorrect.

Notwithstanding this early aberration, the memoir relates Hunter's career to 1800 in a highly positive, praiseworthy and generous fashion, but is also honest in dealing with setbacks to his promotional prospects. This scars-and-all approach could also be a reflection of the essential openness that formed part of Hunter's character. Inevitably it is the major reference source for his early career, beyond which there is a necessity for some speculation.

His first seagoing appointment was in May 1754, as a 16 year old, on the sloop HMS *Grampus*, 14 guns, Captain Thomas Knackston, as a captain's servant on the recommendation of his uncle, Robert Hunter. The *Grampus*, built in 1746, was stationed at Lynn in Norfolk, where

Hunter had attended school. A sloop in the mid-1700s was usually a two-masted vessel with 10–18 guns and a complement of around 40 men, and was employed as an auxiliary in a fleet, on patrol or on message-carrying duties. It usually rated a commander rather than a post captain. The position of 'captain's servant' was not as the name would imply, but rather as a protégé of the captain who would oversee his instruction and prepare him for a career as an officer.

Hunter was described as being nimble and enthusiastic and at nearly 17, he was older than most 'servants' at that time. Admiralty regulations stipulated a minimum age of 13 (or 11 if the son of an officer) but some were taken on as young as eight or nine.[2] Seamen were classified as fo'c'sle, i.e. housed in the forward section of the ship, with the older men looking after the lower part of the rigging, the lead and stowing the stores, and the younger men, or 'topmen', who worked aloft on the masts, yards and rigging. The 'afterguard' attended the quarterdeck, manned the wheel and trimmed the sails, while the 'waisters' manned the capstan and swabbed the decks. The 'idlers' were the barbers, cooks and clerks who did not stand watches. Hunter spent some time as a topman, attending to the topsail which was the second or middle sail on the main and foremast on a square-rigged ship; the lower sail being the mainsail or foresail, while above was the topgallant sail. In some later ships, a fourth sail, the royal, was added above the topgallant on both masts.

Life as a topman required stamina, agility and a cool head for heights, plus an element of luck, as a fall to the deck or into the sea was often fatal. Hunter had a hammock spaced 28 inches (71cm) from the next man and was required to provide his own bedding. Each had two hammocks to allow one to be washed and dried and they had to change their clothing twice a week—weather permitting. Food was allocated equally to officers and men and was supposed to comprise one pound of ship's biscuit each day, plus a weekly ration of four pounds of beef, two pounds of pork, two of peas, one and a half of oatmeal, six ounces of butter, six ounces of sugar and 12 ounces of cheese. Little wonder that scurvy was commonplace with the lack of vitamin C in this diet. There was no designated uniform for seamen in Hunter's time and his pay as an able seaman would have been 24 shillings a month—unchanged since 1653, 100 years before.

Privacy was nonexistent for seamen—the men slept and ate together in cramped conditions. Each had his own mug, wooden bowl and a spoon while the tables were slung between the guns. If the ship was large enough, officers had access to private toilets at the stern (often adjacent to the side of the great cabin windows), whereas the crew used the 'heads', a seat beside or behind the figurehead with a chute to carry the waste away and a knotted, frayed rope as a cleaning device. The Endeavour had two such heads either side of the bowsprit for nearly 100 men. In larger ships, there were a number of urinals which consisted of a funnel and tube built into the side of the ship.

The officers at least had their own small cabins (the actual dimensions depending on the size of the ship) which mostly faced onto a common ward room where the officers ate and conversed. The captain's cabin was located on the uppermost deck level across the stern of the ship in what was known as the great cabin. However, these cabins were only separated by removable canvas screens mounted on wooden frames, which gave the officers visual privacy but precious little protection from noise. These screens could be hastily removed whenever the ship was cleared for action to provide maximum fighting area and to enable the gun crews to man those cannon located at the stern of the ship. This is well illustrated in a drawing made of HMS *Venerable*, a 74 gun two decker, Hunter's last command which he lost in 1804.

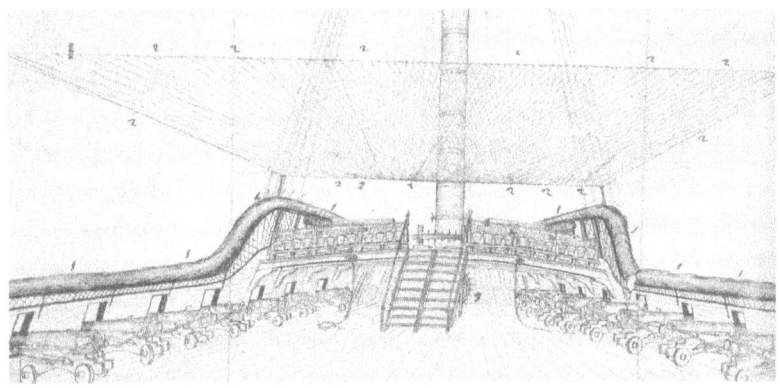

Figure 10. This view of the *Venerable* cleared for action was prepared in 1799 and shows the officers' cabins and the great cabin cleared away for easy access to the rear guns. The stern windows are now visible. The netting was to prevent shot away spars, sails and rigging from falling onto gun crews. Courtesy of the National Maritime Museum, Greenwich.

There was no effective heating or cooling below decks, so in summer especially, the heat generated by perhaps 100-200 men slung close together would have been overpowering. Ceiling heights were another factor, with most decks having less than six feet clearance, causing many of the crew to be perpetually stooping when moving around below. The crew shared trunks to stow their clothes and personal possessions while the officers had their own trunk in their cabin.

As mentioned, during the year Hunter spent on the *Grampus*, he commenced learning the art of navigation under midshipman Mr Allen, who impressed upon him the importance of mastering this art. According to the *Chronicle,* Hunter, who became a competent navigator, was also a very eager student who

> instantly set about this useful and important study, and in a very short time had completely gone through all the common rules of navigation, and soon convinced his teacher that he was

> desirous of going much deeper in mathematical pursuits than it was in his power to lead him.³

Allen could only refer him to advanced maths books, which Hunter could neither gain access to nor afford.

In 1755, Hunter was transferred as an able seaman to HMS *Centaur*, Captain William Brown, a frigate (or sixth rate) of 504 tons, 24 guns and a complement of 155. His abilities as a student and a topman impressed his captain who, 15 months later (in 1756)

> called him from the mast-head one day, from whence he had just sent down the fore-top-gallant yard, and inquired if he had any other clothes than his jacket and trowsers, to which he replied he had; then, said the Captain: "you will take off your jacket and trowsers, put on your other clothes, and do your duty as a Midshipman. I have taken notice of your diligent and active conduct some time past, and I will serve you if you continue to deserve my notice."⁴

The memoir noted Hunter's concern that his close association with the crew might affect his new authority over them, but his fears transpired to be without foundation. These reflections identified Hunter as being sensitive to the reactions and feelings of others and showed he was conscious of the importance of maintaining friendly and correct relations with his peers and colleagues. The fact that his fears did not eventuate would indicate that his promotion was well received and accepted by his fellow seamen, who presumably recognised his eagerness to learn and his potential for advancement. It would also infer that he was popular in the forecastle and was able to get on well with those around him. He had a common touch. The new position permitted him to further his studies of mathematics and drawing, and because he could not afford to buy a quadrant, Hunter designed an instrument to measure inaccessible heights, and proved its accuracy by calculating the lengths of the ship's masts and then comparing his readings with the ship's plans and actual measurements.

Hunter, by now aged 19, was one of six midshipmen on board and would have been entitled to wear a long, single-breasted blue coat with a white patch on the collar, a cocked hat and a dirk. His pay would have been £2 5s a month. The duties of an 18th-century midshipman included standing watch, keeping the log board (the ship's course and speed), signals and usually being in charge of one of the ship's boats. While they were regarded as potential officer material, they lived in the 'cockpit', well away from the officers. Hunter's training involved navigation, firing the large guns, knotting and splicing, leadership and tactics. After 12 months, in 1757, Hunter's proficiency in these skills was sufficient for him to be recommended to Admiral Knowles who took him, then aged 20, as a midshipman into the *Neptune*, a new second rate of 90 guns and 700 men. Who recommended Hunter is not revealed, but logically it would have been Captain Brown of the *Centaur*, who could well have known the captain of the *Neptune*. Favouritism and patronage extended through all levels of the Royal Navy in the middle of the 18th century.

In its broadest, political and social sense, 18th-century patronage could be depicted as 'the system of personal selection from amongst one's kinsmen and connections and was the instrument by which prosperity and rank influenced recruitment to those positions in society which were not determined by property alone.'[5] Political patronage controlled appointments to court and government office, sinecures and pensions, contracts and agencies, bishoprics and excise posts. While government patronage controlled the more lucrative appointments, private patronage controlled the more numerous: salaried county, borough and parish offices, merchants' and lawyers' clerks, estate agents, chaplains, secretaries, tutors and governesses and domestic service. All required the influence of friends, who could range from nearest relations, members of the wider family or household, tenants and villagers to political associates and supporters and those for whom it was useful to recognise special merit. The system was endemic vertically and horizontally across the social spectrum in 18th-century Britain.

Unlike the army, where commissions could simply be purchased and sold without qualification, the Royal Navy (mostly) required a minimum of six years of service before commissioning as a lieutenant, as there were a range of skills required to manage a ship and maintain order and discipline. Interest, or lack of it, could hasten or retard promotions. However, the system was flexible enough to allow talent to shine through and be recognised. Horatio Nelson is a case in point. Interest initially assisted him when his uncle, Captain Maurice Suckling, agreed to take him as a midshipman in 1770, aged 12; while on his mother's side he was distantly related to the Walpole family. He was commissioned seven years later, promoted to first lieutenant the following year (1778), appointed commander later the same year and promoted to captain in 1779, aged just 20 years, after nine years' service.[6] While Nelson's promotions had a strong element of merit within them, interest also played its role. For his part, Nelson was not beyond indulging in some patronage dispensation of his own. Nelson obtained a lieutenancy for his stepson, Josiah Nisbet, when he was under 17. Nisbet was made a commander at 17 and a post captain at 18.[7] Prior to the attack at Santa Cruz on the island of Teneriffe in 1797, at which he lost his arm, the 38-year-old Nelson wrote to his Commander-in-Chief commending Josiah, then a lieutenant, and commenting 'The Duke of Clarence … will, I am confident, take a lively interest for my stepson on his name being mentioned.'[8]

In his book *A Social History of the Navy*, Michael Lewis identified four sources from which naval interest was exercised or wielded.[9]

(i) Captains arranged for the admission of young gentlemen into the service and could rate them midshipman, master's mate or appoint them pro tem as acting lieutenant within their ship. The granting of a commission as lieutenant was beyond their power, but they could recommend them for a commission to the Admiral under whom both were serving.

(ii) The Admiral in command of the region could confirm (or deny) the local appointment of acting lieutenant and could support other captains' recommendations for commissions—unless he had his own candidates whom he would support ahead of the others. An extreme example is that of Admiral Rodney, who during 1780 advanced his son between the ages of 15 and 16 through the ranks from midshipman to captain.[10] Admirals could also gather into their flagships those officers whose promotion they desired to procure. As Hunter was to discover on the *Victory*, once he was a senior lieutenant on a flagship, promotion or command was not far away.

(iii) The Admiralty was the most authoritative repository of patronage, but the Board of Admiralty had two points of weakness; firstly, it was remote from the Admiral who had made the appointments and delays worked in the Admiral's favour, so that Admiralty endorsements sometimes were simply ratifying the status quo where time and events had overtaken the endorsement. Secondly, internal rivalry or politics within the Board, especially if between the Naval Sea Lord and his political master, or Minister, now called the First Lord of the Admiralty, could weaken the resolve of the Board. Much depended upon the character of the individuals. However, the First Lord of the Admiralty generally kept a tight rein on patronage as he also had political considerations to take into account. (Hunter was later inadvertently caught up in such a conflict between his patron Lord Howe, the First Sea Lord and Lord Sandwich, the First Lord of the Admiralty, which delayed Hunter's commission).

(iv) There were other peripheral sources of interest that could apply pressure on the navy when circumstances dictated. These included members of Parliament, retired Admirals and other influential persons.

The prevalence of patronage was inextricably woven into the fabric of the Royal Navy, as with the rest of contemporary society then, but whilst it may have favoured some over others, there were sufficient safeguards to prevent unfit or inept officers from being promoted into positions of critical importance. Inadequate lieutenants were simply not promoted to captain or were given shore-based positions. Incompetent captains might not be allocated a ship. Many officers of ability, but without much interest, usually rose to their level of competence, but at least the navy had many aspirants eager to prove themselves, and so there were many appropriate candidates for all appointments. Hunter's lack of a patron, despite his undoubted abilities, inhibited his chances for advancement for two decades.

During 1757, the French entertained ideas of invading England, spurring Prime Minister William Pitt the Elder to strike first. A large squadron under Admiral Hawke was assigned to neutralise Rochefort, a naval base on the west coast of France, and as part of the operation the *Neptune* and six other vessels were ordered to secure the batteries on the island of Aix near the mouth of the River Charante. This was successfully completed on 23 September 1757, notwithstanding that the larger-scale campaign ended inconclusively. It can be reasonably assumed that Hunter saw some action at this time, whether actively involved on shore, or from the *Neptune*. Either way, he could have been present (perhaps passively) at discussions on how to implement the plan as well as during the post-mortems on the outcome. As there was no reference to any on-shore activities, he was more likely to have been a spectator than a participant. Whichever was the case, it would have broadened his experience.

Hunter remained on the *Neptune* for the next three years and in February 1760, aged 22, passed his examination at the Navy Office for lieutenant, but was without prospects. The fact that he passed his exams on the first attempt is a demonstration of Hunter's scholastic abilities and his aptitude for mathematics, physics, navigation and seamanship. Navy midshipmen sometimes required several attempts before passing these exams while a few never succeeded and remained 'in the midshipman's cockpit' until they left the service. According to the memoir, Hunter continued to develop his seamanship skills, but was not

> from his want of interest, deterred from perseverance; he had now acquired as great a share of professional knowledge as was to be found in the generality of young men at this time of life, and trusted, that by a diligent attention to the improvement of the share he now possessed, and to the increase of it on all the different duties of the profession, he might hope in time to raise some friend sufficiently powerful to serve him. Mr Hunter now assiduously applied to the study of everything which appeared to be connected with the duties of a sea officer, and soon made himself master of the theory of maritime surveying, and of practical astronomy as connected with navigation. Mr Hunter also by dint of diligent application became tolerably expert in drawing views, either on the land or the water; in short, he attained that degree of professional skill, which joined to a steady and unremitting attention to duty, obtained at length the great object of his hopes.[11]

It is hard to escape the conclusion that, in one way or another, Hunter himself had a considerable input into the writing of this passage, since who else would have had the detailed insight into Hunter's motivation? However, the extract does convey the impression that Hunter had done everything in his power to properly position himself for any promotion to lieutenant that may have presented itself; but without the propelling clout of someone with influence to lift him over the barrier to a commission, his prospects were slim. There is a hint of frustration in the words of the memoir but the frustration may not have been fully justified. He joined the navy in 1754 aged nearly 17, became a midshipman two years later and passed his exams aged 23, having the required six years of sea-time. While he might have been slightly older than many of his contemporaries, advancement came slowly.

In 1760, Hunter spent short periods as a midshipman on the *Royal Anne* (a first rate of 100 guns) and the *Princess Amelia* (80 guns), after which he served on the *Royal George* for the final three years, 1760–63, of the Seven Years' War. Once the war ended, the navy reduced its force from 70,000 to 16,000, and so career opportunities diminished accordingly, even for those with connections. For someone like Hunter, now aged 26 and without a patron, openings were virtually non-existent. On the other hand, the early years of his naval career had not been without merit. This experience probably enabled him to secure a midshipman's position on HMS *Tweed*, a fifth rate (or large frigate) of 661 tons and 32 guns, commanded by Captain Hon T. Percival. Who recommended him is not known.

Hunter's proficiency must have been quickly recognised, for soon after joining the *Tweed*, he was appointed the sailing master's mate or assistant. With commission prospects remote at best, Hunter decided that the next best course of action was to accept the offer to become a warrant officer, a position of responsibility in the ship, but a technical rather than a tactical role. Warrant officers were so-named because they (the sailing master and his mate) were appointed under a formal warrant issued by the Navy Board. Other warrant officers were the purser and the surgeon. The warrant officers messed in the wardroom with the commissioned officers and their place was on the quarterdeck, although their cabins were away from the other officers. Their position was perceived as being officers but not quite gentlemen.

The sailing master was in charge of the navigation and pilotage of the ship, as ordered by the captain; he was the best-paid man after the captain, while the standard of accommodation was similar to that of the first lieutenant. He was also responsible for calculating the ship's position and taking noon sightings, supervision of the midshipmen, stowing the hold (as this had a major effect on the ship's sailing qualities) and the condition of the sails, rigging and anchors. Another important function was to maintain the ship's log. The sailing master was assisted by master's mates. It was a consolation prize for the technically competent without influence or connection, 'gentle birth' or social influence. Alan Villiers described a good master as possessing seamanship skills and experience in

> good course-keeping, judgement of leeway (or drift), accurate estimation of speed under sail—for there were no adequate instruments to measure or record it and, the wind being fickle, the sailing ships forward speed varied infinitely—and the assured ability to appraise the performance of his ship in any conditions.[12]

Both Cook and Bligh were masters before their eventual commissioning; in fact Bligh was the master of the *Resolution* on Cook's third voyage 1777–80. While there was never any certainty of gaining a promotion to lieutenant, the master's mate at least gained some respectability along the way, which would be preferable to languishing as a midshipman indefinitely. The position would be likened to a sub-lieutenant in today's naval equivalence. The pay was better too—a master's mate received £2 2s a month, compared to a midshipman's £1 10s, while a master earned £4 a month (more than a lieutenant). The captain of a sixth rate received £8 8s per month.[13]

Cook was a master on the *Pembroke* during the siege of Quebec while, at the same time, Hunter served as master's mate on the *Tweed* and then the *Launceston,* a 25-year-old fifth rate of 44 guns. Considering their similar interests, duties and map-making roles, it is feasible that they may have met at Halifax in the mid-1760s, although there is no record of this taking place. Hunter was confirmed as master in 1768, and as such was entitled to his own cabin and moved from the midshipmen's cockpit to the wardroom with the other officers. The six years Hunter spent as master's mate and master in North American waters undoubtedly advanced his technical skills, but with his duties embracing the direct running of the ship, his involvement in broader tactical matters was still slight. His navigating capabilities were again acknowledged when, in 1769, he sat for and passed the examination at Trinity House (then at Deptford) for navigating officers, where 'he gave so much satisfaction to the examiners, they gave him a qualification for a fourth rate at once.'[14] A fourth rate was the smallest ship in the line of battle, but Hunter was soon afterwards appointed master of the frigate *Carysfort*, Captain William Hay, a sixth rate of 28 guns and 586 tons, which in 1769 proceeded to Jamaica. Frigates were described by Steven Pope as being 'smaller and faster than ships of the line. They generally mounted between 28 and 44 guns on two decks and weighed anything from 500-850 tons and carried 200–300 men'. *Carysfort* was therefore at the smaller end of the scale and there is a black and white print of the *Carysfort* in the Maritime Museum at Greenwich.[15] Pope continued:

> Originally developed as the 'eyes' of a battle fleet on manoeuvres, they could also operate as 'cruisers', patrolling trade routes, watching blockaded harbours or functioning as long-range commercial raiders … they were the most consistently useful warships afloat and the Royal Navy could never get enough of them.[16]

Hunter's draughtsmanship competence was successfully tested in two incidents while serving on the *Carysfort* from 1770 to 1772. The ship sailed from Jamaica to Pensacola in Florida in 1771 (a territory ceded to Britain after the Seven Years' War) where, for three months Hunter worked to make himself thoroughly familiar with the little known harbour and prepared detailed charts for the use of future pilots. His sketching abilities were again in demand when the *Carysfort* arrived at Havana, but the ship's company was not permitted by the Spaniards to land. The Spanish at the time were carrying on some major defensive works on high ground overlooking the city:

a circumstance of such consequence did not escape the inquiring mind of Mr Hunter [and perhaps the captain as well?]; from the mast head, dressed as a common seaman, he made drawings of every thing to be seen from that station, which drawings he afterwards presented to Sir H. Palliser, then Comptroller of the Navy, who during his life-time duly appreciated Mr Hunter's talents.[17]

He was obviously a sketcher of some skill and aptitude, combining a mixture of discriminating observation and clear recording. The sketches may have been sent to Palliser to stimulate his interest and appreciation, but to little avail, as Palliser was never acknowledged as a patron or advocate for Hunter and there is no evidence of any translation of support for Hunter into anything tangible or of any consequence to him. It is likely that Palliser did indeed appreciate Hunter's charting expertise, but this was as far as Palliser went in this regard. Alternatively, Palliser may have subscribed to the view that Hunter's best value to the navy was as a master, rather than as yet another lieutenant.

Hunter's competence as a practical seaman was severely tested on 23 October, 1770, under extreme pressure and hazardous circumstances.

> The *Carysfort* having a pilot from Jamaica for the Gulf of Florida on board, the ship was on her way through the Gulf; and, owing to the perverseness, obstinacy, and ignorance of this pilot, run ashore in the night upon the Martyr Reefs in that passage, where her situation was such as promised little chance of being able to save the ship, and on its first appearance not much hope of preserving the lives of the crew; here all the exertion which could be made by every experienced seaman in the ship became necessary; and on this, as on every occasion where personal efforts or professional skill could aid the public service, we find Mr Hunter very conspicuous; for nine days and nights Captain Hay was not in a bed, nor Mr Hunter off the deck; the masts were cut away, an

anchor was carried out astern, and in letting it go, the night being extremely dark, Mr Hunter's leg was caught in the bite of the cable, and brought the anchor up, but the bone was not broke and he was still able to walk; in cutting the main-mast away, his right hand was lamed in such a manner as to deprive him of its use for some time; but these misfortunes did not relax his ardour for the preservation of His Majesty's ship, a circumstance which, we believe, his Commander, who is still alive, will readily acknowledge. [Hay was, by 1801, a retired rear admiral]. The ninth day after this accident the ship was got out from amongst those dangerous reefs, through a very difficult and intricate passage, which Mr Hunter had buoyed, and was carried to sea under jury-masts, with the loss of her guns, &c.; they were no sooner out of this danger than Mr Hunter's great exertions occasioned the rupture of a blood vessel in his lungs, which discharged so great a quantity of blood as to induce the Surgeon to think he could not live more than two days; being, however, naturally of a good constitution, he surmounted all these misfortunes.[18]

Hunter was 34 at this time.

This account invites some analysis and commentary. The facts of the incident as recorded in the memoir are confirmed by Captain Hay's evidence to the subsequent court martial of the pilot[19] and by Hunter's entry into the log of the *Carysfort* as its master for Monday 22 October 1770[20], but some perspective needs to be introduced. While the captain's and the master's contributions are acknowledged, where were the first lieutenant, the other officers, boatswain, carpenter and crew? As the captain was on deck the whole time, it was he that would have been deciding strategies and giving orders, not the master. Captain Hay would have been directing the overall operation, while Hunter would have been ensuring that the captain's orders were carried out and the handling of the ship and the rigging of the jury masts were properly attended to. It would have been the captain's decision to cut the masts away and to throw the guns overboard, but he could well have been relying on the input of his master (and lieutenants) as events unfolded. There is an inference in the memoir that it was the captain and the master who saved the day. This is not to deny Hunter's aptitude and fortitude, but needs to be put into context vis-a-vis the long and arduous hours put in by other officers and the crew.

Marine pilots, by definition, are presumed to possess an intricate knowledge of the area in which they operate, and should be the last people to have their ship run aground in their region of expertise. Was the accident a result of negligence or outside the pilot's control? What did the charts show? At least when the ship ran aground at 11.30pm the weather was calm, although the winds were of sufficient strength to necessitate the cutting down of the masts to prevent the ship from being further stranded on the reef. Hunter's navigating and charting experience came to the fore when he spent the next week sounding a passage and marking it with buoys for the embattled ship to weave its way through the reef to open water.[21]

At the court martial held on the *Dunkirk* at Port Royal, Jamaica on 18 September 1771, the pilot William Sanderson, was charged with nearly losing the *Carysfort* through his ignorance and obstinacy, his lack of knowledge of the area and his resistance to take soundings, though Captain Hay had urged him to do so. The evidence pointed to both Hunter and Hay being uneasy over the pilot's performance, with Hunter climbing to the masthead to seek a reference to mark the ship's actual position, following the pilot's claim that land could be seen. Hunter saw none. The pilot pleaded that the currents were strong and uncertain at that time and that ten ships had struck the reef over the previous nine weeks—which begs the question, why tempt fate in the face of such uncertainties and not take a safer but longer alternative route? The court martial found that although the charges were partially proven, in view of the contribution of the prevailing currents and the pilot's previous good character[22], he was only dismissed from the navy as a pilot. This was the first of three courts martial Hunter attended during his career, but he was only a witness at this one.

Following the *Carysfort*'s return to England in December 1771, Hunter spent the next three years on the *Intrepid* (a 64 gun third rate, built in the previous year and much larger than his previous ship) in the East Indies, but predominantly in the Indian Ocean, operating from Fort St George at Madras. This quick turnaround between ships was in itself an achievement for Hunter and is perhaps a reflection of his growing reputation as a competent sailor. He appears to have spent little time ashore between assignments, whereas other officers, commissioned and warranted, might have had to wait for some considerable time (months or even years in quiet times) languishing on half pay awaiting their next ship, but at least spending time with their wives and families. Because Hunter was not married, he was under no obligation to spend extended periods ashore and could well have devoted his shore time to actively promoting his availability for another posting.

Hunter's term on the *Intrepid* provided him with an opportunity of extending his knowledge of practical astronomy, and he became a useful assistant to his captain, who taught him how to determine longitude from lunar sights. It would also have been a useful introduction into the astronomy of the southern hemisphere. In addition, during his leisure time, he made himself thoroughly acquainted with the details of every port or anchorage he visited. When Hunter returned home in 1775 he had consolidated an excellent technical reputation, which facilitated his appointment as master of HMS *Foudroyant* in 1775 at the request of Captain Jervis (later Earl St Vincent), who was aware of Hunter's record and capabilities. The *Foudroyant* was a large, two decked, second rate of 80 guns, captured from the French in 1758. Jervis was a strict disciplinarian who demanded nothing less than total efficiency in the operation of his ship. His harsh and unrelenting manner would have made life difficult for those under him, so requesting Hunter can be regarded as a compliment to Hunter's professionalism and an acknowledgement that he could work successfully under this difficult, but successful and well-connected captain. At last he was being noticed and in the following year, at the instigation of someone unknown, he was appointed by Vice Admiral Richard Howe as master of Howe's two-year-old flagship HMS *Eagle,* a third rate of 64 guns, to lead the British fleet against the American colonies revolting against British rule.

Lord Howe was a distinguished naval commander and tactician. Born in 1726, he went to sea aged 14 and served with distinction in the Seven Years' War (1756–63), capturing two French ships. He was also politically inclined and entered Parliament as the member for Dartmouth in 1757. He was Lord Commissioner of the Admiralty from 1763 to 1765 and then served as Treasurer of the Navy until 1770, when he was promoted to Rear Admiral of the Blue. He returned to North America in 1776 as commander-in-chief, resigning three years later over differences with the government in the conduct of the war. He won more fame by his relief of Gibraltar in 1782 and, following a change in government, was back in favour as First Lord of the Admiralty from 1783 to 1788. Lord Howe Island is named after him. His naval policies were austere and doggedly impartial, which resulted in strained relations with cabinet colleagues, as did his handling of patronage, which he complained

> was not so desirable as might be imagined. Whenever a vacancy in the appointments in his nomination happened, there were always twenty candidates for it, at leaSt He was therefore sure to disaffect nineteen, and was not always certain of pleasing the twentieth.[23]

Howe's two greatest naval achievements were his victory of 'the Glorious First of June' in 1794, at which Hunter was present and his successful negotiations in resolving the Nore Mutiny at Spithead in

1797. He became a major influence on Hunter's career until his death in 1799 and was generally respected as a sailor amongst his naval colleagues and popular with the lower deck ranks. Forty years after his death, Sir John Barrow wrote 'His Lordship was universally esteemed by the officers under his command in North America, as the first man in his profession' and quoted a colleague of Howe's, Captain Raynor of the *Isis*, 'He is in my opinion, the first sea officer in the world, and so says every person here.'[24] Howe recognised seamanship qualities and supported Hunter accordingly.

Hunter believed he owed his appointment to the *Eagle* by Lord Howe to the influence of Captain Jervis but Jervis claimed to know nothing of the matter until advised by Hunter. However, Jervis did inform Howe of his support for the move. While Jervis may have been the logical unknown benefactor, it is difficult to identify that person if it was not Jervis. Perhaps it was his *Carysfort* captain, William Hay, Hugh Palliser or the captain of the *Intrepid*, James Cranston who 'mentioned to his lordship (Lord Howe) that he considered Mr Hunter as the most fit and proper person he knows to accompany him as Master of the *Eagle*.'[25] Whoever it was, it meant that Hunter now began to acquire some degree of patronage (to complement his track record) and his service in North America (like Cook during the Seven Years' War in Canada) enhanced his reputation. As master of Howe's flagship, Hunter acted virtually as master of the fleet, more especially in the expeditions to the Delaware and Chesapeake, and in the defence of Sandy Hook.

In the four years he spent in American waters, 1776–79, Hunter was involved in a number of actions, mainly in surveying channels and rivers, and sometimes under fire. On one occasion

> Mr Hunter was employed in examining a channel through which the Americans had never ventured any thing but pilot boats; to this passage there was a bar; Mr Hunter's skill, however, triumphed over all obstacles; and although this

> perilous and difficult enterprize was executed within musket shot of the enemy's centinels, who continually annoyed them, he succeeded in buoying the channel, carried the ship through, and on the day of the attack of this island, she was laid within half a cable's length [one hundred metres] of the fort, and enfiladed the whole line of guns.[26]

The American forces abandoned the position that night, with a loss of 400 men compared to British casualties of 42. During the engagement, Hunter received a severe contusion or bruise on his shoulder, that incapacitated him for some time. *The Chronicle* further relates that Hunter was then employed

> in sounding and examining for a passage through the Cheveaux de Frise, which had been sunk to obstruct the navigation of the river; he succeeded, and buoyed it in so able a manner, that Captain Hammond [who later became Comptroller of the Navy and another useful ally] in the Roebuck, and seventy sail of transports, went through and up to Philadelphia in one flood tide.[27]

In a significant commentary on Hunter's abilities and prospects, the memoir went on to say that

> the services which Mr Hunter performed in the fleet on the American station so firmly fixed him in the good opinion of Lord Howe, that he always, until the death of that great and good man, enjoyed the honour of his friendship and patronage.[28]

At long last Hunter had found his patron, however, Howe's influence on Hunter's behalf was only of use while Howe himself was influential, which was not always the case. Hunter's exertions in North America were undoubtedly of a high order, notwithstanding the almost adulatory tone of the memoir:

> The variety of duties he had to attend, were executed in a manner so creditable to his zeal and abilities, that they were highly approved, not only by the Admiral and his Captain, but

his merit was acknowledged by all the officers in the fleet employed on that difficult and fatiguing service.[29]

Hunter's service in North America was undoubtedly creditable, and although the memoir is one-sided, it does provide sufficient evidence to conclude that he was exemplary in his duties and conduct, and good enough to create a positive impression upon those who mattered. It would seem that Hunter was not an extrovert by nature or one to normally sing his own praises and it was by steady application to his tasks that he set himself above his peers and gained the notice of his captains and others. Whether 'his merit was acknowledged by all the officers in the fleet' is a moot point since there would have been those jealous of his successes as well as others whom he impressed, especially as he was essentially friendly and convivial with his peers. Twenty years at sea in the confines of the ships of those days would generally filter out those who could not relate with their equals and superiors.

When the *Eagle* returned to Portsmouth in October 1779, Howe retired from the navy because he was severely out of favour with the First Sea Lord, Lord Sandwich, and the Prime Minister, Lord North, following his unrelenting criticism of the manner in which the navy had been poorly managed and under-funded. Hunter applied to be commissioned a lieutenant and produced a detailed certificate of support from Lord Howe, outlining his achievements and the exemplary fashion in which he had discharged his duties, which concluded that 'from his [Howe's] knowledge and experience in all the branches of his profession, he is justly entitled to the character of a distinguished officer.'[30] His application was denied, probably because of the adverse reputation of Howe at that time. Several captains then applied to have him made a lieutenant into their respective ships, but without success. These subsequent applications were probably refused because of Hunter's 'guilt by association' with the out-of-favour Howe, or perhaps because his technical competence as a master made him a more valuable asset than being yet another lieutenant. He now had a patron (albeit temporarily *persona non grata*) and a number of supporters, but it could be concluded Hunter had the wrong patron at the wrong time.

To Howe's credit, he wrote to Captain Roger Curtis on 13 December 1779 indicating his displeasure at the refusal.

> The treatment Hunter has met with, indicates a degree of folly equal to the injustice shown to his pretensions and all my friends have the comfort of knowing that it is not through their demerits that their title to consideration is unregarded.[31]

In other words, there was nothing lacking in the application or its supporters, but rather the fault lay with the adjudicators—hardly an approach likely to mend the tear between Howe and the Admiralty.

Patronage or interest was exercised by both the First Lord of the Admiralty or the admirals under him and the First Sea Lord, with the latter having the upper hand through his political connections with the government of the day. Lord Sandwich was First Sea Lord under Prime Minister North from 1771 to 1782 when he was swept out of office with Lord North. While he was pleasant and industrious, good humoured and popular, Sandwich was also reputed to wield his power of patronage in an unabashed manner. Howe not only clashed with Sandwich over naval issues such as the quality of wood used in ship construction and repairs, but from 1775 he also nursed a grievance against Sandwich for having obtained for Hugh Palliser, a junior officer, the sinecure post of Lieutenant-General of Marines which he coveted himself. Later when Howe was offered the position of Commander-in-Chief of the Channel Fleet, his terms for acceptance were politically impossible to meet, which only served to widen the gap between the two men. This antagonism would have worked against any promotion proposals endorsed by Howe, including Hunter's. It was only when Sandwich resigned in 1782 that Howe (and his influence) came back into favour.

For his part, now aged 42 and still not commissioned, Hunter's career seemed to have stalled. He was invited by the Hon Keith Stuart (who only knew him by reputation) to sail as a volunteer on the *Berwick*, a 74-gun third rate. (This ship is not to be confused with the other *Berwick*, a Baltic trader of 511 tons built in 1781 and purchased by the navy as a 22-gun armed storeship and re-named *Sirius* in 1786 to lead the First Fleet. Coincidentally, during the refit at Deptford, the *Sirius* was moored alongside the *Carysfort*). Although not keen on remaining a warrant officer for the rest of his career, Hunter accepted Stuart's invitation. His talents were quickly recognised during the ensuing Channel duty resulting in his appointment as sixth lieutenant on the *Union*, a second rate of 90 guns, by Admiral Sir Charles Hardy, then Commander-in-Chief of the Channel Fleet. Hunter's commander, Captain John Dalrymple, then wrote to the Admiralty requesting confirmation of the promotion, but when the fleet returned to Spithead, all appointments made by Hardy were confirmed, except Hunter's. The memoir states: 'This circumstance appeared so marked that it was supposed to have proceeded from some misunderstanding between the First Lord and Mr Hunter's patron.'[32] This was perhaps a tactful explanation, even a diplomatic one, concealing the real reason behind the refusal, with Hunter being the innocent victim of Howe's antagonism and Sandwich's malice. It was a case of so near and yet so far and Hunter was entitled to experience some bitterness over his misfortune to be caught up in a dispute of this dimension, which was quite outside his control. Hunter's competence at sea, his achievements, his reputation and his supporters all cried out for an overdue promotion, and there were influential people who thought him thoroughly deserving of a commission, but they were outclassed, outgunned and outranked by others even more powerful. Fate had held him back yet again, but Hunter's long sought-after goal was soon to become a reality.

Stuart sympathised with Hunter over his predicament and invited him to sail once more in the *Berwick*, again as a volunteer. He spent 1780 in the West Indies as part of a squadron commanded by Commodore The Hon Boyle Walsingham. A further testimonial to his professionalism is found in the memoir that once more suggests Hunter's hand either guiding or holding the quill.

> It may not be improper here to mention, that such was the opinion Commodore Walsingham had of Mr Hunter's judgement, that whilst he lay windbound in Torbay, (en route to Jamaica) Mr Smeaton, the Civil Engineer, was sent by the Admiralty to fix on a place for erecting the means of watering a fleet here with expedition, and the Commodore was instructed to furnish him with an officer capable of affording Mr Smeaton the necessary information relative to what part of this bay was the most proper for this purpose. The Commodore immediately ordered Mr Hunter on this duty; and Mr Smeaton, when he had finished his plan, thanked the Commodore for the able assistant he had given him on that service.[33]

It is not clear whether Hunter was chosen because of his hydrography and charting expertise, or perhaps because Hunter knew the area through previous visits there, as Torbay was the only convenient shelter on that part of the coast from adverse Channel weather, or a combination of both reasons. The memorial here displays an element of straw clutching by Hunter to present himself favourably, as there is no indication that exceptional knowledge or skills were required by the engineer. This is not to deny Hunter's competence, but rather the possibility that the task was not as complicated or intricate as the narrative may indicate.

Nevertheless, fortunes were about to change for John Hunter.

4
Commissioned without command

In July 1780, at the age of 43, Hunter received a lieutenant's commission for the *Berwick* from Admiral Sir George Rodney, commander-in-chief of the West Indies Fleet. It was a case of third-time lucky for Hunter, for on this occasion the commission was duly confirmed, but it must have been an anxious wait. This important step, aspired to for 20 years, meant that he now had a permanent naval career, as it involved the security of half pay for life at the very least. There was probably a pay drop as a result (masters' salaries were generally above lieutenants) but his accommodation moved to the commissioned officers' section and his duties changed to standing watch duties and assuming responsibility for all or part of the crew on a shift basis. Lieutenants commanded a division of the ship's guns and would be expected to command a ship's boat in shore raids and boarding parties and prize crews.

It is most likely that his friend Captain Stuart of the *Berwick*, recognising his talents and vexed by the denial of Hunter's second attempt for promotion, put up the recommendation to Commodore Walsingham who endorsed it and forwarded it to Admiral Rodney for ratification. The timing for Hunter was fortuitous in one sense, as Walsingham died in the great hurricane of October 1780 (a bare three months later) which swept through Jamaica, Barbados and St Lucia destroying 13 British naval ships and severely damaging many others, including the *Berwick*. Had Walsingham lived, he would quite probably have become another patron of Hunter, while Admiral

Rodney was becoming regarded as something of a naval hero in Britain at a time when Lord North's influence as Prime Minister was weakening. Lord North was described as 'a Tory gentleman of ability and charm, unfailingly humorous and unswervingly faithful to the King.'[1] He was Prime Minister from 1770 for 12 years. However, the failure of the British Government to put down the American Revolution, with consequent dissatisfaction around the country and in Parliament, obliged George III to seek North's resignation in March 1782, paving the way for the emergence of William Pitt the Younger in the following year with a resurgent Tory Party and the renaissance of Hunter's patron, Lord Howe.

The previous two decades had seen Hunter almost continuously at sea, in the Channel, the West Indies, the Indian Ocean and the North Atlantic. He had seen some action and had broadened and honed his seafaring and hydrographical skills, but had never been required to exercise strategic judgement and had always been subordinate to commissioned officers. He could be described as being, by 1780 aged 43, a seaman's seaman. By contrast, Arthur Phillip, a year younger than Hunter, was commissioned in 1761 when aged 23. (Phillip Gidley King was 20 when he was made lieutenant in 1778; he was 20 years younger than Hunter. While Cook was not commissioned until 1768 when he was 40, having started late as an able seaman and rising via the masters' route, his commission was ratified at the first attempt, partly owing to his competence but also due to patronage.) The point here is that Phillip had been a commissioned officer for nearly 20 years when Hunter received his promotion, thus giving him two decades of handling quarterdeck and command issues, an experience he put to good use as Governor of New South Wales. The contrast between the experienced leader and the inexperienced successor becomes even clearer when comparisons are made of their terms of office—Hunter was probably the better seaman, Phillip was undoubtedly the better leader. Importantly, the act of commissioning did not automatically bestow the mantle of leader upon the shoulders of a new lieutenant, but it did enable him to acquire and display his leadership talents, which can take some years to reach full potential.

Phillip was made post captain in 1781 aged 43 (although he had been a captain in the Portuguese Navy from 1774 to 1778) and became governor in 1788 aged 50. Hunter became post captain in 1786 aged 49 and was 58 when he became governor in 1795, while King (who was Phillip's preferred nominee to succeed him) was made post captain in 1798 aged 40 and became governor in 1800 when he was 42. Hunter's lack of senior command experience becomes even more apparent when compared to his predecessor and successor.

Hunter had another three years of almost non-stop sea time before Lord Howe appointed him post captain and second captain of the *Sirius* under Phillip in 1786. The new government came into power in 1782, and Lord Howe was recalled on 2 April of that year and appointed Commander-in-Chief of the Channel Fleet. Hunter's prospects immediately rose when Howe raised his flag on HMS *Victory* on 20 April 1782 and appointed him as third lieutenant, which placed him in charge of signals. A typical entry in his *Victory* log read: 'Moderate and fair weather. Bent the mainsail and made the signal to prepare for sailing. Made many signals for the lieutenants.'[2] This famous ship, a first rate of 100 guns, had been launched in 1765 and weighed 2164 tons, which made her one of the largest British ships afloat at the time. Even today, to inspect the *Victory* at Portsmouth is to marvel at her size for a wooden ship, which was essentially a floating three-decked gun platform. Although she had been modified during her career, she was 40-years old at the battle of Trafalgar and is still technically commissioned today.

Figure 11. HMS *Victory*. In dry dock at Portsmouth—still technically commissioned. Photograph courtesy of the author.

Hunter's rise from sixth to first lieutenant was mercurial, for his term as third lieutenant lasted only from 20 April to 19 June; and as second lieutenant to 25 August, at which time he was appointed first lieutenant. All of these promotions were confirmed by his immediate commanding officer on the *Victory*, Henry Duncan on 2 December 1782. As a result, these rapid rises reflected a speedy turnover of officers on the flagship, mainly through appointments to other vessels, and saw the emergence of Lieutenant Henry Ball, who featured in the early years of New South Wales with Hunter, as commander of the *Supply*. His promotions on the *Victory* were equally as swift as Hunter's but a few levels below him, and with Hunter, would have seen action in the North Sea, the Channel and the relief of Gibraltar during the remainder of 1782.

As first lieutenant, Hunter occupied a unique position. Not only was he fundamentally responsible for the discipline and good order of the ship, he was second-in-command under the captain and the only person legitimately empowered to replace the captain upon the latter's demise or incapacitation at sea. The position of first lieutenant on the *Victory* under Lord Howe was not only a prestigious one, but also signalled that full command was probably not far away. For Hunter, it came soon enough. He was promoted to commander by Howe with seniority dating back to 12 November 1782 and given command of a fireship, the *Spitfire,* of 16 guns and carrying a crew of around 50. This position was short-lived, as before Howe became First Lord of the Admiralty in January 1783, he gave Hunter command of a sloop, the *Marquis de Seignelay,* 14 guns and 232 tons; a small ship but still a true ship of war. The intermediate rank between lieutenant and captain, now called lieutenant-commander, was then known as 'master and commander' until the early 19th century, and then simply as 'commander'. Pope relates that 'in practice, commanders were usually addressed as captain and they were captains in terms of responsibilities and work load.'[3] Their salary was around £200 per year, or £4 per week, and their uniform was different to that of a lieutenant in that they wore an epaulette on the left shoulder; a captain under three years wore one on his right shoulder while a captain over three years wore both.

The Treaty of Versailles, signed on 3 September 1783, ended not only the war with France but also any chance Hunter had of immediate further advancement. There were no sailing opportunities for the next three years until Howe appointed him post captain on 15 December 1786 to serve as second captain under Phillip on the *Sirius* for the voyage to New South Wales in the following year. After 32 years' service Hunter was finally a post captain at the rather advanced age of 49 years. Why would Howe have appointed Hunter to this position? It can only be presumed that Howe believed Hunter deserved and was ready for the promotion to post captain and the expedition to New South Wales would be an appropriate assignment, as his hydrographical skills would be useful for map-making, he had the experience to command the *Sirius* in Phillip's absence, he was unmarried so was freely available for long assignments (Phillip was technically married at the time but separated) as well as possessing the temperament to work with and under Phillip, who was appointed commodore for the voyage. A commodore was a temporary appointment over other captains in a squadron (in this case the First Fleet) who hoisted a broad pennant to signify he was the local commander-in-chief.

More is known of Hunter's seafaring career between 1787 and 1793 because of the information contained in his journal (published in 1793) together with the journals and diaries of others with him during this period, covering the voyages in the *Sirius* and the return journey on the *Waaksamheyd*. While most of these sources cover routine descriptions and narratives of events and proceedings, there are a number of instances when Hunter's seamanship is either alluded to or revealed. For instance, while Hunter could be relied upon to be respectful to his commanding officer, there are two instances when, by reading between the lines of his journal, differences of approach on seamanship issues emerge between Phillip and Hunter.

After the First Fleet left Table Bay on 13 November 1787 on its final long leg to New South Wales, Phillip resolved to split the 11 ships into an advance group, comprising three of the faster transports plus the brig *Supply*, to proceed ahead with some artisans and supplies to prepare for the arrival of the convicts in the remaining seven slower ships, commanded by Hunter in the *Sirius*. Phillip expected to arrive at Botany Bay two to three weeks ahead of the rest to clear land for the settlement and erect store sheds. Hunter believed Phillip had been sailing too far north to best utilize the prevailing westerly winds which blow across the lower third of the Indian Ocean, so once Phillip's ships had disappeared over the horizon, Hunter steered south to catch the Roaring Forties. By steering south then east, he maximised the advantages of these strong and steady winds to the extent that when they arrived at Botany Bay on 20 January 1788, 'the *Supply* had not gained more than 40 hours of us, and the three transports twenty.'[4] In other words, Hunter's keener appreciation of the winds allowed his slower ships to sail almost as fast as Phillip's advance component, so that the whole fleet of 11 ships arrived within a period of two days instead of two weeks as planned. Hunter's technical competence in this instance stood out, aided by his knowledge of the Indian Ocean gained during his service on the *Intrepid* 13 years previously, but there is no record of Phillip's thoughts on this matter.

The second occasion occurred in September 1788 when Phillip, anticipating that the fledgling settlement's ability to feed itself was not going to be realised in the short term, ordered Hunter to Cape Town for additional emergency supplies. Hunter related in his journal that Phillip favoured the shorter westerly route back across the Indian Ocean, whereas Hunter believed it better to again utilize the Roaring Forties and proceed east below New Zealand and via Cape Horn. To his credit, Phillip left the final decision to Hunter, who noted

> I do not say that the passage from Van Diemen's Land to the Cape of Good Hope, by the westwood is impracticable, as that remains to be tried; but from my experience of the prevalence of strong westerly winds across that vast ocean, I am inclined to think it must be a long and tedious voyage.[5]

The other important, perhaps even critical factor was that if the *Sirius* was delayed by contrary winds, her own meagre food supplies would be compromised, forcing her to return to Sydney to replenish from the already precarious state of provisions there, before setting off again. Hunter therefore thought it better to head east and sail the longer but quicker route. This he did but even so it was a close call, as scurvy appeared in the latter stages of the voyage, claiming two lives just prior to arriving at Cape Town. Had he followed Phillip's preference, the outcome could have been disastrous for the *Sirius* and the colony.

By the 1780s, the cause and cure of scurvy were essentially understood by the Royal Navy, but it was slow to institutionalise the issuing of anti-scorbutics to naval ships and the extent of attention given to its containment was, at that time, left to individual captains. It was not until 1795 that the physician Sir Gilbert Blane finally persuaded the admiralty to issue a daily ration of lemon juice to all sailors, thereby virtually eliminating scurvy from Royal Navy ships. In 1808 the American Navy began issuing lemon juice on long voyages, but scurvy was still a problem during the Crimean War and the Irish potato famine of the 1840s. In the 18th century, scurvy was responsible for more deaths at sea than piracy, shipwreck, combat and all other illnesses combined. In his treatise on scurvy, Stephen Bown states that 'historians have conservatively estimated that over two million sailors perished from scurvy during the age of sail'[6] from Columbus to the steam engine. It was prevalent in the West Indies during Hunter's time there, despite the availability of fruit and vegetables, and would have been an issue while in the Indian Ocean on the *Intrepid*.

That Hunter was aware of the need and the methods to treat scurvy there is no doubt. As a compassionate person who had served before the mast and could therefore relate to seamen's needs, he indicated that he was aware of what was needed to combat scurvy but then revealed his frustration at not having anything on board to offer his crew.

> The ship's company now began to show much disposition to the scurvy, and what made it more distressing, we had nothing in the ship with which we could hope to check the progress of that destructive disease, except a little essence of malt that we continued to serve to the ship's company.[7]

However, William Bradley, the first lieutenant, recorded that this practice was stopped on 18 November 1788 as 'the quantity remaining was now not sufficient for those who were attack'd with the scurvy.'[8] Hunter's understanding of what was needed is again shown in his remarks on their diet since leaving the Cape on the outward voyage in 1787: 'During that time (about 13 or 14 months) they had not tasted a bit of fresh provisions of any kind, nor had they touched a single blade of vegetables.'[9]

Matters worsened as they approached Cape Town.

> It was exceedingly fortunate for us that we were so favoured by the winds, for the ship's company were falling down very fast with scurvy; and as I have already observed, we had nothing on board with which we could hope to check its progress, much less to cure it.[10]

Hunter further revealed his knowledge of preventative and curative options.

> Nothing can promise so fair to effect so desirable a purpose as carrying a good stock of various vegetable acids in every ship, but particularly in ships employed upon such service as the *Sirius* was. The elixir of vitriol [the addition of small amounts of spirit of vitriol into sailors' drinking water], hitherto allowed, and formerly considered, not only as a preventative, but as a cure, was found by no means to answer the purpose of the former, far less the latter. The vegetable acids, which might be provided for the use of ships upon long voyages, I apprehend would be found to occasion a very small additional expence, if any; and I am convinced in the end would be found a considerable saving.[11]

His concerns were borne out by one of his lieutenants, Newton Fowell, who wrote of the same outbreak:

> our People now began to grow Sick what for the Want of Fresh Provisions & the Thick Foggy Weather together seized them with Pains in the Breast & Bones / & as soon as they kept their Bed the Scurvy broke out on them & they were then rendered useless for the Rest of the Voyage as there is nothing except the

> Essence of Malt & Portable Soup Allowed by Government which is of the least Service to the Sick / & the Portable soup is never to be given on any account to the Healthy People to prevent their being ill / the Essence of Malt was Served out Daily to the People which prevented their being ill for some time but that did not allways last / we had no place to get any when it was out which was the case before we reached Cape Horn. Some Bourcoal or Dryed Cabbage is likewise to be given to the Sick but in a very small Quantity not exceeding half an ounce a Sick Man which when Boiled he is to eat if he can but it is so very tough that it is not possible for a Man in the Scurvy to get his teeth through it & it is no more palatable than Straw Boiled. Vinegar is the only Acid Allowed & that in a very small Quantity that it is Scarce Possible if the Scurvy once gets hold of any Person to stop its Progress effectually without Vegetables.[12]

Upon their arrival at the Cape, fresh fruit was immediately distributed and Hunter directed that sick-quarters ashore be provided for the afflicted. It would appear that Hunter did all that he could for his crew and that his understanding of scurvy was as sound as could be then reasonably expected.

On a broader health-related matter, Hunter later mused on the need for better medical care on long voyages.

> I cannot help here taking the liberty of saying, that it is much to be lamented, when ships are hired for the service of government, to perform such long and trying voyages to the health of those employed in them, that it is not made a part of the contract and practice, that they carry a surgeon; for I know well, that seamen, when taken ill upon such long passages, are, at the very idea of being without assistance of a surgeon (although careless and void of thought at other times, when in perfect health) apt to give way to melancholy, and a total dejection of spirits; and that many a valuable subject has been lost to the country by such a trifling saving. Out of the nine

transports which were employed on the service [i.e. the First Fleet] only one had a surgeon; and that one, had she not been bound upon some other service, after leaving Port Jackson, would in probability have been without one also.[13]

The ship in question was the *Lady Penrhyn* (Arthur Bowes Smyth, surgeon with John Alltree assistant), one of the transports engaged by the East India Company to collect tea from China on their return voyage. Hunter is incorrect in his statement, as there were actually two surgeons and five assistants spread out amongst the transports, as well as George Worgan, the surgeon on the *Sirius*.

Ship	Surgeons
Alexander	William Balmain (assistant)
Charlotte	John White (principal surgeon)
Friendship	Thomas Arndell (assistant)
Lady Penrhyn	Arthur Bowes Smyth (surgeon)
	John Alltree (assistant)
Prince of Wales	John Irving (convict assistant)
Scarborough	Dennis Considen (assistant)
HMS Sirius	George Worgan (surgeon)

This makes three surgeons and five assistants, a total of eight, for nearly 1500 people, including sailors, or one for about every 187 persons in the fleet, which was probably a reasonable ratio for those times. This is not to say that the general point being made by Hunter was not valid, inasmuch as there were occasions when long voyages were undertaken with inadequate medical care. In the case of the First Fleet, not only were there probably sufficient medical and paramedical personnel, but the health of the convicts and crew remained remarkably well on the outward voyage.

However, when attempting to establish the actual number of deaths on the passage to Botany Bay, a curious range of statistics emerges, which implies that there were no actual official figures. Bateson[14] and Surgeon General White[15] each claim 40 deaths [but a further eight died between embarkation and sailing], the marine Watkin Tench gives the figure of 25[16], while David Collins noted 32 deaths, including one or two by accident.[17] The picture is further muddied by a nameless officer who claimed 25, 'Out of two hundred and 12 marines, they lost only one; and that of seven hundred and 25 convicts put on board, but 24 perished in the expedition, though papers mention 40 which is not the truth.'[18] This last reference is intriguing as it is written by 'An Officer on the *Prince of Wales* who visited Botany Bay with Cook in the Endeavour'. Who was that unnamed officer and why the anonymity? No attempt to date seems to have been undertaken to discover the identity of the author. It is known that the *Prince of Wales* returned to Britain on 30 April 1789, but 'only ten crew members have been identified from the ship's log and other First Fleet documents. The ship may have carried about 25 crew', which seems a small number. Those identified are John Mason (who died on the return voyage), Robert Hosburn sailor, Daniel Butler, Samuel Moore sailor, George Nelson cook, James Porter ship's boy, Joseph Robertson, William Rogers, Joseph Wilkinson carpenter and Yorgan Yourginson (drowned). It would appear that the identity of the other crew members has been lost. None of these names appear on the *Endeavour's* muster books in the Public Record Office (Adm. 36/8569) at Kew Gardens, but a review of the short histories of the *Endeavour's* company by Beaglehole[19] tends, by process of elimination, to solve the mystery by pointing to the probability of the author being Isaac Manley, who was a master's servant on the *Endeavour*. He became a midshipman in 1771 and was appointed post captain in 1790, which means he could well have been a lieutenant on the *Prince of Wales*, and appointed captain on his return. The reason behind the anonymity was probably that the author was anxious to get his account into print as soon as possible to capitalise on public interest and secure good sales, as his would have been the first publication on the voyage and the new settlement, well before any official versions appeared. Anonymity would have also ensured he was not censured or disciplined for going to print ahead of the more senior officers and stealing some of their thunder and sales.

Notwithstanding the discrepancies in the First Fleet's mortality rates, the low figures are a testimony to the care taken by Phillip and White to provide the best diet and living conditions possible under the circumstances, a fact of which Hunter would have been well aware. The mortality figure of around 2.8 per cent is acceptable by contemporary comparisons, especially when viewed against the high rate of 26 per cent in the Second Fleet two years later.

Following the loss of the *Sirius* in March 1790 and Hunter's enforced stay on Norfolk Island for 11 months, the ship's company was repatriated to Sydney in February 1791 when Phillip decided that Hunter and his crew should return to England without delay. His reasoning was he had despatches regarding provisions to go to the Colonial Office and he did not know when the next ship would arrive; Hunter had to face a court martial for the loss of his ship; there was no other work for the crew to undertake in New South Wales; and food supplies were still a problem in the colony. Phillip had sent Lieutenant Ball in the *Supply* to Batavia to obtain further provisions and to acquire another vessel to make the voyage to England. Ball managed to charter a Dutch snow, the *Waaksamheyd* (meaning wakefulness or vigilance), a medium-sized, two-masted square-rigged vessel, not unlike a brig, of some 300 tons (slightly smaller than the *Endeavour's* 368 tons) but a poor sailer. Her sail configuration made it difficult to sail across the wind and one of the *Sirius's* crew members, Jacob Nagle, related that when Hunter asked the Dutch captain how she sailed, he replied 'O, she go eight knots. Oh, said our captain, that is verry well for a merchant vessel. Oh yes, said the Dutch captain, but when she g'dat, it must blow damnd hard, which we found to be true afterwards.'[20] David Southwell, a midshipman on the *Sirius*, but by now a master's mate, recorded that he 'had so great an objection to the ship herself, as considering her ill-calculated etc', but then went on, 'but a much better judge viz. Captain Hunter, entertained a similar opinion; and I understand expressed it in the strongest manner; but reason was in this, as in many other instances, probably overruled by other motives.'[21] Phillip overruled Hunter, who wanted to wait for a British ship.

Once again, Hunter was in the invidious position of not being fully in command, since part of the charter agreement stipulated that the vessel would be commanded by its Dutch master, Captain Detmer Smith, a man of shady character and dubious expertise, plus his crew of 30. Southwell provides an interesting observation on Hunter's unpleasant and difficult situation.

> But what we most complain of in this admired contract is that in every respect the advantage lyes on the side of the Dutchman (Captain Smith) in a manner most degrading to the dignity of our captain. Here it is stipulated that in every operation we shall assist, and only vaguely provided that he (Smith) is to perform the engagement of conveying us to England; thus Captain Hunter is left to have his officers be without the power in any case to enforce them—of this I believe he has often felt and deeply regretted the inconvenience—however there are those who consider him (Hunter) as having himself chiefly to thank for having too tamely engaged in a situation of which he seems to have been or might have been, sufficiently aware.[22]

Hunter made only muted reference to this in his journal.

> A piece of information which I did not by any means feel a pleasure in hearing: for, anxious as I was to reach England as soon as possible, I should with much patience rather have

waited the arrival of an English ship, than to have embarked under the direction, or at the disposal, of a foreigner.[23]

The impression conveyed here is that Hunter should have taken a firmer stand against Phillip's orders. However Hunter's training, long service as a subordinate and sense of duty would not have permitted him to question the orders of a superior and colleague; nevertheless, there is a lingering suspicion that he was perceived by some as being weak or tame. Detmer Smith was undoubtedly difficult; Collins referred to him as impertinent, perverse and ignorant while Tench provided a scathing account of his extravagant behaviour during negotiations for the charter of the ship.[24] Hunter was in an awkward position but the contract agreed to was probably as good a result of Phillip's negotiations as could have been expected in his eagerness to charter the ship.

The addition of 85 members of the *Sirius's* company to the 30 regular crew members would have made the ship extremely cramped. Provisions sufficient for six weeks were supplied, but in fact the voyage lasted six months, largely due to contrary weather and currents plus poor seamanship on the part of the Dutch captain, but perhaps influenced by the terms of the charter, being £1 per ton per month, which encouraged Smith to prolong the voyage for as long as he could, since the more time taken to complete the assignment, the more profit he would make. Immediately prior to their departure on Sunday 27 March 1771, one month after returning from their enforced incarceration on Norfolk Island, a touching event took place which throws some light on how Hunter was regarded by his fellow officers and peers, bearing in mind that, for all intents and purposes, Hunter and his crew were leaving Port Jackson for the last time, with little or no likelihood of ever returning. Hunter recorded that they

Figure 12. Hunter's sketch of *Waaksamheyd*. Biographical Memoir in *Naval Chronicle*. Courtesy of the Royal Australian Historical Society.

> sailed down the harbour, when we were accompanied by the governor, and most of the civil and military officers in the settlement, when we passed the lower point of the cove, all the marines of the NSW Corps, who were off duty, came down and cheered our people, by way of taking leave, and wishing us good passage. Never upon any service, did there a better, or a more friendly, understanding subsist between different corps, than had ever been the case between the seamen and the soldiers employed upon this.[25]

Surgeon John White placed a slightly different slant on the farewell, 'By Captain Hunter's departure, which was regretted by every one who shared the pleasure of his society.'[26] One of the marines, Private John Easty, wrote

> She waid anchor and ran down the harbour. She was again chear'd by the marines which was returned by the Ship's

> Company and thus was two partys of men saparated which had spent 4 years together in the greatest love and friendship as ever men did in such a distant part of the globe … may god send them a good voige I pray.[27]

This would infer a sound relationship between the seamen and the marines and a reflection on Phillip's administrative and diplomatic skills, as well as a strong endorsement of Hunter's relationship with his peers and the respect of those under him.

While Detmer Smith may have been the master of the *Waaksamheyd*, the route to be taken was decided upon by Phillip and Hunter; to avoid Batavia if possible for health reasons, to call at Norfolk Island if practicable to collect the despatches of Lieutenant Governor Ross and to pass to the east and north of New Guinea if the Endeavour Strait proved difficult, then to Timor for provisions and home via Mauritius or Cape Town. Having lost three weeks (of time, water and provisions) trying unsuccessfully against contrary winds to reach Norfolk Island, the ship steered towards New Caledonia where the first incident of note took place. Strong north-easterly winds prevented the vessel from passing to the east of New Caledonia, requiring Hunter (or Smith) to sail to the west of the island where he soon found himself embayed with reefs and small islands all around. Bradley reported that

> we now discovered that we had mistaken the Isle of Pines for Queen Charlotte Foreland and that we had got into the bight between the Isle of Pines and the shoals to the S.W. of it, the wind and a great swell setting right over them, our situation was very dangerous.[28]

After a nervous night under full sail in a ship that did not claw well to windward, the morning revealed they had made progress, but due more to a change of wind. By noon they had successfully weathered the reef. Hunter admitted 'this mistake had nearly proved of fatal consequences to us.'[29] In fact, the *Waaksamheyd* had been embayed and went perilously close to being wrecked on the reef. Hunter had charts of the locality and was at least familiar with Cook's account of the area. So it is surprising he did not undertake more research on the location prior to arriving there, or take more care and precautions, especially as Cook's account related that he too had the same problems in the same bay, 17 years earlier. But he was in unchartered waters.

> Thus we spent the night under the terrible apprehensions of every moment falling on some of the many dangers which surrounded us. Day-light shewed that our fears were not ill-founded and that we had spent the night in the most eminent danger.[30]

As a mariner, near-fatal recorded instances like this would tend to stick in the mind of Hunter more than routine observations. While the Dutchman may have been the master of the ship, his inexperience prompted him to seek Hunter's navigational assistance.

> We steer'd to the northward, and made New Caledonia 23rd April, and passed to the westward of it, [no reference to the near-miss] as the master did not feel himself qualified to navigate a ship in these unknown seas. He had, upon our leaving Port Jackson requested my assistance, which he had.[31]

Therefore Hunter had a major input into courses sailed. That he steered so close to an island he did not know well (but did know something of from charts), suggests that Hunter was not sufficiently versed in the art of staying well clear of unknown shores in a ship of limited sailing ability. There is a suspicion that Hunter may have desired to undertake some explorations of his own during the voyage, like James Cook before him, but he had limited command experience of any description, let alone on a voyage of discovery in strange waters. The *Sirius* under Hunter was embayed before she was lost the previous year and was nearly embayed and lost again the year before that off Tasmania, so one would imagine Hunter to be sufficiently aware of the dangers of straying into a large bay and not being able to extricate himself. One important aspect of seamanship is to always have an escape route if the land ahead begins to surround the ship. This capacity perhaps comes with experience as well as theory, but his undoubted skills in managing a ship did not seem to extend to anticipating suitable alternative scenarios and having appropriate contingency plans ready or taking suitable precautionary avoidance action. Had Hunter steered a course sufficiently clear of the coast, but still keeping it in sight, the near disaster may well have been avoided.

One month later, the *Waaksamheyd* had reached New Britain via Bougainville and on 22 May 1791 was in St George's Channel separating New Britain from New Ireland. Hunter reported being deceived by the distance between Wallis Island and Carteret Harbour and remarked that 'it was our misfortune that the distances marked in the sketch just mentioned did not agree with our judgement of them'[32], while Southwell wrote that

> our intention was to have water'd in Carteret's or Gower's Harbour on that coast, but unfortunately we fell in with the land to leward of the latter, and to our great mortification we overshot the former; there appears to have been some error in the printed chart.[33]

As a master's mate, Southwell would have been working closely with Hunter on the ship's navigation, so his reputation was also at stake, but he was also subordinate to Hunter and would have ensured that his description coincided with his superior officer. Bradley merely noted 'at 2pm bore away for Carteret Harbour which port we unfortunately overshot; having missed both harbours we stood to the nw along the shore in hopes of finding a watering place.'[34] Either Hunter's navigational judgement was at fault or the distances shown on the chart were inaccurate. The fact that Bradley makes no reference to the chart being in error could imply a simple omission on his part, or was it because he thought that the error lay in the navigation rather than in the chart? Hunter undoubtedly prided himself on his navigational abilities, and with good reason; so it would have been difficult to admit a mistake of this nature. On the other hand, perhaps the chart was wrong, but the question remains open.

The voyage was expected to take up to four months, but contrary winds and currents precluded sailing through Endeavour Straits to Timor, then westerly winds and easterly currents prevented Hunter from tracking around the eastern and northern coast of Papua New Guinea. It was therefore resolved to head northwest to the Philippines to replenish. During the journey, there were two incidents involving skirmishes with local tribes during efforts to secure food and water and on both occasions, Hunter's abilities as a strategist, diplomat and leader were put to the test. The first brush took place in late May 1791 at the Duke of York group of islands near present day Rabaul. Hunter recorded that the islanders (who were quite unaware of the power and noise of a gun) became menacing towards the crew as they were refilling the water casks. After some stones were hurled at the shore party, the return fire from muskets and pistols put the natives to flight and the day's watering was duly completed. The next day the ship's guns fired grapeshot into the woods before the crew landed and the watering operation was completed without further trouble. In fact, once the local people realised the superiority of the foreigners' arms, food offerings were made and peace was restored. The implications here are that by waiting until the islanders threw stones before retaliating and raking the shore with grapeshot before the resumption of watering took place, Hunter ensured that the islanders respected the European's superior firepower, and made peace with offers of trade and friendly exchange. Hunter regretted the need to resort to firearms but felt that there was no option and that the reconciliation process was 'harmonious and very pleasing'.[35]

Southwell told the story differently.

> A skirmish with the natives took place, in which ... they were the aggressors. We had a stout party arm'd, part on shore, immediately on the spot where water was filling, and part lay

off in a boat to cover the rest while at work. They never seem'd to like our operations from the first, I lament to think what sad execution probably took place, for, tho' the muskets, of which were near a score, were not sufficient, this inhuman Hollander continued playing upon them with round and grape-shot from the ship till every one that had a spark of anything human in his breast cried shame on it, many of those he fired on them, tho' in the act of aiming at a reconciliation, which, however, his madness would not allow to take place till late the next day, when these poor persequeted beings came down unarm'd, bearing a peace-making present, composed of something of almost every production they had. The morning we sail'd being May 27—many canoes were on b'd, and we parted in a friendly manner.[36]

This version implies an unduly harsh intervention by Detmer Smith and no reference to any role by Hunter. As the Dutchman was technically in charge of the ship, he was probably within his rights to respond as he saw fit, notwithstanding Southwell's dislike of him and his tactics, even if his response may have seemed excessive. Undoubtedly Hunter would have expressed his views to Smith, who generally disregarded them. However, the islanders were kept at a distance, no European lives were lost and all the water needed was obtained, plus some supplies.

An interesting comment was made by F.M. Bladen, the editor of *HRNSW*, in which Southwell's letters appear. After the words 'parted in a friendly manner', Bladen observes in a footnote—'This account does not agree with Hunters.'[37] Actually, the fundamental facts set out by each writer do coincide, but there is a difference in interpretation. As indicated above, on the one part, Hunter's account implies his hand upon events while Southwell's letter points to excesses by Detmer Smith, operating without reference to Hunter. The best Hunter could have hoped for was to modify Smith's aggressive reactions, without influencing him further in the process. Again, Hunter could only suggest and advise and not make the final decisions himself. Would Hunter have acted differently? Possibly. The other two accounts of the events, by Nagle and Bradley, simply lay down the facts without ascribing any responsibilities, but Bradley does note that when the *Waaksamheyd* left the cove, 'the master of the transport with his own officers now took charge of navigating the vessel and of the respective watches, which had hitherto been done by Captain Hunter and the officers belonging to the *Sirius*.'[38] It is unclear who directed operations while the vessel was at anchor. If Southwell is correct, then Hunter's account has been written with considerable restraint. Either way, if Hunter was in charge, his actions achieved the desired result, or if Smith was in command, Hunter probably had a delicate restraining role to play.

The second and more serious event occurred at Hummock Island off the southern tip of Mindanao, in the Philippines, in the following August, where another stop was made for badly-needed water, vegetables and rice. The local Raja or chieftain came on board and agreed to supply their needs. When he returned the following day with a large retinue, the promised provisions were not all forthcoming. Southwell wrote that Captain Smith 'had, with his usual injustice, from the time of our first arrival, hinted that if he found any difficulty in getting what he wanted, he would make the Raja a prisoner, and thus extort it.'[39] Again, Hunter emerges as a conciliator, advising Smith against any violent measures.

> I recommended to him to endeavour to make the Raja understand that unless he sent for the supplies we asked, and he had promised, that he, as commander of the Company's ship, would represent his conduct to the Governor and Council at Batavia, who would certainly take notice of it. I thought a threat of that sort might answer our purpose better than the means he proposed for we were in no respect ready for a quarrel with these people ...

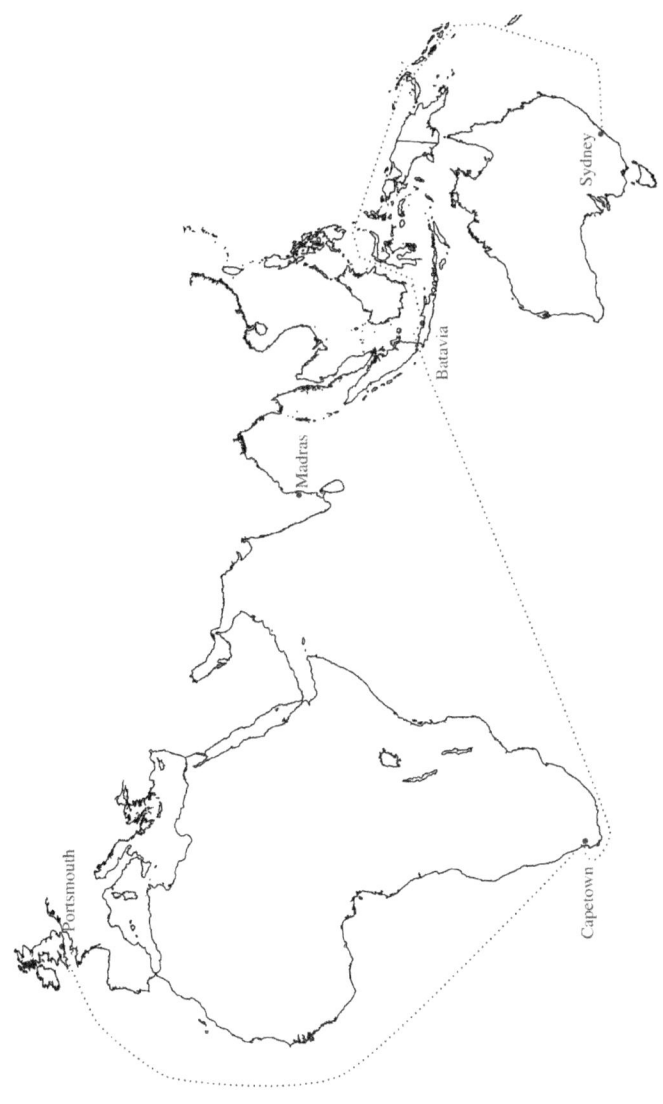

Figure 13. The voyage of the *Waaksamheyd*.

and again later

> I joined them and again recommended prudence and moderation to the master of the ship ... notwithstanding this, the violence and perverseness of his temper was such to dispose him (probably because he was advised against it) to create a disagreement between those people who were all armed and our people who were defenceless.[40]

Hunter was endeavouring to secure a peaceful outcome, being one who preferred consensus to confrontation, whereas the Dutch captain allowed his intemperance to predominate. However, the fault was not solely that of Detmer Smith. Nagle reported that

> About this time there was between 2 and 3 hundred on board in pretense of trade. The Dutch capt. had a Malay girl sitting on the quarterdeck which he kept as a miss, [Hunter made no mention of this] and she was very fond of him. She, understanding the language, heard by there discourse ... that they were then determined to massacree all the whites on board. Of us, was 85 Englishmen, officers and men, 30 Dutchmen and 16 tame Malays ... The girl informed the capt., sent the mate below for an armful of cutlasses. The [Raja's] general drew his dirk half out. The decks being full of Malays, they done as he did, having there eye on him, but the King thinking it was too soon, his son not being on b[oar]d, stopped his arm.
>
> At that moment the mate hove down an armful of cutlasses. Both captains ketched [sic] up a cutlass. The King finding they were discovered made a spring on the gunel of the vessel and from there into his boat and the general with him at the same time. Captain Hunter and Captain Smith made a blow at each of them but mised [sic] them.[41]

The Malays fled in the footsteps of the Raja into their boats and once again, the more gentle and emotional Southwell is scornful of the

Dutch captain's actions (but overlooking the conspiratorial intentions of the Raja):

> upon these unhappy men did our savage, true to his charter, continue firing, willingly assisted by some of my no less barbarous countrymen. The usual doses of round and grapeshot were also liberally administered upon the occasion. Wretched sporting with human lives! and for what? a quarrel—too likely entirely of his own making.[42]

Smith was keen to capture the Raja's boat, but 'Captain Hunter came to the gangway and spoke to Captain Smith and beged [sic] him not to go they being so numerous, and if we had the King's boat in tow, they would kill us all with their poisoned spears.'[43] Smith relented and returned on board, soon after which the *Waaksamheyd* weighed anchor and departed, with the crew unharmed.

Hunter once again emerges as the more experienced, cool headed conciliator over the tempestuous Dutchman, although the accounts of Southwell and Nagle are required to reveal the drama of the moment and the nature of Detmer Smith. The nearest Hunter went in describing his true feelings was when reflecting on 'this unlucky scuffle'. He noted that an armed guard should have been set on the deck and that Smith was reluctant to take advice from others, including Hunter.

> These observations I cannot help making; for they naturally arise from the distressing situation in which I found myself and officers who were placed under the direction of this most ignorant and disagreeable man. If he had felt himself qualified to have navigated a ship in the seas we had to pass through, his conduct would in all probability have been more insufferable, if possible than it was; but our assistance was absolutely necessary, otherwise I believe his vessel had never reached Batavia.[44]

These are strong words for Hunter, but his frustrations were pent up and Smith was neither a colleague nor a superior, so his normal restraints were somewhat relaxed.

Hunter was at a disadvantage in not understanding the language, although even if he had urged a more reasoned approach earlier, it is doubtful that Smith would have listened. Southwell's empathy with the Malays was on this occasion misplaced, as they were plotting to capture the ship and kill the Europeans. Also, they earlier attempted to convince Smith to anchor in another cove, but when he sent a boat to sound the location, it was found to be full of sunken rocks and no passage, which would have incapacitated the ship and rendered it vulnerable to attack. Hunter's preferred bargaining strategy with the Raja for supplies was to threaten to report him to the Dutch authorities in Batavia, and to remain prudent in negotiations. Whether this conciliatory plan would have succeeded is doubtful, considering the sinister intentions of the Raja as overheard by Smith's mistress. At least Hunter would have had an armed party on deck as a show of strength, which may have thwarted the Raja's intentions. Hunter's character and instinct was to promote a more moderate approach, although tellingly, when the daggers were drawn, he had the courage to attack with his sword. There is no hint of Hunter ever being reticent in action.

The voyage must have been an extremely trying experience for Hunter and it is testimony to his acceptance of orders that he sailed in a ship he disapproved of, was under the orders of a captain he neither liked nor respected, was forced into situations of danger because of another's impetuosity, and managed to retain an equilibrium and calmness of manner in spite of the frustrations imposed upon him. It must be conceded that for the ship and his crew to reach Portsmouth on 23 April 1793, 13 months after leaving Port Jackson, was a reflection of Hunter's forbearance, patience, diplomacy and seamanship skills. No one died of scurvy, while illness (fever) did not appear until after they reached Batavia.

Following his arrival in England, and subsequent acquittal four days later at the court martial over the loss of the *Sirius* and having no ship to command, Hunter contacted his patron Lord Howe seeking an appointment. Howe had assumed command of the Channel Fleet in the previous February, which was preparing to blockade the French Atlantic ports, and had hoisted his flag on the recently completed (1790) first rate *Queen Charlotte* of 100 guns (named after the wife of King George III, this ship only had a short life of ten years, being accidentally blown up at Leghorn in March 1800). Howe did not usually accept additional captains as volunteers on his ship, but as he told Hunter's friend and one of the court-martial captains, Sir Roger Curtis:

> Our friend Hunter has urged me with so much cordiality to be received as an associate with us, without any … character, that I cannot refuse myself to the imposition of his friendly interruptions; and, waving my general exceptions to tenders of this kind, assenting to his request to going as a volunteer with us, if no exception is made to it at the Admiralty. His talents and experience will render him a grateful guest on several accounts and supply particularly, the requisites in our contemplation, in search of a well qualified master.[45]

Howe did locate a suitable master and Hunter spent the next 13 months on the quarterdeck of the *Queen Charlotte* as a post captain, but once again in the shadow of a superior officer, in this case Lord Howe and his friend Sir Roger Curtis, the first captain.

The *Queen Charlotte* was actively engaged in the drawn-out battle with the French in what became known as the Glorious First of June, but there is no record of what role Hunter played. Even if he had no authoritative position, it can be assumed that he would have been on the quarterdeck during the engagements and played a committed part in the action. There is no mention of Hunter in Howe's despatches or in his recommendations for awards. The experience undoubtedly broadened Hunter's understanding of naval warfare, but would not have materially expanded his seamanship skills nor added to his command experience. This period could be described as useful rather than developmental.

The fleet returned to Spithead on 13 June 1794 and Hunter's subsequent sea-going assignments added little to his record as a mariner. Following his appointment that year to succeed Arthur Phillip as New South Wales governor, Hunter returned to Sydney in the *Reliance* in 1795. Although Hunter was theoretically first captain, the vessel was effectively commanded by Henry Waterhouse, the second captain and Hunter's appointee and friend. The voyage was uneventful and a biographer of Matthew Flinders (a lieutenant on the *Reliance*) recorded that 'Hunter, a very capable hydrographer himself, seems to have taken time during the voyage to instruct his younger officers in charting techniques.'[46] Hunter spent almost all of his term as governor in and around Sydney and he sailed back to England on the *Buffalo*, arriving at Spithead on 24 May 1801, after another incident-free voyage of seven months. His next and last appointment to full command was to HMS *Venerable* in 1804 (when he was 67 years of age) which he lost at Torbay in November of that year. As with the loss of the *Sirius*, there are factors present on both occasions which throw some doubt on Hunter's command abilities. That aside, his career as a seaman was varied, constant, demanding, sometimes trying and frustrating, undoubtedly interesting and took him to most quarters of the globe. He was extremely, perhaps exceptionally, technically capable, reliable and affable, a dependable subordinate and skilled in navigation, hydrography, sketching and the handling of ships.

Hunter did not deserve the 20-year wait to receive his commission, but the additional time as midshipman and master certainly honed his seamanship expertise, at the expense of gaining leadership exposure. In fact, he had quite limited full-command experience; during his 50 years at sea from 1754 to 1804 he only served for around 15 years as a captain at sea and then much of this time was spent subordinate to another—Phillip, Detmer Smith, Howe and Curtis, while he shared command of the *Reliance* and the *Buffalo*. This deficiency found him wanting at critical times in his career—and it is timely to examine in detail the circumstances surrounding the loss of the *Sirius* and the *Venerable*, as well as the near misses, to ascertain if there are common threads involving Hunter's command and contribution to these events.

5
A veiled alliance

When assessing John Hunter's capacity as a captain, it is only fair to apply a test of reasonableness in relation to the standards and conditions of the day, i.e. what would a reasonable captain have done in the late 1700s. Eighteenth-century sailing ships, though a vast improvement on those of previous centuries, were still far more vulnerable to the vagaries of the elements than modern-day vessels which are larger, stronger and propeller-powered. It is unreasonable to judge Hunter's actions and decisions by today's standards when ships now have engines, electronic communications, better charts and sophisticated navigational instruments, are more manoeuvrable and can therefore better cope with treacherous waters or high winds and seas. While greater allowance needs to be made in understanding the predicaments in which captains could find themselves 200 years ago, through little or no fault of their own, this would imply, however, the need for greater care and caution being exercised by them when entering a situation of potential danger.

While many ships in Hunter's time were lost through general deterioration, hurricanes and other natural causes, there were others whose loss was due to their captains' faulty judgements (sometimes based on inadequate charts), negligence or through inadequate response to approaching storms or dangerous coastlines. In the Western Pacific region alone, there are numerous examples of this. For instance, in August 1791 Captain Edward Edwards lost the *Pandora* carrying some of the *Bounty* mutineers, when the ship came too close to the Barrier Reef and was dragged by swells onto the coral. La Perouse and his crews ultimately perished when both his ships were driven ashore by a storm onto islands north-west of Fiji in 1788. The *Porpoise* carrying Matthew Flinders home (as a passenger) in August 1803 was destroyed while sailing at night beside the Barrier Reef when it struck coral rocks, and the *Sydney Cove* was wrecked on 8 February 1797 when it was caught in a storm and driven ashore on Preservation Island in Bass Strait.

Were these disasters inevitable and would they have occurred irrespective of who was in command? What would a reasonable captain have done under such circumstances? Would he have exercised more caution or incorporated additional factors when weighing up whether to proceed, avoid or await? Many captains never lost a ship in their whole career; Hunter lost two. Was this because of sheer bad luck or was there an element of human contribution as well? If so, how much weight should be placed upon the 'bad luck' component as against the personal contribution portion? This would vary from case to case. Hunter can only be fairly judged against what a reasonable captain might have done in those circumstances at that time, and it is unrealistic to compare Hunter to Cook and Bligh, who were exceptionally brilliant seamen and navigators, and the outstanding leaders in their field. Rather, it is the 'reasonable test' that should be equitably applied to judge Hunter's capacity as a captain.

Hunter did have occasional navigational or judgement lapses involving failure to anticipate events which compromised the safety of his ship. He did not always note these incidents in his journal, while similar omissions relating to these events can be noted in the journals of other naval officers with him, a practise which facilitated Royal Navy courts martial of captains for ship losses to be orchestrated and slanted in favour of the captain on trial. There appeared to exist a code of silence amongst officers in the face of common adversity.

It is an understandable trait of human nature to attempt to conceal an error or mistake, especially when in command of a naval vessel where the consequences of a misjudgement can lead to a loss of life and the ship, as well as adversely impacting upon the person's reputation and promotional opportunities. James Cook had his share of near-misses which were duly recorded (as far as we know) in his journals, but in his favour he had the mitigating factor of being in unknown and uncharted waters where an element of luck and calculated management was required to proceed in the presence of rocks or reefs, as opposed to being in waters previously chartered. For example, after the *Endeavour* struck a reef on Monday 11 June 1770 and was subsequently repaired near present-day Cooktown, Cook resolved to leave the coastal route and continue north outside the Barrier Reef. However, it was essential he remained close to the reef in order to map the coastline as best he could, as well as watching for an opening to the west to proceed to Timor.

At dawn on 6 August 1770, Cook found himself becalmed and being carried by swells at an alarming rate towards foaming breakers a mile away. There was no ground with 140 fathoms of line (so impossible to anchor) and the ship's boats could not pull against the swells. Cook referred to 'this truly terrible situation'[1] and it was only the providence of a slight breeze that blew when they were within 50 yards of being wrecked on the reef that enabled the ship to claw away from 'the very jaws of destruction'[2], a term also used verbatim by Joseph Banks in his description of the incident[3], which infers that he and Cook discussed the event before each put quill to paper. Cook was candid in his narration and could afford to be so, as he had no maps or accurate knowledge of what lay before him, so his navigational and seamanship expertise was not in doubt.

When in charted waters however, there is less excuse for a captain not to manage his ship safely, so any misjudgements become a lapse in seamanship or judgement rather than a misfortune associated with sailing into the unknown. As such, to record such mishaps into the ship's log or the captain's or officers' journals could be construed as an admission of an error and self-defeating. There is also the issue of what other officers write in their journals. If their captain makes a navigational or seamanship mistake of sufficient proportion to jeopardise the safety of his ship, should they record the incident faithfully in their journals and thus 'condemn' their captain, or gloss over it, ignore it or down-play it. If their journal was published or became evidence in a court martial, to what extent would a faithful account be interpreted as disloyalty to their captain? Would such 'disloyalty' compromise their own career prospects? What captain would want an officer upon whom he could not totally rely on to support him in such a situation? Were these incidents discussed amongst officers so that a common approach could be adopted? To what extent did career prospects override consciences? No doubt many officers had to wrestle with these dilemmas, especially when some reference to the incident should be made. In which case, how much should be included? Will it conflict with, or say more or less than, the account of others? The two safest courses would have appeared to be to report fully and truthfully or not at all.

The first circumstance involving Hunter to be considered in the light of these factors occurred on the morning of 26 January 1788 in Botany Bay. The previous day Phillip had departed in the *Supply* for Port Jackson, to be followed by the remainder of the First Fleet under Hunter's command. Hunter recorded that he 'made signal for the transports to get under way' and he himself 'then got under way, and with the transports, worked out of the bay.'[4] Bradley reported that 'as soon as the tide made out of the bay, weighed with the convoy: At noon, working out of the bay.'[5] Phillip, who went ahead in the *Supply* wrote: 'On the 26th, the transports and store ships, attended by the *Sirius*, finally evacuated Botany Bay; and in a very short time they were all assembled in Sydney Cove.'[6] Lieutenant King, who was on the *Supply* with Phillip, simply related from Port Jackson that 'at sun sett the *Sirius* and all the Convoy anchored here'[7], while David Blackburn, the master of the *Supply* wrote to his sister six months later that the *Supply* 'conducted the whole fleet up the harbour to the place where the camp and storehouses now stand.'[8] In similar vein, one of the *Sirius's* midshipmen, Newton Fowell commented that 'at 11 We got under Weigh and worked out of the Bay with all the Convoy / Stood for Port Jackson.'[9] The account of the *Sirius'* surgeon George Worgan is equally brief, 'the Fleet sailed for Port Jackson and in the Evening of the Day of our Departure, We arrived, and anchored in one of the many beautiful coves which it [Port Jackson] contains.'[10] Both the Judge Advocate David Collins[11] and Captain Watkin Tench of the Marines[12] only briefly alluded to the move, while Daniel Southwell, a midshipman on the *Sirius,* recognised the potential danger of ten ships squeezing through the narrow entrance in close proximity, but appeared well content with the departure.

> It must be obs'd that [the] Gov'r had pushed out the day before in the Supply, but this, tho' easily done by a single ship, was not adviseable for the whole convoy of merchant ships, with every circumstance in their favor. However, the W'r being fine and a good breeze, they all turn'd out very well, and by—o'clock they were clear of the bay and standing after us.[13]

Henry Waterhouse, one of the *Sirius's* lieutenants, simply made no reference at all to the departure in his letter to his father dated 11 July 1788.[14]

These accounts would all indicate that the passage from Botany Bay to Port Jackson was without incident and an inspection of the logs of the First Fleet vessels confirms this. For instance, the *Sirius's* log for this passage read 'weighed and made sail in Company with the Convoy, at noon working out of the Bay. Moderate breezes and cloudy at 1. pm clear'd Cape Banks and bore away under an easy sail for Port

Jackson'[15], while the *Charlotte's* log recorded 'prepared and weighed and made sail with the fleet—at noon worked out of the Bay. At 1/4 past 7 pm came to in 5 fath. in Port Jackson.'[16] The *Friendship's* log for 26 January was equally brief 'Got under weigh and turned out of the Bay at 3 pm got safe out and made sail for Port Jackson at 6 arriv'd at the Entrance of the Harbour.'[17] The other logs had similarly bland descriptions, including the *Lady Penrhyn*, whose log merely noted that 'at 7.00am the *Sirius* made signal to get under way. Weigh'd and made sail. At 2 cleared the Bay.'[18]

The first indication that the fleet's departure may not have been without incident was given by the Surgeon General John White, who wrote from the *Charlotte*:

> At ten o'clock the *Sirius*, with all the ships, weighed, and in the evening anchored in Port Jackson, with a few trifling damages done to some of them, who had run foul of each other in working out of Botany Bay.[19]

White does not explain what he meant by 'trifling' damage and whether the damage was trifling by naval standards. A more-detailed description of the departure was given by Marine Lt. Ralph Clark and the surgeon on the *Lady Penrhyn*, Arthur Bowes Smyth. Clark came out on the transport *Friendship* and noted that 'at 8 O'clock gott under way, as did all the ships.' There was

> little wind in the narrow going out there being little wind and the place very narrow and the wind Quite against use—the Prince of Wales and us got foul of each other they carried away our Jibb Boom but what damage we did her I cannot say as I did not lick it I was afraid that we would both have being driven on Shore as the flow fresh—Soon after the Charlotte ran foul of use and struck us very much—I was more frightened than I was when the Prince of Wales was foul of use—if it had not been by the greatest good luck we should have been both on Shore on the rocks and the ships must have been all lost and

the greater part if not the whole on board drowned for we Should have gone to pices in less than half of an hour … we have got clear out as hav all the Ships and hope to be in the course of a few hours at Port Jackson.[20]

Smyth's account is equally vivid.

> We were obliged to work out of the Bay & wt. ye. utmost difficulty & danger wt. many hairbredth escapes, got out of the Harbour's mouth abt. 3 o'Clock p.m.—The Charlotte was once in the most imminent danger of being on the Rocks—The Friendship & Prince of Wales who cd. not keep in stays came foul of each other & the Friendship carried away her Jib Boom—The Prince of Wales had her New Mainsail & Main topmast staysail rent in prices by the Friendships yd. The Charlotte also afterwards ran foul of the Friendship & carried away a great deal of the Carv'd work for her (the Charlotte's) Stern, & it was wt. the greatest difficulty our Ship avoided the same fate. however at last the whole fleet got clear of the Harbour's mouth without any further damage being sustain'd, Every one blaming the Rashness of the Governor in insisting upon the fleets workg. out in such weather, & all agreed it was next to a Miracle that some of the Ships were not lost, the danger was so very great.[21]

While it is difficult to reconcile these two accounts with the others, there was no reason for Clark and Smyth to either fabricate or invent the chain of events they described, nor was there any need for them to exaggerate or embellish the incident. Clark was accountable to Major Ross while Smyth's superior was the captain of the *Lady Penrhyn*, which escaped damage, so neither had any loyalties to any of the captains involved. The collisions were hardly 'trifling' as inferred by White since any accident involving three ships and causing damage in light winds in confined waters to the extent of putting them in some danger is scarcely 'trifling'. While the jib boom and torn sails could be replaced and their loss would only have mildly affected the ships' performance on a short voyage, there is always potential danger in collisions of this kind in narrow, crowded and shallow waters. Was 'trifling' White's own word or one suggested by another person? Why were the collisions ignored or swept under the carpet by the naval journalists and those close to or dependent upon them? How could Daniel Southwell write that 'they all turn'd out very well'[22] in the light of the collisions and the damage to yards, sails and superstructure? Instead of remaining silent on the matter, was Southwell in his youthful enthusiasm, going too far the other way and claiming that the departure was executed successfully and without incident? Perhaps this was part of a conspiracy or code of silence to protect the superior officers in the event that the Navy may have required these accounts to be submitted for inspection and possible evidence.

Phillip had left for Port Jackson the previous day and had ordered Hunter to bring the remainder of the fleet as soon as the weather permitted. Contrary winds prevented them from leaving later on 25 January, so Hunter decided to depart the following morning. Smyth's reference to people blaming Phillip for ordering the fleet out in such weather overlooks four factors. Firstly, Phillip was keen to assemble everybody at Sydney Cove as expeditiously as possible; secondly, the surprise arrival of La Perouse's two ships, the *Boussole* and *Astrolabe*, delayed the fleet's departure; thirdly, Phillip (and Hunter) would have wanted to have all ships safely anchored by dusk (as it happened, it was not until the end of the day before the last ship dropped anchor in Sydney Cove); and fourthly, Phillip would have relied upon Hunter to oversee the fleet leaving Botany Bay in an orderly and safe manner. It would seem that Hunter underestimated or did not fully anticipate the complexities of getting ten ships as an entity out of the relatively narrow confines of Botany Bay. It would have been embarrassing and even demeaning for these collisions to have occurred in front of the French.

Hunter did at least plan to affect an orderly and safe departure from Botany Bay. There was a meeting of commanders on 25 January, as Captain Gilbert of the *Charlotte* noted in his log: 'Answered the signal for all masters on bd the Agent'[23] which would infer some briefing by Hunter on Phillip's overall plan and arrangements regarding the move from Botany Bay to Port Jackson. It would appear however, that Hunter's plan for their embarkation was not explicit enough, not detailed enough or not followed adequately. As the senior captain, Hunter should have issued clear and practicable instructions to keep the ships suitably separated, but in a fashion that still had them all at Sydney Cove before nightfall.

The two principal issues emerging here are that the incidents did not appear in any navy log or diary, and the extent to which Hunter was responsible for the confusion during the ships' departure. It is only possible to speculate upon whether the omissions were the result of an agreement between the captains not to mention the matter, the collisions were genuinely not regarded as sufficiently serious to record, each involved a captain who did not want the events recorded because of possible adverse impact, and respective officers were diplomatic and careful enough to not mention it in their diaries so as not to implicate their captains' (and possibly their own) reputations. The real reasons remain hidden but it does seem strange that collisions or incidents of this nature were not recorded in ships' logs or officers' diaries. As second captain of the *Sirius*, Hunter would have been the nominal commodore in Phillip's absence. It was therefore his responsibility to supervise the fleet's safe and systematic withdrawal from the bay. Notwithstanding the appearance of the French, the need to be at Sydney before nightfall and the contrary winds, Hunter could have just as easily delayed their exit until the following morning. His inexperience in tactical command could well have contributed to the problems of that day. It is not possible to claim that there was not a cover-up to shield Hunter and the other affected captains.

An underlying question here is whether the naval accounts were actually a whitewash or deliberate omissions with a malevolent intent, compared to the impressions of two non-naval witnesses, albeit a surgeon and a marine lieutenant. Observers frequently see and interpret events in different ways, so that what may be frightening to one could be more routine to another. Had this been an isolated occasion, then it could well be asserted that the differences in interpretation were simply in the eyes of the beholder. The fact that similar differences appear in the recording of subsequent events however, could well indicate a pattern rather than an isolated instance. These discrepancies were less likely to be merely a series of differing interpretations by naval officers compared to other observers, a veiled alliance to downplay events which might have a deleterious impact upon the senior naval officer. While a conspiracy theory cannot be proved, there is evidence that one may have existed. Hunter appeared to be at least partly responsible in that he had overall responsibility for the welfare of the fleet and had to properly plan accordingly. It is very easy to be wise in hindsight and dangerous to pass judgements with the possibility of not being in possession of all the facts. On the available evidence, however, it is possible to query Hunter's leadership capacities over this incident, unless additional information to the contrary emerges.

The next incident reflected detrimentally on Hunter's navigational abilities. This took place off the south-east coast of Tasmania (or Van Diemen's Land as it was then known) during the return voyage of the *Sirius* from Cape Town in April 1789, bearing much needed supplies for the colony. Hunter was an excellent navigator and seaman in a technical sense, borne out by an endorsement of John White, the surgeon general, as the First Fleet rounded Tasmania in January 1788.

> Indeed, ability and experienced nautical knowledge were never more fully evinced on all occasions than by Captain Hunter; who is, I may venture to pronounce, without much risk of

having any veracity called in question, one of the most assiduous and accurate observers, and able navigators, the present day furnishes.[24]

This view was supported a few years later in the review of Hunter's journal, published in 1793, with comments describing 'the care with which the observations of longitude have been made, and the Tables for the Winds and Weather kept', and referring to Hunter as 'this able navigator'.[25]

The episode occurred as the *Sirius* was sailing east from Cape Town and preparing to round the southern tip of Tasmania for its final leg north to Port Jackson. On 19 April 1789, Hunter plotted the ship's position at 144° 30' east and 44° 29' south, putting it about 100 nautical miles south-west of Tasmania on an easterly course to pass almost 30 miles south of South East Cape, the most southerly point of Tasmania. The weather then deteriorated, the seas rose and the wind assumed gale proportions from the south, so much so that three days later three staysails (fore and aft sails between the masts) were split. At 3.30pm on 21 April, the haze lifted and they saw land ahead to the east, not far from the *Sirius*. Hunter immediately turned about and headed west. Three hours later, with the wind blowing violently from the south-east and the ship on a westerly course, land was then seen off their bow, with a prodigious surf breaking on the shore. At this point, Hunter admitted 'I now found that we were embayed'[26], a serious admission at any time. In fact, the *Sirius* was at the entrance to the D'Entrecasteaux Channel between Tasman Head at the southern end of South Bruny Island (the land they had seen to the east) and South East Cape to the west. They were not technically embayed, as they were at the entrance to a large channel (but Hunter was not to know this) between Bruny Island and the Tasmanian mainland, but they were well off course. The strong southerly gale had blown them northwards into the channel area, whereas if Hunter had been more cautious and plotted to sail further south to allow more than the 30 miles leeway, which was not a large clearance considering the strong southerly storms, he would have compensated for the southerly forces and passed comfortably south of Tasmania as originally intended, and not have set up his predicament.

Once the heavy surf had been sighted, Hunter immediately veered away and, with the aid of a slight wind shift in his favour, set all sails and headed south, notwithstanding the enormous strain put on the ship's masts, sails and rigging and which caused some structural damage to the ship's bow. They sailed out of danger, passing perilously close to a rocky point in the process. While Hunter's technical navigational expertise was not the issue, it was his inexperience as captain that nearly cost him his ship and his crew, but his seamanship qualities shone through in extricating the *Sirius* from the very real perils it faced. Hunter attempted to justify himself by writing:

> I still flatter myself that we were so far to the Southward, as not to have a doubt of passing some distance to the Southward of Rock Swilley [rocks south of South East Cape] and consequently at a sufficient distance from the South Cape,

and

> It may not be improper to observe, that three days had now elapsed without the sight of the sun during the day, or a star during the night, from which we could <u>exactly</u> determine our latitude; but as every allowance had been made for the drifting of the ship to leeward [this is the crux of the issue], under a very low sail, and an exceedingly heavy sea, and for every other disadvantage attending such a situation; there remained not a doubt with me, or any officer on board, but that we were near half a degree [thirty nautical miles] to the southward of the South Cape, and as the distance from west to east, across the promontary, is not more than a degree and a half of longitude [ninety nautical miles], or about twenty or twenty two leagues [i.e. about sixty-six nautical miles] in distance, we had every reason to think we were near round it.[27]

There is a considerable difference between 66 and 90 nautical miles representing the width of southern Tasmania, and it is difficult to understand why Hunter would equate the two. Is this simply a slip on Hunter's part or did this differentiation contribute to their subsequent near-loss, or did different charts show different distances? Modern maps indicate a width of nearer 90 miles or 150 kilometres.

Hunter's basic mistake was deciding not to clear the southern tip of Tasmania by a greater margin, in view of the southerly gales at the time when he did approximately know his position. Hunter remarked that he believed they were half a degree or 30 nautical miles below South Cape and that the other officers were in agreement with his claim. Midshipman Newton Fowell observed 'we Supposed ourselves not far from the South Cape'[28], which is not quite the same thing. He then made an interesting comment, 'Swilly was only 9 Miles Distant and the Weather so very Hazey that we could not see it.'[29] If they could not see it, how could they be sure of its proximity? The first lieutenant, William Bradley, confirmed that sightings were taken on 16 April but made no reference at all to their position in relation to South Cape three days later.[30] Their reticence on this issue was more likely deliberate than accidental. Perhaps they agreed on a cautious approach to the matter which was of some importance and pride to Hunter and therefore they made minimal or no reference to it. Fowell's word that they 'supposed' themselves not far from the Cape is vague but perhaps deliberately so. Southwell makes no reference to their position other than describing their very narrow escape from shipwreck. Hunter's claim therefore to have the agreement of his officers on the ship's position is not as strong as he might have wished and this could be construed as an attempt at self-justification.

The seriousness of the danger and the narrowness of their escape becomes clear when scrutinising the accounts of others on board at the time. Southwell tactfully captured the anxiety of the moment by describing:

> being driven on that part of the coast call'd Tasman's Head, in thick weather and hard gals of wind, and embay'd being twelve hours before we got clear, the ship forced to be over-pressed with sail and the hands kept continually at the pumps, and all this time in the most distressing anxiety, being uncertain of our exact situation and doubtful of our tackling holding, which has a very long time been bad; for had a mast gone or Topsail-sheet given way, there was nothing to be expected in such boistrous weather but certain death on a coast so inhospitable and unknown.[31]

It was indeed a period of high drama and a close call. Newton Fowell's account also paints a dramatic scenario and praises Hunter's seamanship.

> We were at this Time in a very dangerous Situation nor could we tell when we might expect to be out of Danger ... So heavy a press of Sail was on the Ship that the Sea made a fair Breach over her which obliged every person to be very carefull in holding fast for fear of being Washed overboard / indeed the Forecastle was constantly under Water / at 12 the Weather was very Dark and not seeing any Land made us Suppose ourselves out of Danger / however Capt. Hunter did not think it proper to shorten Sail till Daylight / this was a very lucky precaution for at 2 OClock all of a sudden Land was seen close on the Lee Beam We had not room to Ware so was obliged to Stand on / We thought at this time we were among Breakers and several heavy Seas were Shiped some of which broke above half way up to the Fore Yard.[32]

Bradley remarked that 'the hand of Providence now interfered' when the wind changed direction slightly to assist them and he then related the drama in more technical terms, but still left the impression of a narrow escape[33], evidenced by the fact that the force of the water washed away the ship's figurehead and other parts of the forward superstructure. Bradley was usually more eloquent in his descriptions; perhaps there was a reason to be more constrained on this occasion.

All of these diarists were Royal Naval officers. Their accounts were generally vivid and highlighted the extreme peril they and their ship endured. Their versions of the story essentially coincided and while they may not have supported Hunter to the extent he may have wished, neither did they criticise him for drifting too far north into potential disaster. They were perhaps deliberately non-committal to protect their own reputations as well as Hunter's. What their inner thoughts might have been is open to speculation—possibly a mixture of anger that he did not exercise sufficient caution in keeping the *Sirius* well south of Tasmania, mixed with admiration and praise for his skilful handling of the ship afterwards.

There is another, even more vivid and descriptive account of this incident however, which throws extra dimensions into the episode, written by one who had no vested interest in relating the sequence of events other than openly and honestly, without fear of any implications to his naval career. Seaman Jacob Nagle later wrote:

> The capt. thinking to give a wide berth to the five sunken Rocks, we got nearer the land, and a gale coming in from the Sotherd, till we ware under a reefed fore course in the night, and so dark you would scarcely now the next man to you, the see flying over us and the pumps going, though she did not leak, and the hatches battened down, but the lookout forrod cried out 'Land a head'. We then had to ware ship and stand to the westward, In about half an hour there was land ahead again. We then had just room to ware again. Though dark it was, we could then see the surf breaking over the rocks, and appeared higher than our mast heads. We found now that we were embay'd, and a heavy gale, and a heavy sea rolling in upon us, and nothing but high cliffs of rocke under our lee. The Capt. ordered close reef topsails to be set and loosed the

mainsail and set it. He said she must carry it, or capsize, or carry a way the masts, or go on the rocks. The men at the lee pumps were standing to their nees in water and every man in his station. If she had not a spar deck upon her, [i.e. a single deck, unlike many frigates] she could not have carried the sail without filling hur gun deck, the see flying over us under such a press of sail, standing on, expecting every moment the masts to go over the side, and I dont suppose their was a living soul on bd that expected to see daylight.

About half an hour before day light, she struck upon the reef, a bank that run as good as two miles to windward of us. She lay motionless for the space of two or three minutes when a most tremendous see struck hur under the quarter and hove her over the reef and a way she went in full sail and smooth water, the reef keeping the heavy see off. We carried a way our fore top gallant mast and split the uper part of hur stern and lost the figure head. At day light it fell calm, and the ship lay two sheats to port, or on the left side, our backstays and riging all carreing away, with the sails flaping to the mast, they were so strained by the gale. We turned too righton the ship by putting much flower as we could on the opposite side between decks; spliced the riging. Through God's assistance, we were saved, where we had no hopes but in him.[34]

The ship's grounding, a truly hazardous incident, is not alluded to in any of the other accounts, but surely it was sufficiently critical and potentially disastrous not to overlook or omit from these reports. The others did not mention it because this would have adversely impinged upon Hunter's reputation and taken the gloss off his successful efforts in saving the ship. It is difficult to accept that Nagle would have concocted the episode, as he would not have gained from so doing. There were no career or promotion interests to protect, nor was there any evidence that Nagle wanted to impugn Hunter's image. In fact, Nagle would have been kindly disposed towards Hunter, following an incident at Cape Town the previous January in which one of the midshipmen badly treated a boat's crew (including Nagle) while on shore. On learning of this occurrence, Nagle related that Hunter then 'confined him [the midshipman] to his cabbin for three weeks and told me to go to my hammock and get some rest.'[35]

Nagle's journal was not written up until some years after these events took place, so there is the risk of memory loss or blurring with the passing of time. Some details could have become hazy or misplaced in Nagle's mind over the intervening years, however, momentous or hazardous experiences are more likely to be remembered more vividly. The clarity of Nagle's account of the *Sirius*' grounding, combined with the similarity of his description to those of the naval officers' versions of other aspects of this incident, provide strong grounds for credibility.

There is no evidence to indicate why Nagle wrote his journal, whether he had a particular audience in mind or what ultimate plans he had for it. Nagle died in the United States in 1841 and the journal was not published until 1988. The detail of some of his observations (corroborated by other diarists' accounts and ships' logs) would suggest that perhaps he kept a pocket diary which he later wrote up as a journal. While Nagle may have had only limited education, he did have a gift for descriptive and accurate detail.

The essential issue is whether Nagle's account should be preferred over the descriptions (or omissions) of the others. Nagle had no interests to protect or any known scores to settle, so there are no compelling reasons to discount or disbelieve his version of events. His diary does not contradict the accounts of others, but rather includes supplementary details as well as views from another perspective. Again, there is no strong ground to discount this additional information, while there is a suspicion that the naval diarists' omissions to any reference to the grounding were to protect their captain.

Hunter emerges from this incident with a mixed scorecard; a 'fail' for not keeping the ship sufficiently south of Tasmania in the face of the strong southerly gale, a 'pass' for his handling of the ship once it was nearly embayed, a 'fail' for not reporting the grounding and another 'fail' for attempting to justify his actions by implying the support and endorsement of his officers. On balance, Hunter has to bear the responsibility for the near loss of the *Sirius*.

The third episode took place on 6 March 1790 as the *Sirius* and *Supply* were sailing through Sydney harbour heads en route to Norfolk Island. Hunter simply recorded that 'We sailed from Port Jackson on 6th March'[36], while Bradley noted 'Saturday 6. Wind fresh from the S'ward. Sail'd out of Port Jackson. Supply in Co.'[37] Newton Fowell's letters briefly related that 'On the 7 We went to Sea with the Supply in Company.'[38] The date discrepancy here probably is a consequence of ships' time commencing each day at noon rather than midnight. Daniel Southwell was stationed at South Head lookout and would have had a clear view of the departure. 'They left this port on 6th of March 1790, and I from the flagstaff followed them with my eyes 'till out of sight.'[39] David Collins and Watkin Tench, neither of whom witnessed the ships' passing through the heads, and therefore reported second-hand, respectively wrote: 'On the 5th the *Sirius* and the *Supply* left the cove, but did not get to sea until the following day, when at the close of the evening they were scarcely to be discerned from the south head'[40] and 'she sailed on 6th March.'[41] In a letter to his sister dated 12 August 1790, David Blackburn, the master of the *Supply*, merely noted: 'In March 1790, the *Sirius* and Supply sail'd for Norfolk, with 300 convicts—men and women.'[42]

Once more, it is necessary to turn to the accounts of the non-naval officer diarists (the seaman Jacob Nagle and Marine Lt. Ralph Clark) to learn of the more likely scenario. Nagle wrote:

We sailed for Norfolk Island. Going out of the heads, we had a narrow escape of loosing our ship on the rocks, being light winds, and a heavy swell setting in for the rocks, but a little more wind springing up, we got safe out to see.[43]

Evidently it was not the uneventful occasion that the naval accounts would infer. A more graphic picture was painted by Lt. Ralph Clark.

> Fine Moderate weather little wind—about Six o Clock got under way a great swell setting into the Harbour—just as we came abreast of the outer South Head it fell calm and the Swell was Setting us fast to leward on the North Head which, had not a puff of wind fild the Sails we should have been drove on Shore on the North Head and every body on board would have been in pices in a few minutes from the great Sea that was breaking on the Rocks and the most of use on board would have been lost but by great good fortune the puff of wind shoved use clear out the harbour as it did the *Supply*.[44]

Again, an edited account is given by the naval writers on the one hand, while on the other, a fuller, more descriptive and complete version is offered by others. It was a potentially serious matter luckily averted by a fortuitous breath of wind—or perhaps Nagle and Clark were exaggerating. No one could predict a loss of wind at that, or any other, critical time, but an experienced captain may well have anticipated the likelihood and have planned ahead accordingly. In this case, as the winds (such as they were) were blowing from the south-east, as was the swell, it might have been prudent to steer a course as close as safely practicable to the South Head to compensate for any northerly drift across the heads emanating from the south-easterly swells, which might take precedence over the ship's slow forward movement from the light winds. Two years before, Hunter had estimated the distance between the heads at one and three quarter miles and had recommended to mariners entering the harbour to 'steer in between the heads.'[45] The entrance was therefore wide enough and sufficiently deep to plot a course nearer to South Head, but Hunter appeared to have steered nearer to midway between the two heads, with potentially disastrous consequences.

This would therefore seem to be another instance of Hunter's failure to properly anticipate conditions ahead, compounded by the omission of any reference to the episode by the official diarists. Hunter probably did not know of Clark's diary and Nagle did not write his account until later. As both Clark's and Nagle's versions are essentially similar, and they were unlikely to have conspired, it may be reasonably assumed that the incident took place as they related it. What is not clear, however, is why once again the matter was not recorded by the naval officers. Nearly being washed onto the rocks below North Head seems to deserve a mention at least—unless it may adversely affect the reputation of those in charge at the time. It is not intended to suggest that Hunter and his officers were alone or pioneers in suppressing embarrassing information. The fact that it happened is more a reflection of a presumably established, but unofficial, practice widespread throughout the navy, rather than a code of silence introduced or imposed by Hunter. The excuse that 'others do it' is no justification for perpetrating a bad practice or a deception, but the fact that Hunter and others did engage in selective reporting needs to be seen in this light.

The final instance when Hunter found himself embayed and was lucky to escape occurred at New Caledonia in 1791 when he and the crew of the *Sirius* were returning to England in the *Waaksamheyd*. The ship itself was technically under the command of Captain Detmer Smith, but Hunter did have some input into the courses sailed and had to bear some responsibility for the crisis.

While near-misses could, to a certain extent, be swept under the carpet, the loss of a ship was an entirely different matter, requiring a court martial as a matter of course. Hunter had already appeared as a witness at the court martial against the pilot of the *Carysfort* in 1771 so he was aware of the requirements and processes. He was to face two courts martial over the loss of ships under his command, the *Sirius* in 1790 and the *Venerable* 14 years later in 1804.

The loss of HMS Sirius

Having nearly been lost at Sydney Heads on 6 March 1790, the *Sirius* arrived off Norfolk Island seven days later. Bad weather precluded landing personnel and provisions at Sydney Bay, on the south side of the island near the settlement, so Hunter landed all the marines and some of the convicts at Cascade Bay on the north-east coast over the ensuing couple of days.

On the morning of 19 March 1790, the *Sirius* entered Sydney Bay to land the remaining convicts and stores and worked around to the anchorage near the settlement. By 9.00am she was positioned with her bow pointing out to sea to the south-west, with the wind on her port bow and the reef about a mile away at the western end of the bay, and then commenced unloading her cargo. The *Supply* lay nearer to the reef. The currents pushed both ships towards the rocks and around 11.30 Lieutenant Ball on the *Supply* drew Hunter's attention to this by waving his hat and pointing. The *Sirius* soon afterwards trimmed her sails and gathered way on a port tack towards the south-west and the open sea. The *Supply* was closer to the reef when the alarm was raised and after failing to clear it on the port tack, went about and successfully cleared it on the starboard tack, passing close to the bow of the *Sirius* in the process, at which time Ball called out to Hunter to emphasise the extent of the danger. This was corroborated by Lieutenant Newton Fowell, who wrote 'As the *Supply* passed us on the other tack, Mr Ball informed Capt. Hunter that both vessels were much too near in shore and recommended to him to get out of his situation as fast as he possibly could.'[46] (Hunter claimed that he had already realised he would not clear the reef and had begun to change tack before the wind changed.[47]) At that moment, the wind veered more southerly which forced the *Sirius*, still on a port tack, to fall away towards the reef.

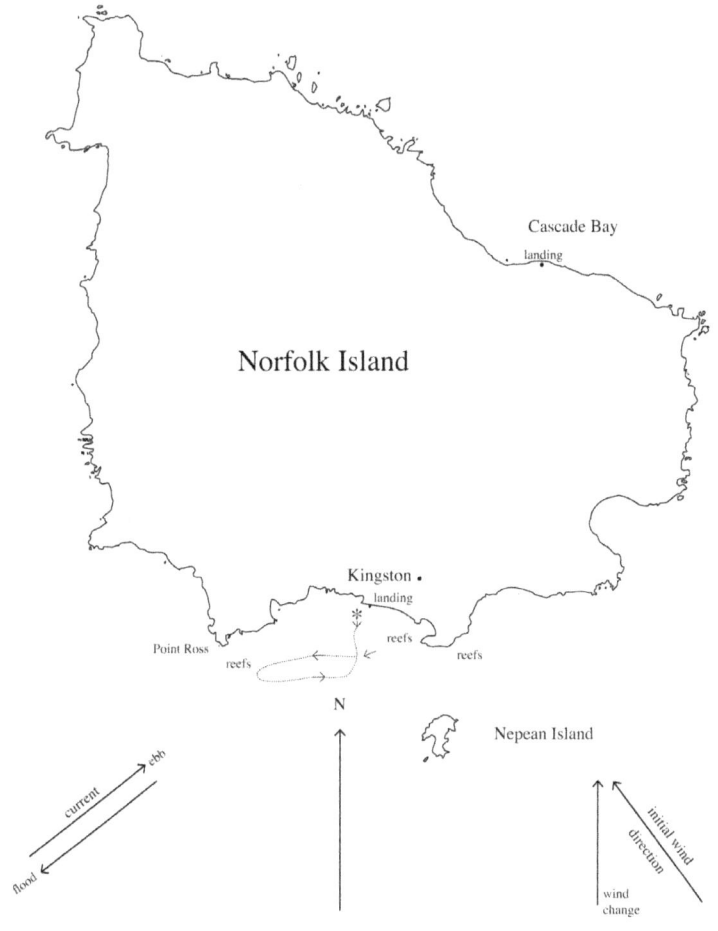

Figure 14. Last movements of HMS *Sirius* on 19th March 1790.

The situation was now desperate as the *Sirius*, requiring sufficient momentum to turn around, had been permitted to run perilously close to the reef. The ship drew almost beside the reef near the shore, but managed to turn downwind onto a starboard tack without striking. More sail was set to increase her speed as Hunter hoped to proceed through a rock-infested channel to the open sea, but the *Sirius* was now on a course parallel and close to the rocky coastline. The ship continued to drift closer to the shore so the helm was put down (i.e. full opposite rudder) in a frantic attempt to go round and head back in a westerly direction, but further out from the shoreline. In so doing she lost the wind and forward speed and started to move backwards towards the rocks. The sails were loosened to spill some of the wind and the anchor was let go, but before the cable's slack was taken up, the *Sirius* hit the rocks and was holed in the bottom. John Bach, the editor of Hunter's journal published in 1968, observed:

> the entire episode is a classic example of the gravest of all dangers that confronted the sailing ships; embayment on a lee shore with no sea-room to work out. The identical situation had been rapidly developing off the Tasmanian coast when the change of wind, ironically also to the south, had saved the ship.[48]

The fine line once more arises: when does prudence and caution take precedence over the need to complete the task? This decision may involve some element of fortune or luck but should fall well short of rashness. Hunter could have anchored further out or further away or he could have waited, thereby further delaying the landing of the balance of the cargo and convicts. The correct decision may not be clear cut but does require judgment based on experience and knowledge of the options and their consequences.

Hunter made no reference in his journal to any communications from the *Supply* and justified his decision to proceed into the bay because the *Supply* was already there and the signal from the shore indicated no danger from the surf to boats landing supplies. He then 'steered in as far as judged safe'[49], which transpired to be a critically important judgement. Bradley recorded that, while they were loading the boats, 'Mr Ball hailed from the *Supply* then on our lee bow and waved his hat towards a reef of sunken rocks which lay off the West point of Sydney Bay'[50], after which the *Sirius* made sail. This would suggest that Hunter did not want to admit that the *Supply* recognised the dangers before he did and that his pre-occupation with landing arrangements and other matters distracted his attention from the safety of his ship.

Figure 15. The wreck of the *Sirius* in Sydney Bay, Norfolk Island. Watercolour from the Journal of William Bradley, Mitchell Library, State Library of NSW.

Bradley is almost contradicting Hunter in implying that Ball was ahead of Hunter in his anticipations and had tried to warn Hunter accordingly.

One interesting interpretation of the reasons for the loss was made by E. McHugh in his book *Shipwrecks* when he wrote 'She'd tried to sail for open water, but her hull was so fouled with weed that she barely responded to the helm.'[51] This speculation is not borne out by those involved in overhauling the ship in Sydney after the damage sustained during the narrow escape off Tasmania ten months before. Newton Fowell wrote that the *Sirius* was taken to the north side of the harbour for repairs and

> This Same Opportunity was taken to Examine the Places where She leaked on her Passage Round Cape Horn Two Streaks of Copper was ripped off for the Purpose of Examining her Bottom which was found in a very Sound State.[52]

If the *Sirius's* hull was in the condition McHugh claimed, some reference would most likely have been made and corrective action taken. Jacob Nagle was involved in the overhaul and also made no reference to a badly barnacled bottom when relating details of the repairs, and the intervening time period up to the loss was too short for any significant barnacle or weed growth on the hull.[53] This theory can be safely discarded.

Daniel Southwell, who witnessed the departure of the *Sirius* on 6 March from the South Head lookout, recorded on 14 April 1790 that

> The Supply bro't an account that on the 19th March about noon the *Sirius* had in course of loading the boats drifted rather in with the land. On seeing this, they, of course, endeavour'd to stand off, but the wind being dead on the shore, and the ship being out of trim and working unusually bad, she, in staying—for she would not go about just as she was coming to the wind—tail'd the ground with the after part of her keel,

and with two sends of the vast surf that runs there was completely thrown on the reef of dangerous rocks.[54]

While Southwell's version is second-hand, he would have discussed the loss with officers from the *Supply* on her return to Sydney. No one else made any reference to the ship being 'out of trim and working unusually bad.' She could well have been out of trim as a result of being part way through unloading the baggage and provisions which would account for her 'working badly' and may partly explain McHugh's misinterpretation as to why she did not respond well to the helm. The officers could well have been so preoccupied with the unloading process that they missed the drift of the ship, although this is no excuse and does not absolve responsibility for her safety. Further, unloading a ship would normally involve systematically removing cargo from various parts of the hold to minimise or reduce any imbalance arising from emptying the ship unevenly. Perhaps the *Sirius* was not being unloaded properly and was out of trim or even listing somewhat and the officers were not sufficiently attentive to the operation and therefore did not disclose this as a factor.

From the *Supply's* perspective, Master David Blackburn simply (and tactfully) noted in a letter to his sister:

> On 19th the *Sirius* was unfortunately drove on shore by the violence of the sea and in ten minutes she was a wreck. She went on shore directly opposite the town and thank God no lives were lost.[55]

Lieutenant Ralph Clark had been put ashore at Cascade Bay five days previously and witnessed the loss from the shore. His account adds nothing new to what has been disclosed so far, other than to observe that

> about 11 o Clock the *Sirius* been well in the [bay] hoisted her Boats out and Sent them on shore with Provisions—at this time she was laying too under Nepean Island—Soon after She

made Sail and was endeavouring to get father out of the Bay, for she was too near the Shore.[56]

The two issues of note raised thus far are that Hunter was sufficiently at ease with the ship's location and safety to allow the boats to commence unloading, and the ship was too near the shore to effectively escape. What might have happened if Hunter's attention (and that of Bradley and the other officers) to the ship's drifting towards the reef had not been drawn by Ball; most likely the grounding would have taken place sooner. An inexorable conclusion begins to emerge that the *Sirius* had already reached her point of no return before Hunter began evasive action. A more alert captain should have anticipated this. Lieutenant Phillip Gidley King, the island's commandant, had noted 'Moderate Gales at daylight made the Signal that landing was very good and that the large Boats could land.'[57] Hunter appeared to have relied on this signal as evidence that he could proceed into the bay, but currents and undertows are not always visible from the shore. In any event, the *Supply* was successfully able to complete the operation, so it is feasible to conclude that, properly managed, the *Sirius* ought to have been able to accomplish her unloading tasks as well.

Once more, it is Jacob Nagle's diary which reveals the extent of the current and a state of affairs sufficiently casual on board the *Sirius* as to paint a damning indictment on Hunter's command abilities that borders on a dereliction of his duties.

> In shore the current is verry strong, running six hours to the west and three to the eaSt We making all sail, and the current shifting, we are up with the island by a leven o'clock in the day and sent the boats on shore with baggage.
>
> Having a fine pleasant day, with a light breeze off shore, all the seaman that could muster hoks and lines was ketching groopers, not thinking of any danger. At 12 o clock, when thinking of going to dinner, Captain Ball of the Supply Brig

> hailed us and informed Captain Hunter that we are too close in, the swell of the surf having holt of us though it did not brake. Capt. Ball, being at a distance outside of us, perceived it sooner than we did. Immediately we made sail that we could set, and a light breeze off shore, but it all availed nothing. The swell was stronger than the wind, and the swell still driving us in, we let go an anchor, thinking to warp out, but the curl [coral] roks cut the cable the first and second time we struck.[58]

This conjures up a picture of Hunter, then aged 52, having released some of the crew (while the others were unloading) to undertake some fishing, and about to go below for lunch, being told by the commander of the *Supply* that his ship was drifting too close to the reef and in increasing danger. It would have been bad enough to be preoccupied with the unloading operation and not notice the ship's deteriorating position, but to have relaxed to the point of standing down some of the crew and disappearing below for lunch under such conditions could be construed as negligence and a gross lapse of judgement and command. Hunter had been embayed before, so he should have recognised the impending dangers. The weather was clear, visibility was good and the *Supply* was able to perceive the trap and work her way out in time. It is virtually inconceivable that the *Sirius* could not also have escaped if her officers had been more alert to the conditions around them. This was a major blunder by Hunter since, as captain, he had overall responsibility for the safety and preservation of his ship. He should have been more aware of the hazards surrounding his ship, as Lieutenant Ball was. Needless to say, none of the naval officers' accounts made any reference to the fact that Hunter did not correctly read the forces acting on his ship and it can only be assumed that they too were either unaware of, or underestimated, the force of the swell and the proximity of the rocks. It is highly unlikely Hunter would have ignored or dismissed any warning cries from his own officers. It is difficult to escape the conclusion that Hunter was fundamentally responsible for the loss of the *Sirius*. It is equally difficult to identify any extenuating circumstances that could exonerate or excuse Hunter from his apparent negligence. His lack of independent command experience probably was a factor, while his age may well have contributed to the lapse in concentration. While 52 was an advanced age in the 18th century, Hunter was apparently physically quite fit judging by the overland excursions he undertook around Port Jackson. His skill and judgement as a seaman were still of a high order, but the unavoidable conclusion resurfaces that Hunter's abilities as a captain were found wanting once more, largely for the same reason—his impaired ability to anticipate.

Knowing that a court martial was inevitable, Hunter had plenty of time to prepare his report and to contemplate how best to present his defence. In fact, two years elapsed before the court met. Hunter and his crew were marooned on Norfolk Island for 11 months, while the voyage home in the *Waaksamheyd* took another 13 long months. Hunter was obviously anxious for the hearing to take place as soon as possible, for he wrote to Secretary Stephens on the day of his arrival back in England in April 1792.

> I have now Sir to request that you will be pleas'd to move their Lordships for an order, that the usual Court-Martial be assembled to enquire into the cause of the loss of His Majestie's late Ship the *Sirius*—as soon as it may be convenient to their Lordships.[59]

The speed with which the court martial was convened once Hunter returned was remarkable. Judging by its length, Hunter's letter to Secretary Stephens was more than likely prepared prior to the *Waaksamheyd*'s arrival at Portsmouth on 23 April, and received by Stephens within 24 hours. Stephens replied on the following day, 24 April, acknowledging receipt of Hunter's letter and advising that an 'order for assembling a court martial to enquire into the loss of the *Sirius* was sent to Vice Admiral Roddam, commander-in-chief of His

Majesty's ships at Portsmouth, by this last post.'[60] Presumably Roddam would have received the order by the next day, 25 April, and the order to those captains in Portsmouth at the time to attend the hearing would have been despatched to them later that day or early on 26 April. The court martial was held the following day 27 April.

One possible explanation for the haste could be that, as it was desirable to have the whole crew of the *Sirius* present, an early date was arranged before they dispersed. As well, if an acquittal was likely, it was better to have the matter dealt with expeditiously so that all concerned could resume normal duties, or in the case of the crew move on to their next assignment.

Naval courts martial were usually held on board a naval vessel, often in the great cabin of the senior officer's ship and, in the late 18th century, could be described as 'a very imperfect instrument of justice'.[61] It consisted of between five and 13 captains or admirals, together with a secretary, none of whom were lawyers. Defendants were permitted to be represented by counsel. However, few ever were because of cost and availability and the proceedings were not according to the procedures of the civil and criminal courts. They could be lengthy processes, as each statement had to be recorded in longhand and read back to the witness or defendant. Those charged were judged by their peers without any legal training or guidelines, with the judge advocate or his deputy being in effect the court's secretary. The defendant's fate generally relied more on a sympathetic hearing than any formal consideration and testing of evidence. Courts could sentence for treason, mutiny, cowardice or murder, as well as for loss of ships. Commissioned officers found guilty of major crimes could be executed by shooting (although this practice ceased in the 1790s) while other ratings might be hanged from the forward yardarm, which Pope regarded as being more humane than land-based hangings, as 'the victim was hauled aloft by a party of sailors at high speed, and died almost instantly.'[62]

For a warship lost other than in battle, the entire crew was tried automatically, although attention was focused on the captain and officers whose career and reputation were then at stake. If found guilty, the captain could expect at least a demotion to the bottom of the seniority list or up to two years imprisonment, depending upon the degree of negligence. Few were ever found guilty, which would indicate a degree of leniency or even bias shown towards the captain or officers on trial. As the normal rules of legal evidence and cross-examination were not strictly followed, the proceedings were directed by a presiding officer (the most senior of those assembled) with a number of captains against a fellow captain, many of whom would have been friends or at least acquaintances. The system was biased in favour of the defendant in these cases, since any of the judging captains could inadvertently find themselves on the other side of the table sometime in the future. Setting harsh precedents could rebound to their own disadvantage.

Upon examining the minutes of Hunter's court martial, it is not difficult to conclude that, by modern standards, the procedures bordered on a cover-up in favour of the defendant, especially when that person was a brother captain. The transcript reveals that Vice Admiral Robert Roddam and seven captains, including a friend of Hunter's, Sir Roger Curtis, assembled in the great cabin of HMS *Brunswick*. The judge advocate formally convened the court 'to enquire into the cause and circumstances of the loss of His Majesty's Ship *Sirius* and to try Captain Hunter her Commander, his officers and Company for their conduct upon that occasion.'[63] The court was advised that Arthur Phillip had submitted a letter dated 18 April 1790 to the admiralty advising that he had ordered the *Sirius* and *Supply* to

Norfolk Island the previous month and on 5 April 1790, the *Supply* returned to Sydney with a letter from Hunter detailing the loss.

The relevant section of Phillip's letter read

> the *Sirius* was hove to in the Bay and the boats were employed in landing of provisions, when finding the ship dropping fast to leeward, he made sail to get out of the Bay, but the wind shifting they could not clear the Reef and the ship having missed stays, [lost the wind and momentum while turning] although the anchors were let go, and everything done that was possible, she struck and was lost on the Reef.[64]

As Phillip was relying on Hunter for this description, it can be presumed that Hunter omitted any reference detrimental to himself.

The court then asked Hunter: 'Have you any objection or complaint to make against any of the Officers or Ship's Company respecting the loss of His Majesty's late Ship *Sirius*,' to which he replied, 'None at all. They did their utmost to assist my endeavours.' The court then addressed the officers and crew: 'Have you any Objection or Complaint to make against the Captain respecting the loss of the *Sirius*?' The transcript recorded the response as 'None at all, on the Contrary everything that could be done was done.'[65] The court asked Captain Hunter: 'Have you any Narrative of the Facts relating to the loss?' Hunter responded 'Yes, I have.' It was then noted that 'Captain Hunter delivered a paper written which he signed and which was read by the judge advocate and is hereto annexed.'[66] This important ten-page report (see Appendix 2) was probably written by Hunter on Norfolk Island or during the return voyage and outlined in some detail the events leading up to and surrounding the wrecking. The relevant extracts are [with comments attached]:

> *On the 6th of March everything being embark'd, I sailed from Port Jackson. [No reference to the near loss.]
>
> *This day appearing by signal from the shore to be a favourable one in the passage of the surf thro' which the boats

had to pass to the landing place. [As outlined earlier, the flag only indicated a safe surf; it could not indicate currents or rips, sometimes invisible from the shore] I stood in as far as I judged safe, [a critical component of Hunter's competency] and brought the Ship too with her head off shore in the S.E. or windward part of the Bay. Got the boats out, loaded and sent them in. [No mention of standing the crew down or preparing for lunch.] The Supply was at this time close in and to leeward of the *Sirius*, as soon as the boats were despatched or rather before the second boat quitted the Ship, observing that she fell part to leeward, and settled in upon the shore. [But it was the Supply that alerted Hunter to this, according to Bradley[67] and Nagle.[68]]

*She pay'd short round on her Hull, but altho she went round in as little room as any ship could, yet being disappointed in stays in this particular situation and the ground consequently lost by that accident, I consider as the original and principal cause of our misfortune. [But if Hunter had more keenly assessed the currents, he could have stood further out from the shore. On the other hand, the fact that the *Supply* escaped would suggest the *Sirius* could have escaped also. Hunter appeared to have either underestimated the dangers or relaxed his vigilance.]

Hunter then pleaded inadequate knowledge of the reef area.

Here I must observe that the ship's striking where she did was rather unexpected by me, for I had never understood that the water was so very choal at such a Distance from the surf on the Shore, so very imperfect had the information been which we had from time to time receiv'd of this place.[69] [But this merely reinforced the need for additional caution in areas of uncertainty.]

Once the narrative had been read by the judge advocate, the court asked First Lieutenant William Bradley whether the account just read was true. He replied, 'They are, every part of them.'[70] Lieutenant Henry

Waterhouse was asked the same question and responded, 'Perfectly true, every part.'[71] The master and the remaining crew, including Nagle, then answered, 'It was very just and true.'[72] The court was then cleared and agreed that the *Sirius* was lost by 'an unexpected Westerly Current' and that 'her loss was not in any respect owing to the mismanagement or a want of proper attention to her safety'[73] by Hunter and the crew and they were duly honourably acquitted.

The proceedings of the court martial appeared to be a formality with no effort made to test Hunter's account, which is now known to be at best incomplete and at worst omitting vital details which would reflect badly on him. Bradley did not contradict Hunter's assertion that it was he who noticed the current rather than it having been pointed out to him by Lieutenant Ball. No reference was made to preparing for lunch or releasing some crew members to fish as the dangers approached. There could well have been a dangerously relaxed state of mind on board the *Sirius* as the boats were unloading, instead of a watch being kept on surrounding conditions. None of the officers would have dared dispute their captain's line of defence for fear of being perceived as disloyal or a troublemaker, with disastrous consequences for their own careers. The captains sitting along the *Brunswick*'s great cabin table could have been more rigorous in their questioning of Hunter and the crew, but equally they could well have been thinking 'there but for the Grace of God, go I' and that some time in the future they may also have to answer for losing their ship. There was a code of silence operating amongst all concerned.

Courts martial closing ranks around fellow captains were not unusual 200 years ago, especially as they were in effect closed shops with little need or regard for transparency. The court martial of William Bligh on 22 October 1790 on board HMS *Royal William* at Spithead, over the loss of the *Bounty*, could only have one outcome; notwithstanding Bligh's reputation as a vindictive and draconian captain. Bligh and those with him were honourably acquitted of responsibility for the *Bounty*'s loss, although only three witnesses were called and the questioning of them was perfunctory.[74] In this case, to have even vaguely or indirectly implied that any contribution or fault may have rested with Bligh would have given some encouragement or validity to the mutineers (who were yet to be tried) with the possibility of serious disciplinary problems arising in the future as a consequence. As it was, there was a naval mutiny seven years later in 1797 at the Nore over seamen's wages and conditions. In this instance, while the ringleaders were hanged, there were improvements as a result of negotiations by Hunter's patron, Lord Howe, but as a rule, the navy could not tolerate the slightest hint of acquiescence to any mutineers, no matter how severe their captain. Courts martial at that time were indeed a flawed system of justice.

The final aspect to be considered is that of collusion. It is inconceivable that Hunter did not discuss at length the chain of events with Bradley, Waterhouse, King and even Ross (with whom Hunter fell out) during their 11 months on Norfolk Island and on the long voyage home. How regularly did Bradley update his journal in his immaculate copperplate hand? How soon after the loss did Hunter write up his journal, and then edit it before publication? Did Hunter discuss his version of events before they wrote up their diaries? It has already been demonstrated that Cook and Banks did. Bradley and the other officers would have been aware, either firsthand or second-hand, of what actually happened on board the *Sirius*. As the officers also failed to note the growing danger, before it was too late, for their own preservation as well as Hunter's, the less said the better. Such collusion may well have been by unspoken agreement or mutual understanding of the need to present a united and consistent front to the court and to be totally supportive of their commanding officer. There was what appeared to be a veiled alliance between the captain and his officers in the evidence presented. It served no one's benefit to break ranks. In similar vein, the captains comprising the court also had a vested interest in the softness of their approach. The acquittal was a convenient outcome for all concerned, and it can be presumed that this code of silence operated throughout the Royal Navy at this time.

The transcript leaves a strong impression that the hearing was more of a necessary showpiece formality than an exhaustive enquiry. Prima facie, Hunter's narrative would seem to exonerate him from negligence and mismanagement, but after peering below the surface, there is also a lingering notion that the loss was in fact avoidable had Hunter been more aware and alert, i.e. a better captain, and that, had the court proceedings been more rigorous and impartial, the truth may have emerged.

The loss of HMS Venerable

The somewhat tenuous peace treaty between Britain and France signed at Amiens in 1802 collapsed in May 1803, after which the Royal Navy responded by increasing its numbers and upgrading the readiness of its ships. In late August 1804, Hunter, four years after his governorship of New South Wales, became captain of a 20-year-old, 74 gun, third rate battleship HMS *Venerable* of 1669 tons. She was part of the Channel Fleet under Admiral Sir William Cornwallis, employed in blockading Brest to assist in preventing a French invasion of Britain. It is not known precisely when Hunter joined the *Venerable*, but as he was not on the ship's muster roll on 21 August 1804 and signed a roll dated 1 September 1804, he would have come on board between then.[75] Hunter's appointment is surprising in one sense, given that he was 67, with limited command experience and had lost one ship. Conversely, the navy was short of senior captains due to the ravages of disease and the wars against France and the rebel American colonies.

The weather in the channel with the approach of winter was often bad, which made blockading a risky undertaking. Squadrons ran short of food or had to avoid being driven perilously close to the French coast and were sometimes forced to seek shelter and provisions in protected waters along the south coast of England. One such haven was Torbay, a large, fairly open, south-east facing bay on the Devon coast between Exmouth and Plymouth, the latter port at that time not having the protection of its mile-long break water built some time later. Hunter knew Torbay quite well, having called in there on several occasions during his seafaring career, but more importantly, having assisted in its survey in 1781 while serving on the *Berwick*. When the wind blew from the east into the bay, sailing ships had difficulty in leaving, notwithstanding the four-and-a-half mile distance from the north headland to Berry Head in the south, and ran the risk of being blown onto the western shore by the wind or the swells, i.e. embayed. Cornwallis adopted the system of all ships being ready to put to sea immediately the wind turned easterly and before the heavy swells rolled into the bay. On 23 November 1804 the Channel Fleet was anchored in Torbay, forced through contrary winds from blockading Brest. The following morning, 24 November, saw heavy, continuous rain with light westerly winds. At about 2.30pm, the wind suddenly turned from the west to the north-east with the heavy rain continuing unabated, so Cornwallis elected to go to sea without delay. The respective ships' boats were recalled from the shore and at about 4.00pm, Cornwallis' flagship *Ville de Paris* made signal for the squadron to weigh anchor and proceed into the Channel.

The events leading to the destruction of the *Venerable* are outlined in four extant contemporary sources. The first and most detailed is Hunter's own report to the subsequent court martial[76], a brief account of the loss in 3 December 1804 edition of Avis' *Birmingham Gazette*[77] and two extracts from the Bonwick Transcripts, one being a summary of the evidence given by one of the officers at the court martial[78] and the other, a one-page description of the incident written by a Mr Heaton.[79] To this can be added a 15-page booklet written by Colonel

Gerald Boyle just over 100 years later in 1913, based upon the court martial proceedings, and who possessed good local knowledge.[80]

The *Venerable* was anchored near the middle of the bay—marked A in the following diagram.

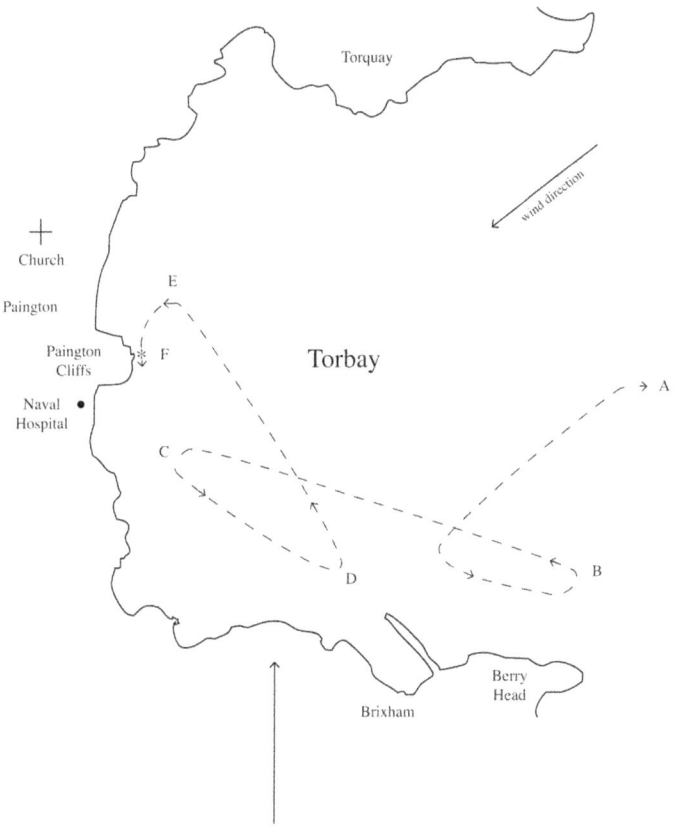

Figure 16. Last movements of HMS *Venerable* on 24 November 1804.

When the wind increased and shifted to the north-east and the rain blotted out the shore marks, Cornwallis made the order to sail. Once the boats had returned to their ships, the crews raised their anchors and were in the process of securing them as the ships began to manoeuvre out of Torbay against the rising wind and swells. On the *Venerable*, just as the crew were 'hooking the cat' (lashing the anchor to the hull) one of the men fell overboard from his perch on the anchor. The cry of 'man overboard' sent a crew to quickly launch a boat, but in their haste and approaching darkness one of the boat's ropes was let go too quickly. The boat tipped, throwing midshipman Frederick Deas and two seamen into the water, drowning all three. Another boat was lowered from the other side of the ship which managed to pick up the original seaman who fell from the anchor.

While the rescue and retrieval was underway, the *Venerable*'s foresails and topgallants were being set, but all the time the ship had been drifting back into the bay and was then unable to weather Berry Head—marked B on the diagram. They tacked and headed north-west but found themselves in danger of running into other ships of the fleet also attempting to leave. To avoid collisions, they lost more ground and suddenly on tacking once more, found themselves near the lights of Paignton Hospital (C). They attempted once again to round Berry Head (D), but were unsuccessful and headed north-west as before. Another ship loomed out of the gloom and in avoiding her, they lost more ground (E). At about 8.30pm the wind died and as it did, the ship touched bottom and then grounded hard. The rain stopped momentarily and they could see they were under the Paignton cliffs (F). The *Venerable* was held by rocks fore and aft. However, the lull did not last and the wind came back from the east with increasing velocity and the seas rose up with it. The crew attempted to cut the masts away so they would fall between the ship and the shore to provide a means of escape, but the attempt failed. As the ship was now likely to capsize, distress signals were fired and by 10.00pm the water had reached the lower gun deck inside and large waves were breaking over the hull. Having heard the distress signals, HMS *Impeteux* anchored close by and worked her way back to within 600 metres of the *Venerable*. HMS *Goliath* did likewise and both sent their boats to the stricken ship. The *Venerable*'s crew dropped into the boats from stern ladders in a wild rescue relay amidst high winds and a pounding surf. By midnight, the ship was almost on her side and soon after the last man was taken off, she broke in two and disintegrated. The loss of life was only eight (including the midshipman and the two sailors drowned earlier) which was a tribute to the courage and skill of the crews of the *Goliath* and *Impeteux*.

From the safety and with the benefit of hindsight, there would appear to be two occasions when Hunter could have taken different steps to save the *Venerable*. Firstly, while the boat was rescuing the seaman (and presumably the overturned boat and her drowned crew were being retrieved) the ship's drift should have been noted. When this drift began to compromise the ship's safety, the boat could have been ordered to proceed to the shore, or another ship, once its mission had been accomplished, while the *Venerable* made haste to get under way. Hunter should have been more aware of the circumstances surrounding him and taken earlier corrective action so that the ship could have cleared Berry Head on her first attempt. Secondly, other ships were still in the bay while Hunter was manoeuvring around them, and all managed to clear the bay, except the *Venerable*. Had Hunter tacked differently, earlier or more often, he might have extricated himself as the other ships did. There was probably a combination of bad luck and bad management involved.

Hunter had not independently commanded a ship since the loss of the *Sirius* 14 years earlier (although he was in charge of the *Waaksamheyd* on the last leg of her voyage home) as his time on the *Queen Charlotte*, *Reliance* and *Buffalo* was always in the company of another captain. He had not been to sea for three years (since returning from Sydney in the *Buffalo*) before taking up his appointment to the *Venerable* in August

1804. Under such circumstances and taking into account his age, it is feasible to speculate that Hunter was not perceptive enough or not able to react quickly enough to make the series of rapid decisions necessary to preserve his ship. It is also possible to postulate that, once again, his inadequate command experience took its toll. Hunter knew Torbay better than many of the other captains, all of whom got clear, notwithstanding the poor visibility with which the other ships also had to contend. For the second time, a perception emerges that the loss of the *Venerable* was not unavoidable or inevitable.

The court martial of Hunter and the crew was held 16 days later on board HMS *Salvador de Mundo* on Monday 10 December 1804 at Plymouth, under Vice Admiral Cuthbert Collingwood (not on 11 December under Vice Admiral Young as claimed by Hoyle[81]) together with Rear Admiral John Sutton and nine captains. After a letter from Captain Thomas Martin of the *Impeteux* was tendered, a narrative of 'the circumstances of the getting under weigh and loss of His Majesty's late ship *Venerable*'[82] was read to the court. The account was written in the first person plural (we) and appears in the minutes in the handwriting of the Deputy Judge Advocate, Robert Liddel, but Hunter's name appears at the foot of the report. At one point however, after the ship had gone aground, the narrative relates 'we were then ordered to quit the ship as fast as the boats could come near enough to the stern ladders.'[83] Who issued the order if it was not Hunter? Perhaps it was Captain Martin of the *Impeteux* or a senior officer in one of the boats.

Following standard procedures Hunter was asked by the court if the statement just read was true, to which Hunter affirmed yes, after which he was questioned whether he had any complaint to make of any of the officers or ship's company. Hunter replied that he had none at all. The officers and ship's company were then asked if they had any knowledge whether any officers or crew were guilty of neglect or disobedience on the night of the loss, which Lieutenant Thompson and the officers answered that they had not. Thus far the proceedings were similar to those of the earlier hearing, however Hunter then proceeded to question Captain Martin on weather conditions in the bay and the extent to which his own ship was at risk. Martin agreed there was great risk, 'not only from the hazard in crossing on difficult tacks, but the impossibility of seeing the land and the consequent uncertainty of our situation.'[84] Martin also admitted his ship was at one point probably near where the *Venerable* went aground, but he did not see any land to verify this; all of which was supportive of Hunter's position. Lieutenant Thompson of the *Venerable* was then called and corroborated Hunter's account. Thomas Hodgson, the master, another lieutenant, the boatswain, quartermaster and several seamen were also called; all of whom testified along the same lines as Hunter's statement. The questioning of the witnesses by the court simply confirmed Hunter's version of events and the minutes then recorded that

> The Court having heard Captain Hunter's Narrative of circumstances and examined the surviving officers and company of the *Venerable*, and very maturely and deliberately weighed and considered the said Narrative and Evidence, was of the opinion that no blame whatever attached to Captain John Hunter or any of the surviving Officers and Company of His Majesty's late ship *Venerable* for their conduct and proceedings—as it appeared that every possible precautionary measure was adopted.[85]

Hunter was duly acquitted.

Once again, it can be conjectured that the questions raised by the court lacked vigour or insight and were more concerned with endorsing Hunter's statement than probing beneath the veneer to establish whether there was any culpability or incompetence on anyone's part. Perhaps there was also a veiled alliance in this instance, not only between Hunter and the officers but also between the captains embodying the court for reasons outlined in the earlier court martial. Although not recorded in the court minutes as such, it is alleged that, at the time of his trial, Hunter 'was said to have pleaded his belief that the King preferred the life of a subject to the safety of a ship.'[86] Considering that Hunter lost eight crew members plus his ship in order to successfully save one life, this logic does not justify his

Figure 17. Inscription: 'Loss of HMS *Venerable*. To Captain Hunter, his officers and company. This representation of their unfortunate Shipwreck of the night of 24th November 1804 on the rocks in Torbay is most respectfully inscribed by their obt. Servant Robt. Dodd.' Painted by R. Dodd from a sketch by J.T. Lee. Courtesy of the National Maritime Museum, Greenwich.

actions. With the advantages of hindsight, Hunter could have taken different courses of action and still saved his ship as well as the seaman and the boat crew, even though they may have been separated in the process. The tipping of the boat was an accidental by-product of well-intentioned haste so the loss of Midshipman Deas and the two sailors was no direct fault of Hunter's. However, it cannot be equally claimed that the loss of the other five crew members as well as the *Venerable* was beyond the control and responsibility of John Hunter.

In reviewing the two near misses and the loss of the *Sirius*, the Botany Bay mishaps plus the narrow escape in the *Waaksamheyd* and the loss of HMS *Venerable*, a pattern emerges pointing to a deficiency in John Hunter's judgement capabilities. When confronted with command decisions of a tactical nature, Hunter sometimes displayed an inability to anticipate the consequences of his actions or inactions. Hunter did not see the dangers confronting the *Sirius* as it drifted towards the rocks, as Lieutenant Ball could. Hunter did not realise quickly enough the hazards arising from drifting back into Torbay, an area he knew well. Potential embayment appeared to be Hunter's Achilles heel and there is an element of causal similarity between the losses of the *Sirius* and the *Venerable*. Hunter's lapses were possibly a mixture of both inadequate experience and simply the failings of a man of advancing age. It needs to be emphasised however, that Hunter's seamanship expertise was never in doubt and was again put to good use after both ships went aground. He undoubtedly did all that he could in cutting the masts, seeking assistance and saving the crew. It is an endorsement of these skills that he lost none of the *Sirius* crew and only eight from the *Venerable*. The toll could well have been much higher. Had Hunter been tried exhaustively with all the evidence produced and tested, it would appear likely that he could have been found negligent on both occasions and perhaps have been demoted down the seniority list or even lost his hard-won commission as a result.

Hunter lacked sufficient broad-based independent command familiarity while his seamanship strengths probably best suited him as a master or second captain, but his technical expertise was acknowledged and recognised. Perhaps he became a captain too late, at a time when his capacity for assessing situations and making speedy decisions had not fully developed or was diminishing. The delays in his promotions, while not of his doing, almost certainly contributed to the problems arising from his later command decisions, both at sea and in New South Wales.

6
Whence came the pox?

Just over a year after the First Fleet arrived at Sydney Cove, an outbreak of smallpox crippled the local Aboriginal population, but left the white settlers unscathed. The source of the epidemic remained a mystery for the ensuing 200 years, with historians and medical practitioners periodically debating whether it really was smallpox, if it was already present in Australia or whether the Europeans brought it with them in 1788 or 1770, or even earlier. The question has not been conclusively or convincingly answered to date but it might now be possible to definitively respond to queries of 'whence came the pox'.

Following the return of the *Sirius* on 9 May 1789 to Port Jackson from its voyage to Cape Town, John Hunter wrote:

> I expressed much surprize, at not having seen a single native on the shore, or a canoe as we came up in the ship; the reason of which I could not comprehend, until I was informed that the small-pox made its appearance, a few months ago [actually the disease manifested itself the previous month] amongst those unfortunate creatures. As we had never yet seen any of these people who have been in the smallest degree marked with the smallpox, we had reason to suppose they have never before now been affected by it, and consequently are strangers to any method of treating it: and, if we consider the various attitudes which the different dead bodies have been found in, we may easily believe that when any of them are taken ill, and the malady assumes the appearance of the small-pox (having already experienced its fatality to whole families) they are

immediately deserted by their friends, and left to perish, in their helpless situation, for want of sustenance.[1]

John Hunter had an inherent interest in people and activities around him. As a kind, caring and compassionate man, his diary indicates that he gave the epidemic considerable thought and his inquisitive nature, combined with his observational skills, ensured that he analysed the origins and implications of the calamity in some depth. The possible causes would have been discussed with others over lunch or after supper in front of a fire (it was the beginning of winter) on many occasions, while his concern over the effects of the outbreak on the health and welfare of the local population caused him genuine distress.

These discussions with fellow officers revealed a variety of differing interpretations regarding the origins of the disease. Bradley recorded, 'How this disease came among them, or whether they were strangers to it before, is doubtful.'[2] Newton Fowell, a lieutenant on the *Sirius* wrote to his father from Batavia on 31 July 1790, 'How this disease got among them it is impossible to tell, but it is supposed that they had it among them before any European visited the country, as they have a name for it.'[3] This last important point is confirmed by Collins, but not raised by Hunter, possibly because Hunter did not discover the local word for it until later.

> Whether it had ever appeared among them before could not be discovered, either from him [an aborigine living in the settlement at the time] or from the children; but it was certain that they gave it a name (gal-gal-la); a circumstance which seemed to indicate a preacquaintance with it.[4]

This linkage is overlooked by the proponents of the camp favouring the European infestation theory. It is also worth noting that while Hunter makes no reference to this connection, the word 'gall gall' appears in his vocabulary as meaning smallpox, but this is possibly due to his learning of this word at a later date.[5] He therefore eventually knew the native name for the disease but did not draw, or at least record, the conclusion at the time that the Aborigines already knew of smallpox. It is unlikely that they would have had a word for a condition that was unknown to them. King was prepared to make a judgement on the matter upon his return from Norfolk Island in 1790 when he wrote, 'This dreadful disorder, which there is no doubt, is a distemper natural to the country, together with the difficulty of procuring a subsistance, renders the situation of these poor wretches truly miserable.'[6]

There is no reference to smallpox in *The Voyage of Governor Phillip to Botany Bay* as it was published in late 1789, but Phillip does refer to it in his letter to Lord Sydney dated 12 February 1790, nine months after the outbreak.

> Whether the smallpox, which has proved fatal to great numbers of the natives is a disorder to which they were subject before any European visited this country, or whether it was brought by the French ships, we have [not] attained sufficient knowledge of the language to determine. It never appeared on Board any of the ships in our passage, nor in the settlement, until some time after numbers of the natives had been seen dead with the disorder in different parts of the harbour.[7]

Interestingly, only one of the new arrivals succumbed to the disease, a native American seaman on the *Supply*, who died a few days later. This would imply a degree of inherited immunity by those of the First Fleet. On the following day, 13 February 1790, Phillip contemplated the extent of the impact of smallpox on the indigenous community.

> It is not possible to determine the numbers of natives who were carried off by this fatal disorder. It must be great, and judging from the information of the native now living with us … one half of those who inhabit this part of the country died.

He went on, 'it must have spread to a considerable distance, as well inland as along the coast.'[8]

The cause of the outbreak remained a matter of conjecture, as evidenced in a letter Elizabeth Macarthur wrote two years after the catastrophe to her friend in England on 7 March 1791. 'In the winter 1789 (which you will recollect is summer in England) a dreadful smallpox was discovered amongst the natives. How the disorder was introduced cannot be discovered.'[9] Thirty years after the event in 1819, William Charles Wentworth wrote in his description of New South Wales,

> Some few years, indeed, before the foundation of this Colony, the smallpox committed the most dreadful ravages among the aborigines. This exterminating scourge is said to be introduced by Captain Cook and many of the contemporaries of those who fell victim to it, are still living; and the deep furrows which remain in some of their countenances, show how narrowly they escaped the same premature destiny.[10]

The *Sirius*'s surgeon George Worgan left the settlement before the outbreak occurred but makes no reference to smallpox during the voyage out in his letters up to July 1788. Interestingly, although John White was the Surgeon General to the colony until his departure in the *Daedalus* on 16 December 1794, he left no mention or reference to smallpox in his writings which have survived. While his narrative concludes in November 1788, the notes he wrote concerning the next five years he spent in Sydney have unfortunately been lost. Rex Rienits wrote a biographical introduction to the 1962 publication of White's Journal and stated that 'no evidence of the disease had previously been seen among either natives or whites, and the cause of the outbreak remained a mystery.'[11]

The most detailed analysis at that time was proposed by Captain Watkin Tench of the marines, 'how a disease, to which our former observations had led us to suppose them strangers, could at once have introduced itself, and have spread so widely, seemed inexplicable.' He added as a postscript,

No solution of this difficulty had been given when I left the country, in December, 1791, I can, therefore, only propose queries for the ingenuity of others to exercise itself upon: Is it a disease indigenous to the country? Did the French ships under Monsieur de Peyrouse [sic] introduce it? let it be remembered that they had now been departed more than a year; and we had never heard of its existence on board of them.—Had it travelled across the continent from its western shore, where Dampier and other European voyagers had formerly landed?— Was it introduced by Mr Cook?—Did we give it birth here? No person among us had been afflicted with the disorder since we had quitted the Cape of Good Hope, seventeen months before. It is true, that our surgeons had brought out variolous matters in bottles; but to infer that it was produced from this cause were a supposition so wild as to be unworthy of consideration.[12]

When Phillip took an exploration party up the Hawkesbury River in July 1789, a month after the outbreak, Tench reported that 'natives were found on the banks in several parts, many of whom were labouring under the small-pox', indicating the swift spread of the disease.[13]

Until recently, it has not been possible to be conclusive about the source of the smallpox epidemic. However recent research has enabled fairly explicit conclusions to be drawn. As there has been little detailed attempt to date to piece together all the available scientific and historical data on the outbreak, it is proposed to answer Hunter's query, especially as his observations form part of the fabric of evidence used by some observers to clothe their theories.

The matter remained one for (muted) technical discussion in medical journals and occasional references to it by historians for nearly 200 years until the press seized upon a book by Butlin published in 1983 titled *Our Original Aggression*[14] and popularised its essential finding that it was indeed the first settlers who introduced smallpox to the

Aborigines—'How English settlers waged biological war on the aborigines'[15]—a view then promoted by the media and some sections of the community leading up to and during the bicentenary celebrations in 1988. There had been, however, some limited references before this.

Prior to 1914, medical notes on smallpox were confined to technical descriptions in medical journals and occasional reflections on earlier outbreaks. In the first edition of the *New South Wales Medical Gazette 1870-71* there is an article by Dr George Bennett who described a report written by a Dr John Mair in the 1830s.

> As far as our information at present extends, it appears not to be an introduced disease, or at least we have no facts to prove such being the case ... As far back as the year 1789, an eruptive disorder, resembling the small-pox, broke out amongst the aborigines, and proved extremely fatal: its marks were still to be seen on the bodies of several of them of very advanced age, corresponding in appearance with the pits left by the small-pox.[16]

Australian history books of the later 19th century made passing reference to the incident, for example James Bonwick in his *First Twenty Years of Australia*, published in 1882, remarked:

> Shortly after the English landed, a fearful pestilence set in among them (the aborigines) and very many bodies were left unburied in the bush. The disease—Gal-gal-la—is termed a sort of smallpox, though the affection was unknown among our own people there. According to their own account a similar desolation visited them the year before we came.[17]

Opinions on the cause of the disease were still mixed 100 years after the event. Hunter's views in 1789 were still feasible a century later. The two main points made by him were that no natives had been seen with smallpox marks or pits prior to the outbreak, and therefore they had not been exposed to or affected by it before and had no knowledge of any treatment.

The first exacting attempt to analyse the outbreak of 1789 was published by J.H.L. Cumpston in 1914, but drawing upon work done by Mullins in 1879, Tidwell in 1898 and Cleland in 1912.[18] Cumpston reviewed most of Tench's five propositions. Was it indigenous to the country? Did La Perouse introduce it? Did it travel across the continent from the west? Did Cook bring it on the *Endeavour*? Did it come with the First Fleet? Cumpston further wondered whether it was really smallpox (or possibly chicken pox) and if it could have been introduced by Macassan fishermen (travelling from the Indonesian island of Sulawesi) into northern Australia and spreading to central New South Wales (which was Cleland's 1912 hypothesis).

Based upon the data and knowledge available to Cumpston in 1914, he concluded that

> It does not appear that the evidence advanced by Cleland in favour of his hypothesis is very convincing and pending the discovery of more satisfactory information, the safest course would seem to be to follow the generally accepted theory that the introduction of the disease amongst the aborigines was in some way associated with the arrival in Australia of a comparatively large number of Europeans.[19]

But he conceded that 'an unusually long interval'[20] had elapsed between the arrival of the First Fleet and the French expedition and the appearance of the outbreak and that there were no signs of smallpox on the voyage out. He then appears at odds with himself by stating that

> the hypothesis that the French fleet was responsible has some support in a statement made in 1804 by a Dr Jamieson who said 'It is generally accredited by the medical gentlemen of the colony on its first establishment that the small-pox had been

introduced among the natives by the crews of the French ships then lying in Botany Bay.'[21]

He does not speculate on how this could have occurred. Later evidence will discount this theory. Cumpston does agree that the disease was smallpox, 'it is abundantly clear that there was a very extensive epidemic of smallpox amongst the aborigines'[22], but he does not address the possibilities of Cook's or Dampier's involvement. He does admit that the 'variolous matter cannot be dismissed lightly as a possible source' but offers no explanation of how it could be the case.[23]

While Cumpston's conclusions are incomplete and somewhat insubstantial, they did form a useful basis for later investigation. Little of real analytical note appeared for the next 70 years until Butlin published *Our Original Aggression* in 1983, in which he came to a number of radical and controversial conclusions which grabbed media attention. Butlin dismissed the Macassan fishermen theory as having 'a low probability of occurring'[24] and attacked the First Fleet settlers for engaging in 'a conspiracy of silence' regarding the demographic consequences of the pestilence (i.e. the number of Aborigines killed) and

> there are some possibilities that might lead one to believe that epidemic disease could have been used deliberately as an exterminating agent. Although one cannot be certain, the most reasonable judgement seems to be at the least, that there was a failure of responsibility by British authorities, very likely with catastrophic consequences for Australian aborigines.[25]

He expanded on this concept, 'the whites had control of a virus known to be extremely potent and failed in their responsibility. It is possible and quite likely that they deliberately opened Pandora's Box.'[26] Butlin also refuted the notion that smallpox was an indigenous disease because Hunter declared 'the absence of pock marking'[27] and since the French left 13 months before, they would not have been implicated and that 'the Dampier hypothesis may simply be ignored and Hunter again negates the Cook hypothesis' (no pock mark signs).[28]

Butlin develops his deliberate transfer theory by claiming that 'although one might exclude Phillip as a matter of judgement, no similar exclusion applies to other senior authority; it cannot be beyond reasonable bounds that Phillip was pressured into action'[29], however this assertion has been undermined by subsequent writers. Two years later in 1985 P.H. Curson published a book *Times of Crisis* in which he ponders on Butlin's claims, but does not reach firm conclusions of his own. He poses more options than answers. 'Tench's reference to variolous matters remains highly suspicious and cannot be dismissed out of hand as a possible source of the epidemic'[30], followed by a cautious conclusion. 'While Butlin's case largely rests on circumstantial evidence as well as the assumption that the disease agent in question was smallpox, it nonetheless provides a plausible explanation of how the disease might have spread to the aboriginal population.'[31] Even the argument over whether the outbreak was smallpox or chicken pox is not assisted by Curson's each-way bet. As to whether the disease was an indigenous pox, Curson is again vague, relying on Cumpston's conclusion that it could have been a spurious kind of chickenpox. Notwithstanding that the French left over a year before the epidemic, well beyond smallpox's incubation period, Curson provides no opinion himself but relies on others (Cleland) to discuss the proposition. The general debate on the subject was continued but not advanced.

In 1988 John Goldsmid published *The Deadly Legacy* in which he was at least prepared to take a stand on some of the questions under review, including the points made by Hunter, albeit without providing substantiating or new information, 'There seems little doubt that smallpox was not endemic in Australia before the Europeans arrived and suggestions to the contrary lack any really solid foundation.'[32] He does gently tackle Butlin's theme of deliberately infecting; the suggestion that this was done in Australia has recently been resurrected in the press, but there is no evidence for this accusation[33], but concentrates more on airing issues than solving them, e.g. 'It has been suggested that smallpox was introduced not with the Europeans at all, but that it spread from the north from Macassan traders', tantalising the reader with the concept but then failing to pursue it.[34]

It was not until one year later, in 1989, that Butlin's claims began to be effectively tested and reasoned conclusions started to emerge. Alan Frost first entered the fray via a joint contribution to *Studies from Terra Australis to Australia* with J. Hardy, in which he stated 'the evidence for smallpox (versus chickenpox) is by no means conclusive'[35], but five years later he had changed his mind to 'it seems sensible to conclude that the disease that struck the Aborigines about Port Jackson in April 1789 was indeed smallpox.'[36] Further, Frost claimed in 1989

> It was clear that the surgeons had no active variolous material available when the epidemic occurred, for they feared smallpox so much that their first act would have been to inoculate all who were at risk, especially the children. This they did not do.[37]

However, there is no evidence to support these contentions. Tench certainly refers to the surgeons having the material at that time, but did they know whether it was active or not? If they knew it was useless, why keep it? None of the surgeons' notes of this time are extant, but it is reasonable to conclude that they would not have been aware of the variolous material's life-span nor of the effect that hot summer weather would have had on its viability. To inoculate children after the onset of the outbreak may have been too late, but no white child (or adult) died from smallpox. As Tench himself said 'nothing which medical skill and unremitting attention could perform, were left unexerted.'[38] These children could well have inherited the immunity from their parents, even if they were inoculated with inert 'variolous material'.

Frost's next foray into the debate appeared as *Botany Bay Mirages* in 1994. While his points are made with strength, using a range of convincing historical and demographic evidence, there is a lack of scientific verification to support some of his claims, but at least some of Butlin's assertions were being seriously contested. Referring to the origins of the outbreak, Frost wrote 'adopting his characteristic mode of fearless pronouncement wrapped in seductive but misleading prose, Robert Hughes has stated that cholera and influenza germs [sic] from the ships began the work [of destroying the Aborigines] ... Noel Butlin went a good deal further when he suggested not only that the infection came from the Europeans, but also that it was deliberately conveyed.'[39] Frost then proceeds to demolish the theory, commencing his case by saying 'it is extraordinary that a serious scholar should have raised this mirage, for there is no documentary evidence to support it. Let us examine the record with a dispassionate eye.'[40]

He then outlined, using reason and logic, why this could not have happened. The Aborigines did not have access to the medical supplies so that accidental infection was not possible; in fact the Aborigines rarely ventured into the settlement; access to the medical store by Europeans, let alone the Aborigines, was restricted; and when the outbreak did occur, the surgeons did their best to treat those Aborigines brought in—an unlikely scenario if the policy was to exterminate them. Most importantly, Frost reviews the evidence indicating that it was unlikely or virtually impossible for the virus to have remained alive in those conditions for the two years since the First Fleet left England in May 1787 and to have survived two hot Sydney summers, as it was temperature sensitive. (Hunter records a maximum of 80 degrees F [26.6 degrees C] in January 1788 and 102 degrees F [44.4 degrees C] the following December).[41] Frost concludes that 'there are no grounds whatsoever for supposing that they deliberately opened "Pandora's Box".'[42]

Was it really smallpox? Contemporary opinion would seem, on balance, to say yes. Collins stated 'that it was the small-pox there was scarcely a doubt, for the person seized with it was affected exactly as Europeans who have that disorder.'[43] Hunter wrote, 'I was informed that the small-pox had made its appearance.'[44] Frost described the onset and appearance of the disease as described by the observers and decided 'on the balance of things then, the process of the disease seems to conform to that of smallpox infection.'[45] This conclusion is borne out by comparing smallpox symptoms described by the actual observers with those outlined in a modern medical diagnosis text book. The two descriptions conform, with the textbook version issuing an interesting caution. 'The pre-eruptive stage may be mistaken for an acute respiratory infection; the eruptive stage may be mistaken for chicken pox'[46], a mistake either made by or seized upon by commentators such as Cumpston, Curson and Goldsmid. It is worth noting that most contemporary observers would have seen smallpox (especially the surgeons) far more frequently (notwithstanding immunity levels) than those coming 100 or 200 years later, while the surgeons would have been better able to distinguish it from chickenpox, as opposed to later medical practitioners with less experience of both diseases.

Frost also examined the question of whether smallpox was endemic or introduced by the white settlers. He considered the demographic data and discovered that there could well have been sufficient numbers of Aborigines to convey the disease from the northern coastline to central New South Wales and beyond. While Butlin and others clung onto Tench's comments that their observations led them to believe the Aborigines were strangers to it and Hunter's assertion that no sign of pock marks was proof that it was not endemic, Frost remarked that 'in doing so, those historians simply did not read far enough'[47], and pointed out that King, Hunter and Collins demonstrated that the Aborigines had a name for it, which is a fairly strong indicator of preacquaintance. As Newton Fowell put it, 'it is conjectured that it was among them before any European visited the Country as they have a name for it.'[48] Why would they have a name for a condition they did not know?

Did the smallpox come with the First Fleet or with the French? Frost dismisses this concept on the grounds that there is no evidence by any diarist that the disease was present on the voyage out, and discussions with the French at Botany Bay revealed no evidence of smallpox on either ship, added to the fact that all ships had been away from Europe and other potential contact points sufficiently long for any variolous material to have died long before the disease outbreak. Similarly there is no evidence of any smallpox on the *Endeavour*, 19 years before the 1789 incident, and none of Cook's crew died of disease before arriving in Batavia. For smallpox to have originated from Dampier's landings on Australia's arid north-west coast in 1688 and 1699 would have required the disease to be transmitted from west to east across the continent. Aboriginal numbers in that region were insufficient for smallpox to spread in a north-easterly or south-easterly direction, especially when having to cross over the vast stretches of emptiness now known as the Great Sandy, Gibson and Great Victoria deserts, which form a barren barrier extending more than 1200 kilometres eastwards into the Northern Territory and South Australia.

Frost concluded that the remaining option was transmission from the Macassan fishermen who visited northern Australian shores each year for trepang, or *bêche-de-mer*, to sell to the Chinese. He demonstrated the voyage duration, from Sulawesi to northern Australia, of ten to 15 days would enable the smallpox to incubate and allow carriers to infect natives they came in contact with. Frost then argued that demographic evidence now shows that there were in fact sufficient Aborigines to transmit the disease to New South Wales and that Aborigines had more contact with other groups (thereby spreading the virus) than

Butlin suggested. Frost supported this contention with evidence of the spread of smallpox in Africa and experiences of later smallpox epidemics in Australia in the 1860s where its source can be sheeted home to the Macassans.[49]

It would seem reasonable to conclude that Frost's arguments are logical and compelling and that the disease did not come from the Europeans in 1789, but rather was transmitted from the north along aboriginal paths south and east. However, as definitive and as thorough as Frost's deductions may appear, they lacked scientific collaboration and it was left to Judy Campbell in 2002 to close this loop. Her work, based on 20 years' research, produces convincing scientific evidence that not only did the epidemic kill about half the existing aboriginal population (thus confirming Phillip's estimation based on Bennelong's information), but also that the source was indeed the Macassan region of the Indonesian Island of Sulawesi.[50]

The crux of her findings revolves around the enormous amount of research on smallpox gathered during 1967–79 in the World Health Organization Intensified Smallpox Eradication Program, published in 1988. She was also able to show that the other two major smallpox outbreaks of the late 1820s and 1860s also killed about half the Aborigines in the respective catchment areas, which would go far in explaining the low numbers of Aborigines in those regions seen in later years, 'their small numbers astounded newcomers'.[51]

Her arguments in favour of the Macassan theory are supported by evidence of the disease in South Sulawesi in the 1780s; and that it spread south and east from the points of contact on the north Australian coast, 'by the mid-19th century, it was clear to older migrants in South-Eastern and Southern Australia that small-pox had occurred before settlement' and 'when the country was settled in the 1830s, 1840s and 1850s, well-informed British and German migrants saw elderly pockmarked aboriginal people in districts they occupied.'[52]

The scientific as well as anecdotal data quoted by Campbell, plus the fact that the Aborigines already had a name for the disease, corroborates the historical and demographic proposals put up by Frost. This leads to a reasoned and tenable conclusion that the smallpox outbreak in New South Wales in 1789, as described by Hunter, did in fact predate the First Fleet and was not of European origin, but rather emigrated from the Dutch East Indies and was brought to Australia by Macassan fishermen.

7
The challenge of New South Wales

The highlight of John Hunter's career should have been his five-year term as the second governor of New South Wales from 1795 to 1800. It would have been the pinnacle of an almost astonishingly rapid series of promotions (after a prolonged gestation period) within only 15 years from receiving his commission as lieutenant. Instead, it became a period of frustration, torment, confusion and bewilderment, culminating in an ignominious recall with his reputation and future seemingly compromised and being persona non grata at the Colonial Office. To appreciate what went wrong with his governorship requires an understanding of why the colony had become such a difficult place to govern, together with the nature and extent of the opposition and the issues he faced. In particular, the actions of the New South Wales Corps require scrutiny to ascertain whether its image and reputation was justly warranted.

Manning Clark described Hunter as 'a man of incorruptable integrity, unceasing zeal and a sound and impartial judgement'[1], to which Ritchie added 'Hunter possessed a toughness which strengthened his power to endure hardship and pain'[2], which would have indicated a person well positioned for a successful term in office. On the other hand, he has also been described by other historians as being 'out of his depth as Governor of New South Wales'[3] and 'a sensible, pleasant, friendly old salt, brave and honest, but not perhaps tough minded enough for the position'[4], as well as 'a weak but well-meaning sort of man who made feeble and inefficient attempts to put down the infamous traffic [of rum] ... He seems to have been a muddle-headed person.'[5]

These seemingly contradictory descriptions of Hunter are symptomatic of a general lack of awareness of the depth and extent of the virtually intractable problems which confronted him during his five-year term of office—the monopolists' domination of trade; the trafficking of spirits; the allocation of labour; law and order and the acquisition of land. The entrenched forces opposing him were determined that their power should prevail and played all the cards they possessed to win, including disobedience, subversion, sabotage and innuendo. Clark described Hunter's failure as 'a public one, written over the pages of the history of New South Wales, the impotence of the good man before men with evil and malice and madness in their hearts.'[6] It would therefore appear that, in part, Hunter has been misjudged because of the insufficient consideration given to the magnitude of the problems which beset him. He may have been ill-prepared and even unsuited to break the stranglehold of the New South Wales Corps, but its power and influence at that time was insidious, pervasive and extensive. Each of the assessments quoted above are intrinsically correct, but they do not represent a comprehensive picture of Hunter's character and abilities, nor do they take into account the tenacity of his opponents.

Hunter's inability to control the monopolists should be contrasted with the actual contribution played by the New South Wales Corps officers to the economic development of the colony and whether their poor image was fully deserved. Perhaps another person (naval or military) could have better retained control of the colony and crushed the power of the New South Wales Corps. For instance, had Phillip's health permitted him to return to Sydney in 1794 or 1795, he may have been able to untangle the economic web woven by members of the Corps. A military officer may have been able to succeed instead of another naval captain.

Phillip's farming experience, his knowledge of the Corps and his proven leadership abilities would have enabled him to resume a reasonably dominant role, although the challenge of turning ex-convicts and unsuited and unskilled settlers into successful farmers would have been daunting. Phillip had been essentially a benevolent dictator, but Hunter found himself in a more 'mixed' economy and had to deal with military officers resentful of his corrective attempts and vigorously defending their new-found privileges. Similarly, a military officer may well have been able to reinstate some order and discipline into the activities of certain Corps officers, but their resentment at this interference would have been just as great, and therefore may have prompted equivalent reactions.

The New South Wales Corps was raised in 1789 to relieve the Marine detachment of its garrison duties and arrived in Sydney in 1790 and 1791, under the command of Major Francis Grose and included the 23-year-old Lieutenant John Macarthur. (Grose was succeeded by Captain William Paterson in late 1794). Upon Phillip's departure in December 1792, the Corps officers, under the then Lieutenant Governor Grose, soon assumed effective command of the colony's economy to their own financial advantage. By the time Hunter arrived in September 1795, their grip was widespread and profound and they had been joined by some senior civil officials such as the surgeons William Balmain and D'Arcy Wentworth. The Corps had the added advantage that, as the enforcers of the law, its members could delay or subtly deny any order or regulation of the governor which compromised its own position, thereby negating any remedial proposal that Hunter attempted to impose. This was a critical factor in the dispute between Hunter and the New South Wales Corps.

The essence of Hunter's problems during this phase of his life involved three fundamental factors, the first two external and therefore beyond his immediate control and the third Hunter's own character, personality and background. The first factor was the three year interregnum between Phillip's departure in December 1792 and Hunter's arrival. This period allowed the New South Wales Corps to establish a number of dubious practices which shaped the politics and the economy of New South Wales for the ensuing 18 years. This was described by the boat builder Daniel Paine, brought to New South Wales in 1795 by Hunter, as a monopoly of trade

> by the Principal Officers to the very great hindrance of the industrious settler and the total prevention of any Commercial Speculation, the Crops of many Settlers having been sold or mortgaged before the Harvest to supply their wants and spirits.[7]

This could well have influenced the Duke of Portland's later decision in 1799 to send Philip Gidley King to succeed Hunter, armed with Hunter's recall in order to succeed him immediately, to prevent any recurrence of the previous long hiatus of command.

While the three year interlude, 1792-95, was sufficiently long to enable Corps officers to develop trade and labour management practices to their own financial and social advantage, the reasons for the extended gap can be explained by examining the series of events which occasioned the interval—a project which seemingly has not yet been thoroughly attempted. In the first place, Phillip requested leave of absence as early as 15 April 1790, citing personal reasons to Lord Sydney for returning. 'As the settlement is now fixed, whenever his Majesty's service permits, I shall be glad to return to England, where I have reason to suppose my private affairs make my presence necessary.'[8] Not perceiving any urgency in the request, Sydney referred this letter to Lord Grenville, who replied to Phillip on 19 February 1791 (11 months later) asking him to defer the request.[9] However at the same time, Phillip wrote to Grenville on 25 March 1791, this time indicating it was poor health that prompted the request, 'A complaint in the side, and from which, in more than two years, I have seldom been free, has impaired my health.'[10] This was an ongoing severe complaint, confirmed by Surgeon John White, who noted on 4 June 1788, being the anniversary of the King's birthday,

> The day passed in cheerfulness and good humour, but it was a little dampened by our perceiving that the governor was in great pain, from a return of his complaint … his countenance too plainly indicated the torture which he suffered.[11]

This was possibly due to stones in his kidney or calcium deposits in his urinary tract, brought on by eating highly salted meat at sea for many years; an occupational hazard of the day.

Phillip acknowledged receipt of Grenville's 19 February 1791 letter on 21 November of that year, but this time stating that his illness caused him 'to request permission to resign the government that I may return to England in hopes of finding that relief which this country does not afford.[12] This letter would not have arrived in London until the middle of 1792, by which time another six to eight months would have elapsed before Phillip could have expected a reply. His health would not allow him to wait, so he left Sydney on 11 December 1792 on the *Atlantic* which arrived in Spithead on 23 May 1793. His health not improving, Phillip formally resigned the governorship on 23 July 1793, at which time Hunter was serving as second captain under Lord Howe on the *Queen Charlotte* in the Channel.

This news reached Hunter when they were anchored in Torbay, Devon, a couple of months later. On 8 October 1793, the First Captain of the *Queen Charlotte* Sir Roger Curtis, (a friend of Hunter's who was part of the court martial which exonerated him over the loss of the *Sirius*), wrote to Under-Secretary Evan Nepean promoting the suitability of Hunter as a candidate to succeed Phillip.

> I believe that if incorruptable integrity, unceasing zeal, a thorough knowledge of the country, and a sound and steady judgement are qualifications desirable in the governor of New South Wales, they will not to be found in a higher degree in any man living.[13]

Six days later, Hunter wrote to Henry Dundas, then the Secretary of State for the Home Department, setting out his credentials and offering himself for the position.[14] On the very next day, Lord Howe wrote to the Earl of Chatham supporting Hunter's application.[15]

These three targets had undoubted influence. Sir Evan Nepean (1751–1822) was appointed Under-Secretary for War in 1793 and the following year succeeded Sir Philip Stephens as Secretary of the Admiralty, a position he held until 1804. He had earlier served in the navy in North America from 1776 to 1781 and could well have met Hunter there. Henry Dundas (1742–1811), the first Viscount Melville, was Treasurer of the Navy and Home Secretary in 1793, a fellow Scot and a member of parliament. Lord Portland succeeded him as Home Secretary in mid-1794. The Earl of Chatham was John Pitt (1756–1835), eldest son of William Pitt the elder, first Earl of Chatham and brother of William Pitt the younger, the prime minister who appointed John Pitt First Lord of the Admiralty from 1788 to 1794. He was a friend of King George III as well as Lord Howe. The patronage game was being played at the highest level with some vigour, but this time on behalf of John Hunter.

The sequence of these letters is of interest; since it would appear that it was orchestrated so that Curtis wrote first, followed by Hunter's letter and then supported by Lord Howe, rather than Hunter applying without endorsement. The careful spread of approaches to these three important figures, who would have had an impact on the appointment, indicates a calculated, coordinated and deliberate plan of attack. Phillip's only letter to Dundas proposing his preferred nominee, Philip Gidley King, was not sent until 26 October 1793.[16]

Hunter's selection was not only based upon some element of familiarity with the region plus intrinsic merit, but was also due to his seniority over King (who was still only a commander in 1793, having been promoted only two years previously) and the strength and influence of his supporters. Further, while King was 20 years younger than Hunter (35 compared to 56), he was in indifferent health with gout at the time.

There is no evidence to indicate whether any other candidates were considered. While there was no formal position description for the office, it can be assumed that the Colonial Office would have sought a person who was a naval officer with a knowledge and understanding of the colony and its requirements, together with an ability to lead its development. As Hunter's commission[17] was similar to Phillip's[18], who was highly regarded by the decision-makers, the government would have probably used Phillip as a role model. This would have considerably limited the number of candidates eligible for consideration. At the same time, the position may not have appealed to many serving naval captains, with war against France having broken out the previous February, thus providing better prospects for active service, prize money and promotion, especially for those with 'interest', rather than disappearing into a remote corner of the Empire.

Hunter's appointment was not formally gazetted until 30 December 1793[19] and his commission as Governor was dated 6 February 1794.[20] Dundas did not write to inform Lieutenant Governor Grose of the succession until 15 February 1794[21] and did not issue Hunter with his instructions until the following 1 July[22], 12 months after Phillip's resignation and 18 months after his departure from Port Jackson. The time span was further extended by preparations required for the voyage out, with supplies for Hunter and the colony to be identified, located and brought to the *Reliance* and *Supply*. These included a wide diversity of items large and small, such as navigational equipment and books, surveying materials, food and medicines, stationary and the appointment of officials such as purser, boat builder and governor's secretary[23], in all of which Hunter was intricately involved.

Although Hunter was on board the *Reliance* at Spithead by September 1794, they did not actually sail until 16 December, being further delayed for another two and a half months by the threat of the French Fleet in the channel. They were required to be part of a convoy that spent time sheltering at Portsmouth, Torbay and Plymouth before finally leaving the English coast on 1 March 1795, arriving in Sydney on 7 September of that year, two years and nine months after Phillip's departure. While the intervening period was excessive by modern standards, there was no indication that any urgency was required to replace Phillip, as the reports sent home by Grose and Paterson inferred that the colony was developing slowly but satisfactorily and that the shortages of items such as clothes, tools, utensils and building materials were more of nuisance value than major catastrophes, and while food supplies were still an issue, the starvation days of 1790 were behind them.[24] There were some tensions between people such as Grose and Reverend Richard Johnson over religious observances and the provision of a church, but overall there appeared no reasons or pressure for any inordinate haste for Hunter to assume control.

In addition, during the years 1792–1800 (i.e. the interregnum and Hunter's term as governor), the British Government had more important issues to contend with than the problems of a small and distant outpost. Early in 1793, England was drawn into war with France after the French attacked the Netherlands. Pitt sent a large naval and marine contingent to seize control of the French West Indies, losing 40,000 soldiers in the process, mainly due to disease, thus crippling and handicapping England's military efforts in Europe. Notwithstanding Howe's victory over the French on 1 June 1794 (at which Hunter was present) by May 1797 England stood alone against

France, with a navy at Spithead and the Nore in mutiny against the neglect and harsh treatment of the sailors. The mutinies were quelled (by Lord Howe) and a re-invigorated navy was successfully involved in the battles of Camperdown on 11 October 1797 and the Nile on 1 August 1798. England still needed to re-enforce its presence in India and was simultaneously dealing with a recalcitrant Ireland.

Domestically, it had to confront the economic problems of a sharply rising population, the early stages of the industrial revolution with the relocation of industry from the village to the town, the agrarian revolution and the feeding of the increasing populace, and the political struggles between the Whigs and the Tories. All of these challenges were more immediate and urgent, demanding prioritised government attention over the distractions of a remote corner of the empire.

These preoccupations also probably contributed to the second factor affecting Hunter's governorship—the lack of any real understanding by the British government of conditions in New South Wales. Dundas and Stephens were only as informed as the information from Sydney allowed them to be. Details or incidents were slanted, emphasized, downplayed, muffled or even omitted, according to the values placed upon them by the various writers, or where there was a vested interest in what, or how much was reported. This was compounded by the rivalry and interplay between the New South Wales Corps and the settlers and the emergence of a monopoly by some Corps members in spirits, food supplies and convict labour allocation. It was not in the interests of the emerging elite in Sydney to raise any alarms or suspicions in London over their activities or conditions in the colony, and most of the various reports reflected this.

In his first letter to Dundas on 9 January 1793, a month after Phillip's departure, Grose recorded that he had been 'obliged' to purchase a cargo of spirits (7597 gallons at 4/6 per gallon according to Collins which could be sold at profits up to 2000 per cent) from an American trader (it is unlikely Phillip would have felt the same obligation) and that he was experiencing difficulties with some of the settlers, but 'I am happy to add that the colony in general is healthy, and that we seem daily to improve in the cultivation of the country.'[25] On 12 October 1793, Grose advised Dundas that, in spite of some crop failures,

> I am at present safe in assuring you that, what with the public ground and private farms, there is but little doubt of our reaping as much corn this harvest in the colony as will supply us the ensuing year.[26]

His communication to Dundas dated 29 April 1794 revealed there was a diminishing need for imported flour as 'I have the satisfaction to say that there is now indian corn enough remaining in the Colony to serve us with bread until our next harvest'[27], and that the allocation of ten convicts per landed Corps officer as servants was in the public good.

> The public labour is very little interrupted by their accommodation, as nine hundred and sixty acres of ground have been cleared in one year by the officers only, and as the produce of that ground has been of much public utility, I have hope that on this representation they may be suffered to keep their convicts.[28]

Grose's favourable report on the Hawkesbury settlers on 31 August 1794 was echoed by his successor, Captain William Paterson, expressing confident predictions one year later of livestock expansion, 'Their numbers are daily increasing.'[29] Elizabeth Macarthur reinforced the positive tone of the colony in a letter to a friend in England written in 1795. 'This country possesses numerous advantages to persons holding appointments under Government' and 'we enjoy here one of the finest climates in the world. The necessaries of life are abundant and a fruitful soil affords us many luxuries.'[30] This is not to infer that shortages or quarrels were never reported, but the general impression conveyed was one of overall harmony, steady growth and slowly increasing prosperity. The lack of haste in servicing the fledgling settlement is therefore more understandable, considering the generally encouraging reports received and the other more pressing pressures on the British government.

The third factor was John Hunter himself and his competency as a governor. However, it does seem appropriate to consider firstly why Hunter applied for the position and what his expectations were. While Hunter has not specifically answered these questions in any available correspondence, it can be deduced that while he was not avaricious, he was ambitious and felt himself qualified to take on the task, although he had no idea of the extent of the changes that had taken place since he left in early 1791. He was 56 years old and in the lower half of the captains' seniority list. He had no immediate family ties to England and did possess an understanding of the locality and the nature of the settlement. While he had been a post captain for seven years, independent command prospects appeared bleak, and this was an opportunity for him to demonstrate his abilities as a leader and administrator, and to perhaps open doors to other senior appointments. He had witnessed how Phillip had developed the settlement and felt that he could pick up where Phillip had left off, but he was unaware of the changes which had actually occurred in Sydney after Phillip departed.

When Hunter left there in 1791, the settlements at both Port Jackson and Norfolk Island were penal in nature and Phillip was, in effect, the chief jailor. This made the colony far easier to rule, with an authoritarian system reflecting naval customs and practices which Hunter had lived with for the previous 35 years. The captain's (or governor's) authority was all-embracing and final and everyone was under his jurisdiction. There were few free officials and even fewer free settlers. Only a small number of the convicts had served their time and were therefore due for release. Phillip exercised virtual total control, subject to the laws and regulations applicable to the colony.

Up to 1793, the governor controlled food supplies, labour allocation, the militia, land grants and the building programme, in fact nearly every aspect of life in Sydney. Hunter expected to pick up the reins of a penal colony.

His disillusionment becomes clear when he compared his tasks to those of Phillip in one of his defensive letters to the Duke of Portland dated 15 November 1799.

> There was a time, my Lord, in this settlement, and that was when I was formerly employ'd here its service, when a Public Order answer'd every end propos'd—the Governor had no further trouble; the various persons then upon service here had no objects of a private nature to withdraw them from a due attention to every public regulation, orders were attended to by all in authority—they felt the public interest theirs. If that be contrasted with what I have experienced, and have had some occasion to represent to your Grace, how different will appear the situation of the first governor of this colony and mine. In those days to be employ'd here was like a party of amusement; in the present it requires an incessant labour of the mind, and a strength of body equal to that of a lion to struggle with to counteract these difficultys.[31]

In other words, while Phillip enjoyed total control over his colony, Hunter was not able to handle the different circumstances that existed on his return. This disenchantment of reality to the detriment of expectation is further illustrated in a private and revealing letter Hunter wrote on 20 May 1799 to a friend, Sir Samuel Bentham (brother of Jeremy Bentham, the political economist and lawyer) who was a noted naval architect and author.

> This, be assured, my friend Bentham, is a most irksome command. The fatigue to which the governor of this territory must submit, both mental and corporeal, is far beyond any idea you can have of the nature of his duty, rendering such fatigue necessary to the Commander-in-Chief. I may venture,

> however, to assure you, that had I been gifted with the power of looking into future events, I should never have covetted that which now occupys my endeavours; in short, altho' I possess not a shilling in the world besides my commission in the Navy, my present salary would not have been an object sufficient to have inclined me to return to this country, for after all I have suffered formerly in its service my troubles then were by no means equal to my fatigues now.[32]

Hunter went on to claim that part of his problem was that the New South Wales Corps was disappointed that another naval officer should be appointed to the governorship (instead of one of their own) and that some were determined to resist any effort to reduce their power, influence and growing affluence. He then confessed to being disenchanted with the obstacles put in his path.

> My former knowledge and acquaintance with this country encouraged me in a hope, which, however, has, in some respects, proved delusive, that I should with ease to myself and with proper effect and advantage to the public have been able to manage all the duties of my office; but I had not been long entered upon it before I was awakened from that dream of comfort and satisfaction the prospect of which I had so vainly indulged; the seeds of those vexations, which had so disappointed me, had been sown for a very considerable time [i.e. the interregnum] and being rather of a prolific nature amongst such a people had gained so much strength that it will require immense labour to grub them up by the root.

Hunter then indicated his determination to persevere in his attempts to reduce the power and influence of the New South Wales Corps, but which

> cannot amongst such characters be a very popular one; that however, will be a matter of no immediate concern to me if I succeed only in a small degree to check the growing profligacy and abandoned turn of the lower classes of people, altho' I may

> be censured on the spot by those whose views and interests may be effected by my endeavours.[33]

Hunter was not to know that as he wrote this letter, his own recall was already on its way from Portland.

While Hunter expected to pick up where Phillip left off, it took some months before the realisation set in that the rules had changed, the scenario was different and the people he had to deal with (or work with) had other priorities to his. He could not properly impose his will or his orders by force, because the very people he was challenging were the enforcers themselves, i.e. the New South Wales Corps. Nothing in Hunter's naval career had quite prepared him for such a situation where his authority could be questioned, undermined or disobeyed. His power as governor turned out to be not absolute and he was not sufficiently experienced in the art of political persuasion or diplomatic manoeuvrings to be able to out-think his adversaries.

While it was (mostly) some officers of the New South Wales Corps who oversaw the emergence of monopoly purchasing of food supplies and goods, the trade in spirits, land and labour allocation to their advantage and the usurping of civil power to the military, in some instances a number of these practices turned out to be to the advantage of the colony and its economy. The Corps has been rightly criticised, but has it been fairly condemned? As Brian Fletcher has remarked,

> The claims that the officers purchased their farms in exchange for liquor, deliberately prevented them marketing produce so as to guarantee an outlet for their own, or bought their crops cheaply, subsequently reselling them at a profit, cannot be substantiated. There may have been individual instances of such abuses and there is certainly evidence of some small holders having disposed of assets other than land in exchange of liquor. But the effects of this appear to have been

exaggerated by writers unduly influenced by the suspect observations of Grose's opponents.[34]

Hunter regarded Macarthur and his fellow officers as his bête noire, and it is worthwhile to analyse the Corps' activities to ascertain if Hunter's complaints were valid, since it does not appear that a detailed defence of the Corps has been mounted to date.

Within a year of his return to Sydney, Hunter described the Corps to Portland as soldiers from the Savoy [a military prison] and other characters 'who have been considered as disgraceful to every other regiment in his Majesty's Service ... often superior in every species of infamy to the most expert in wickedness among the convicts.'[35] Strong words for Hunter. This view supported the opinion of Robert Murray, a junior officer on the *Britannia*, who recorded in 1794 that 'Tyranny Oppression and Fraud had arrived at their meridian in Port Jackson under the auspiceies [sic] of the officers of the New South Wales Corps.'[36] Two years after his recall in 1800, Hunter produced a publication outlining his views on needed reforms and cost reductions in New South Wales. Amongst his concerns were 'the iniquitous monopoly established by a combination of the officers, to the great injury of the fair trader, and total exclusion of all the other inhabitants of the country'[37] including the distribution of spirits, 'which involved charges for provisions and spirits issued to "parties on command", civil as well as military, in the commissary's accounts.'[38]

These views were reinforced by later historians who, in a cacophony of criticism, condemned out of hand the Corps and its actions. Shaw asserted that 'they merited almost any unsavoury soubriquet they received.'[39] Clark believed 'they were ruthless and vindictive'[40], while Evatt stated that the Corps was 'a permanent hindrance to the peace and good government of the colony.'[41] In a book for school children written around the time of World War I, Walter Murdoch claimed 'the NSW Corps was a curse to the colony' and was 'so unscrupulous that we can only call them a pack of sorry swindlers.'[42] Little wonder that the Corps acquired a disreputable reputation. However, while these criticisms undoubtedly had some justification, those associated with the Corps saw the situation differently. Elizabeth Macarthur attempted to justify the actions of her husband and others in a letter to a friend soon after Hunter's arrival in 1795.

> The officers in the Colony, with a few others possessed of money or credit in England, unite together and purchase the cargoes of such vessels as repair to this country from various quarters. Two or more are chosen from the numbers to bargain for the cargo offered for sale, which is then divided amongst them, in proportion to the amount of their subscriptions. This arrangement prevents monopoly, and the impositions that would be otherwise practiced by masters of ships.[43]

This was a fairly feeble defence of a practice designed to produce quick and easy profits for the officers concerned and to shut out any other person or group, with resultant high prices causing hardship for the poorer free settlers. Ships' masters were hardly in a position to sell competitively when the officers presented themselves as the only purchasers of the cargoes at their prices, which the master could either accept or take his cargo elsewhere. Having purchased the goods, the monopolists could resell them at whatever price the market would bear. If demand was low at the time, they could hold onto the goods until demand rose and higher prices could be levied. Elizabeth Macarthur's claim that this prevented the masters from imposing monopolistic prices (which some may have considered) overlooks the fact that it was the officers who exacted the monopoly upon the masters, so the settlers would lose either way. Hunter's plan was for the authorities to purchase the imported goods and resell to all settlers at reasonable prices, but he was unable to put this into operation because of the power of the Corps and his inability to enforce the idea. Similarly, Hunter's attempts to open up the market equally to all inhabitants failed because of the economic and financial dominance of the monopolists, illustrated by the First Fleet convict from the *Scarborough*, Mathew Everingham, who in August 1796, wrote

> This monopolizing trade of purchasing the whole cargo of the vessell in shares is very much hurt since the arrival of Governor Hunter in this Country who gave leave to all free persons to go on board and purchase according to their Circumstances but he has not been here above fourteen months and the Trade in a manner does still remain in their hands for this reason: the settlers who were the only people who could have it in their power to purchase independent of the Gentlemen were by them so drawn into debt before the arrival of Govr. Hunter, that this order was of no service to them.[44]

Everingham also related the method that the monopolists employed in achieving their mark-ups in the spirits trade.[45] After purchasing the spirits for around five shillings per gallon, they would considerably water down the rum to produce six bottles per gallon and sell them for up to 6 or 7 shillings each, thereby earning a profit in the order of 150–200 per cent, depending upon the extent to which the raw spirit was diluted; not quite the 2000 per cent quoted by Phillip Lisle[46], but the variations in profit margin may well have depended upon the concentrated strength of the rum or brandy and the degree to which it was broken down.

Claiming that it was the Corps officers who had the monopoly in rum traffic and trade conceals the fact that, once these activities commenced, they were joined by other civilian inhabitants (including some emancipated convicts), as evidenced for example by a petition to Hunter in 1798 seeking 'to permit us to become the purchasers of a proportionate part of a ship's cargo.'[47] Hunter actually encouraged settlers to form purchasing cartels to off-set the trading influence of the Corps officers and in 1800 another petition was put to Hunter by other settlers, including seven ex-convicts, three ex-soldiers and sailors and two former missionaries, but no Corps officers, seeking his approval to purchase a cargo of spirits from the *Minerva*.

While it is clear that although some Corps members (but certainly not all) did engage in monopolistic practices, encourage the rum trade and distort the distribution of convict labour (which did cause suffering to some), their activities did accelerate farming and food production which materially contributed to the economic growth of the settlement. The principal activists appear to have been the paymaster John Macarthur and the commanders of each of the Corp's four companies, Paterson, Johnston, Foveaux and Rowley, with the addition of Lieutenant Abbott and surgeons Harris and Balmain. As the Corps, under Major Grose, initially comprised four companies—each under a captain, one lieutenant and three sergeants, three corporals, two drummers and 67 privates—the hard core of the traders consisted of only a small fraction of the total Corps strength of just under 300 men. While some additional members did take part in those activities later on, perhaps no more than 20 per cent of the entire Corps was ever actively involved.

Hunter described the Corps as being 'disgraceful to every other regiment' and 'superior in every species of infamy.' Some excuse can be made for Hunter's uncharacteristically candid comments because of his frustration which was developing into a siege mentality. However, the New South Wales Corps cannot be fairly compared to other military units for two reasons. Firstly, England was preparing for war and needed its best men for active service (hence the recall of the Royal Marines by 1792) so the Corps was always a second-string body. Secondly, the Corps was raised for garrison duty only, which, as the Select Committee on Transportation noted, was distasteful to them as well as demoralising. Their prime object was the supervision of the convicts rather than the protection of the settlement. In any event, the conduct of the Royal Marines before them and Macquarie's 73rd

Regiment after their departure was far from exemplary. Hunter recorded in May 1789 that 'six Marines had been tried by a criminal court and found guilty of robbing the public stores: they were sentenced to death, and executed accordingly ... and all originally occasioned by some unfortunate connections they had made with women convicts.'[48] The Corps' successors under Macquarie, the 73rd and 46th Regiments, both earned dubious reputations in New South Wales. Several murders were committed by the men of the 73rd, one of them by an officer. Finally, with respect to the Corp's general image, it should be remembered that since the majority of those they guarded were convicts or had a convict background, and because of the duties they had to perform, the military naturally was extremely unpopular, regardless of their trading activities.

On economic grounds, the land-grants policy of Grose and Paterson did have merit, in so far as while they may have abused the spirit of their instructions, their actions benefited the economy in both the short and long term, and undoubtedly accelerated the formation of a capitalist economy in New South Wales. Cattle numbers and production rose more quickly because of the superior farming skills of the larger land holders. The land-grant system itself does not appear to have been the disaster so often espoused, but rather it was its sequel that was the problem, as there were no effective controls over subsequent land ownership and subdivision. This did bring hardship to some, but on many occasions as a result of the smaller landholders' own incompetence and laziness.

The small number of early settlers who arrived in New South Wales was, in Grose's view, quite worthless. 'I am sorry to report that I am much plagued with the people who become settlers, and who have evidently no other views than the purpose of raising a sufficient supply to pay their passage to England.'[49] There was a high turnover of some farms as good arable land was in limited supply and some blocks were sold or transferred up to three times during Hunter's term. For example, one block was leased on 11 July 1796 to Thomas Crowder. It was then 'transferred on 29th March 1799 to Martha Burkett and sold the same day by her to Dennis Geary. Half of the farm again sold on 22nd May 1799 to Edward Bisbey. Another part transferred on 8th July 1799 to James Ormond.'[50] Grose recognised that the officers and some senior officials were the only class of settler anxious to secure and develop larger tracts of land and who were capable of fully exploiting it and had the ambition and incentive (profit) to achieve economic prosperity for themselves and the colony.

The general and popular criticisms that Grose and Paterson generously distributed land[51] warrants some qualification. In the first place, Phillip's original instructions empowered him to grant land to emancipated convicts and settlers only (not to the military), on the basis of 30 acres per man or 50 acres to married couples plus an extra ten acres per child of the marriage.[52] This formula was devised before the poor quality of soil surrounding Sydney was known and it was only around Parramatta and the rich but flood-prone banks of the Upper Hawkesbury River that 50 to 100 acres could produce viable crops using a small labour force. Phillip set a precedent for exceeding his authority by granting to a number of settlers, emancipated convicts, former seamen and ex-marines, many of whom were unmarried, 60 or more acres of land around Parramatta in 1791.[53] To facilitate those non-commissioned officers and enlisted men of the marines who wished to remain in New South Wales after their three year tour of duty, Phillip was authorised by Grenville on 22 August 1789 (and acknowledged by Phillip on 17 June 1790) to grant 100 acres to every non-commissioned officer and 50 acres to each private 'over and above the quantity dictated by Our General Instructions to you, tax and rent free for ten years.'[54] This cuts across the statement by Brian Fletcher that 'Lieutenant Governor Grose began giving 25 acre holdings to privates and NCO's of the New South Wales Corps—a practice that was implicitly accepted though never formally sanctioned by his superiors.'55 In fact the grants made to these ranks were both authorised and within the limits stipulated. There was no mention by Grenville of any other class of settler, to whom Phillip also bestowed larger blocks than allowed, because as mentioned above, farms of less than 50 acres were hardly viable.

The exclusion of the Corps officers from these benefits caused considerable discontent and resentment, especially as they were aware of the land grant policy for marines in North America, as illustrated by the complaint of Captain William Hill of the New South Wales Corps in July 1790, soon after arriving in Sydney.

> In America, the officers and settlers had grants of land in proportion to their rank, but those of the marines who are now here, and have born every hardship, have no such thing, neither is there any intention of giving each their portion. In my humble opinion, nothing can be more impolitic.56

Phillip had no authority to grant land to officers (nor did he) and referred this to Lord Sydney in February 1790 and again to Lord Grenville in November 1791 seeking guidelines to redress the problem. While acknowledging Phillip's request on 15 May 1792, Dundas did not specifically address the issue (possibly on the grounds that there were more pressing matters to deal with and he needed more time to consider the subject), but in his next despatch to Phillip dated 14 July 1792, he did approve the request to grant land to officers. 'I do not forsee that any inconvenience can arise from your complying with their requisitions' (a poor prophecy as it transpired), the condition being that 'the allotments are not made with a view to a temporary but an established settlement thereon.'57 No reference was made to any limitation of the area of the land allotted. This permission was received by Lieutenant Governor Grose on 15 January 1793, just over a month after Phillip's departure.

Phillip had recommended to Sydney that each settler be given between 500 and 1000 and have not less than 20 convicts to clear and cultivate the land.[58] There were sound reasons for these recommendations; Australia was not generally suited to small peasant-type farming. Successful wheat and livestock production for example, required much larger holdings than those normally granted to New South Wales' settlers and demanded more capital and labour than the small emancipist and free settler farmers had at their disposal—even if they were competent enough to successfully manage their holdings. Another reason for the proposed large number of convict labourers was that there were no ploughs available (the first plough did not arrive in Sydney until 1796) and so all clearing and farm work had to be undertaken manually with basic hand tools, spades, hoes, picks and axes.

Further, many of the free settlers and emancipists, as alluded to by Grose, had no idea about clearing and working the land and were often unwilling or unsuited to apply themselves to the task. As an example, of the 274 settlers granted land in New South Wales in 1795, the vast majority of them (251) being ex-convicts, only 89 were still farming their land in 1800; in other words, during Hunter's term, only about one in three was able to make a success of their land allocation. The holdings of the other two-thirds were acquired by the more successful farmers, including Corps officers, who also had the advantage of being able to choose the more fit and able convicts to tend their lands, thus aiding their chances of increased income and acquiring additional holdings at marked-down prices. Large-scale farming was proving to be more appropriate for local conditions, but this is not to imply that all ex-convict farmers did not succeed with their small holdings. Mathew Everingham, a First Fleet convict, was given, after his term expired in 1791, 50 acres near Parramatta. Fifteen months later, in August 1792, he wrote to a friend in London

> I have 5 acres of Indian Corn one of English wheat about half an acre of Barley Pumkins Melons callavans etc in abundance,

all seem to thrive well. I have two Sows big with Piggs some poultry and a hive of this Country's bees they are exceedingly small. In three months I am to maintain myself and family independent of the public store, and do the best I can for myself. Next year I hope I shall be able to maintain two men off the store, I have now one and then I shall be able to live a little comfortable.[59]

He was in the minority and remained a successful small farmer until his death in 1817.

There has been criticism of Grose for granting land with undue haste to fellow officers as soon as Phillip disappeared over the horizon, but an examination of the facts does not to support this. Between 11 December 1792 (when Phillip left) and 15 January 1793 (when he opened Dundas' letter approving land grants to officers), Grose allocated only one small parcel of land, being 25 acres to William Cummings, an ensign with the Corps, and well within the limitations set down by Dundas to Phillip.[60] Between 7 February and 1 April 1793, Grose made 21 more grants, only three of which were to Corps officers (John Macarthur, George Johnston and Thomas Rowley—100 acres each), the remainder being to ex-convicts, free settlers and non-commissioned officers plus the chaplain, commissary and the principal surgeon, and all within the allotment size stipulations.[61] It could well have been that pressure was exerted on Grose by the officers to allocate more (Grose was not a confident person and could normally be easily persuaded, and he was of indifferent health) but on this occasion he acted in accordance with his instructions.

As to criticisms that the military monopolised land grants, it should be noted that land was also granted to senior civilians such as the chaplain and surgeon, as well as emancipists, free settlers, other corps ranks and ex-marines and seamen.[62] In addition, the amount of land allocated to the military—to the officers—does not appear to be out of proportion to that given to other groups collectively within the colony, although subsequent mergers and acquisitions did result in some larger estates. For instance, the assistant surgeon D'Arcy Wentworth had accumulated 1800 acres by 1800.[63] Of the acreages granted, Hunter estimated that a total of 10,674 acres were apportioned by Grose and 4965 by Paterson, a total of 15,639 over three years (or around 5000 acres per year).[64] This cannot be regarded as excessive since Phillip's grants approximated 6000 acres (with restrictions applying to the time required to locate and open the land and the smaller numbers of those eligible and able to establish farms), while Hunter himself distributed 28,279 acres over five years, at an average of just under 6000 acres per annum, including a parcel to his nephew Lieutenant William Kent.

The New South Wales Corps' practice of allocating land for private usage was not exercised at the total expense of government farming as has been alleged.[65] John Macarthur did advocate the abandonment of government farming at Toongabbie, saying that 'it was a most disadvantageous system for Government to cultivate grain.'[66] Grose was not inclined to completely close down public agriculture, although acreage sewn did decline to 340 acres in 1795; in fact he authorised the opening of a new farm near Sydney in 1795.[67] The reasons for Grose not abandoning public farming were three-fold. Firstly, the farms were meant to provide both a source of food and a place of labour for the convicts. Secondly, the authorities in London were committed to a policy of promoting public agriculture and neither Grose nor Paterson was prepared to disobey. Actually, Hunter himself shut down public farming in 1796, on Macarthur's advice, pleading scarcity of labour, but was instructed to re-open it immediately the news reached London. Thirdly, while the government not only continued to produce grain between 1792 and 1795, with crops increasing despite a drought, there was never any real danger of competition with private farms or of over-supplying the market.

Of the New South Wales based population of 4958 in September 1800, 3545 were victualled from the public stores and only 1413 supported themselves.[68] These figures would imply that many convicts employed on private farms were still being sustained from the public purse. The colony was becoming slowly but increasingly self-sufficient in spite of droughts, floods and pest disease, but at the expense of public infrastructure such as roads, bridges and buildings, because of the Corp's diversion of the labour supply to their farms. In September 1796 however, the government cropped 1700 acres, the officers 1172 and the settlers 2547 acres—hardly a monopolistic hold by the Corps.[69]

To whom belonging	Mares and Horses	Cows and Calves	Bulls and Calves	Oxen	Sheep	Goats	Hogs	Land in cultivation acres
Government	14	67	37	46	191	111	59	1700
Officers—civil and military	43	34	37	6	1310	1176	889	1172
Total Government and Officers	57	101	74	52	1501	1287	948	2872
Settlers	-	-	-	-	30	140	921	2547
General Total	57	101	74	52	1531	1427	1869	5419

Table 2. Account of live stock in the possession of, and land in cultivation by Government and the Officers, Civil and Military, and Settlers, 1 September 1796.[70]

However, it was in livestock production that Corps officers were more prominent. Hunter's own returns of livestock and farming as at 1

September 1796 clearly show that it was not farming that the officers monopolised, but rather the possession of sheep, goats and hogs. This point appears to have escaped many writers.

It is of interest to note that no settler possessed any horses or cattle, but this is most likely because they could not afford them and their land holdings were not large enough to cater for them. Settlers had almost as much land under cultivation as the government and officers but they did not generally work their land as well as Corps members did, because of lack of skills and supporting labour. There were also many more settlers holding smaller allotments. The principal issue here is that the Corps monopoly was not in every sphere of agriculture, a caveat which needs to be taken into account when considering Hunter's attitude towards them.

On balance, the influence of the New South Wales Corps upon colonial society and its economy had some positive as well as negative aspects, notwithstanding the criticisms of Hunter, and later King and Bligh. Its behaviour towards some convicts and settlers alike during the interregnum and beyond was reprehensible at times and probably engendered a dislike of authority amongst the population which subsequently developed into a national trait. By the same token, however, the 1837–38 Select Committee on Transportation seemed convinced that the convicts had a more profoundly negative impact on their guards and overseers than the soldiers had on those they were supervising.

> The nature of the duty imposed upon the military in guarding the chain gangs has the worst effects upon the character and discipline of the soldiers ... it produced the greatest demoralizing among the troops and the men became reckless ... demoralization was likewise produced amongst the troops by their intercourse with the prison population which could not be prevented.[71]

Some Corps members abused their positions for personal wealth and gain, while others abused their authority over the convicts. The introduced dependency on rum and the financial hardship imposed upon some small farmers properly deserved censure. But not all Corps personnel were equally involved in these practices. Hunter's concerns over the activities of John Macarthur in particular, plus some others, was quite justified, but prudence needs to be applied in blaming all for the deeds of some, as Hunter did, while balancing the evils they created with the economic benefits their activities brought to the colony.

By 1795 New South Wales had become a difficult place to govern for a variety of reasons—personality clashes, isolation, labour shortages, entrenched interests and a Colonial Office preoccupied with a war against Napoleon. To untangle this knot required a person possessing a mixture of skill, diplomacy, perseverance, firmness and tact, plus the determined support of the British Government. John Hunter did not possess sufficient quantities of these ingredients to mount a successful challenge against these obstacles, especially those of an economic nature, but there were other aspects in which his administration had some measure of success.

8
A governor under siege

> After the departure of Govr. Phillip from this colony a general change took place, all his plans and regulations were completely laid aside, the civil magistrate was superseded entirely, and all the duties respecting the distribution of justice and every other concern of that office was taken into the hands of the military.[1]

The Sydney that Hunter arrived to administer in September 1795 was still small and primitive (as was Parramatta), with parochial factions, deep social divisions and constant personality clashes; typical of any small and isolated community. Everyone knew everything about everybody, with slights magnified and gossip rampant. From its original population in 1788 of just over 1000, by 1795 there were still only 1858 souls in and around Sydney, 880 at Parramatta, 473 on the Hawkesbury—a total of 3211—plus another 1000 on Norfolk Island.[2] There was no dedicated court house, church or granary; the only fresh water supply for Sydney, the Tank Stream, was becoming polluted; there were only rude tracks around the town and most buildings were still basic. It had become a military establishment ruled by the New South Wales Corps leaders, who had a vested interest in maintaining the status quo, and Hunter became a threat to their power base.

Hunter's initial impressions of the colony and the Corps were generally favourable—'the state of agriculture and the breeding of livestock wears the most favourable appearance; it far exceeds any expectation I cou'd have had'[3], and he noted 'the very great success attending both the raising of grain and the breeding of livestock in the hands of private individuals.'[4] He even confirmed the appointment of John Macarthur as Inspector of Public Works 'for which he seems extremely well qualified'[5], and praised the benefits of Grose's convict labour allocation.

> The number of convict labourers allowed by Lt. Governor Grose to the civil and military officers, who have farms, appear to me to have been the principal means by which this colony has arrived at that state of improvement in which I have found it. I have, therefore, thought fit to continue them.[6]

This was the inexperienced, trusting, gullible and naive Hunter.

However, cracks soon began to appear in the facade. Four months later, John Macarthur resigned his official position because of 'a want of support in the measures I have recommended' and 'the loss of that confidence which your Excellency was once pleased to express'[7], largely occasioned by Hunter not agreeing with Macarthur's recommendations on labour and land apportionment, which would have in effect, bestowed his official imprimatur on Corps practices. Henceforth, the divide between these two men steadily widened.

Within nine months of Hunter's return to Sydney, the battle lines had been drawn. On 12 November 1796, Hunter wrote two long letters to the Duke of Portland[8] (which must have occupied most of the day), outlining the difficulties he was encountering. They ranged from a shortage of public labourers (skilled and unskilled) resulting in a lack of attention to maintaining and developing public buildings and roads; diversion of convicts from public works to private farms and servants; the traffic in spirits in spite of his orders to suppress it (on 22 March; 18 June and 11 July 1796)[9]; unscrupulous trading practices by a self-interested militia and some senior civil officials; the lack of competent administrative support; the usurpation of the judicial system by the Corps; the relaxed discipline within the colony with the subsequent difficulty of maintaining order; the rush to get rich by certain individuals; land grants and their consequences; attacks on Hunter's authority (especially by John Macarthur) and particular problems with the Irish convicts. These were compounded by the 18 months to two years it took to get advice or instructions from London, compared to three or four months for mail to cross from North America to London and return.

Hunter soon identified the attitude of his principal antagonists.

> After the attention shewn by me to the different officers civil and military, since my arrival—an attention mark'd from the beginning by every proof I cou'd give of my having the most perfect confidence in each individual in their respective situations—often such assurances of a disposition to make them as happy as possible—to find that, instead of receiving that assistance which it was the duty of every officer to give, every means was practic'd to frustrate the endeavours I saw necessary to use for correcting various tricks, and to remove customs which had been too long establish'd, and for want of timely attention consider'd as licens'd.[10]

Hunter had also realised it was not only parts of the Corps who opposed him, but some senior civil officials as well, such as Surgeon Balmain.

These were the fundamental problems that confronted Hunter, but there was no doubt in his mind that he could successfully affect the necessary reforms.

> From these few circumstances your Grace will be able to judge how difficult my task is; yet, be assur'd my Lord, that, having entered upon it, thro' it I will go, nor shall any difficulty whatever arrest my progress; nor do I despair of being able to re-establish that order, discipline, and regularity on which our prosperity as a colony must depend.[11]

Self-confidence is an essential ingredient of leadership, but it is a moot point whether his confidence was justified.

Contemporary descriptions of him were generally positive, ranging from 'The governor is a pleasant, sensible old man'[12], and 'whose virtue and integrity was conspicuous as his merit'[13], to 'He's a man devoid of stiff pride, most accomplish'd in his profession and, to sum up all, is a worthy man.'[14] He earned the approbation of Reverend Samuel Marsden who commented to him

> Some months after Your Excellency succeeded to the command of this settlement, and had learnt from your own knowledge and observation the true state of its concerns, exertions were made to arrange its distracted affairs, and to establish order and subordination and quiet amongst the inhabitants'.[15]

To his credit, Marsden indicated that Hunter had been able to remedy some of the malpractices which had developed, although not without some stiff resistance. In addition, Hunter took a particular interest in the education and care of the colony's children and was essentially responsible for the establishment of Sydney's first orphanage as well as seeing two new schools opened during his term.[16]

Hunter did manage to restore the civil magistracy and made some reductions in the number of convicts assigned to the larger land holders and to at least curtail additional land grants to those with large estates. He attempted to lead by example in reviving religious observances but was thwarted with non-cooperation by the Corps officers, who employed a measure of civil disobedience by not attending themselves and not enforcing attendance on the convicts. The boat builder Daniel Paine, brought out by Hunter in 1795, recorded that

> Religion has very few advocates for its cause here, more particularly when under the Government of the late Military Commandant Major Grose, who held Religion in Contempt

and caused the Drums at times to parade round the Town in the time of Devine Service for no other reason than to disturb Mr Johnson. But to the praise of Governor Hunter, he sets the Example of a constant attendance twice every Sunday at Church, which is not much followed by the Officers in general, particularly the Military.[17]

Hunter was handicapped by poor administrative support from his assistants, and undoubtedly regretted the departure of the efficient David Collins the year after his arrival. His Deputy Judge Advocate Richard Dore floundered in his official role and was incompetent and self-seeking in his role as the governor's secretary. Dore soon fell out with Hunter, who told Portland that Dore 'had very soon cause to observe that he was determin'd to be govern'd by his own views and interests in the line of his profession, and to follow, or rather to establish, such rules as best suited those objects.'[18] Hunter was not alone in his views, as he reported to Portland, 'The very persons whom he has chosen to consider as his best friends are the most loud in other places in proclaiming his conduct improper.'[19]

He was not able to eradicate the rum trade or reduce the self-interests of the Corps and civilian officers any more than he was able to break their trading monopoly. Hunter's deficiencies played a large part in these failures. He was unable to cope with difficult people like Macarthur and Balmain who were outside naval rank and discipline spheres and he lacked independent leadership experience and the hardness which this sometimes required. As well, he could not plan longer-term strategies for the colony, as he was pre-occupied with a range of assaults on his authority which precluded forward thinking and planning. He failed to understand and relate to Corps officers' aspirations and to be able to negotiate a suitable land and trade outcome which, while perhaps involving some mutual compromise, could have been for their mutual benefit. On the other hand, Corps officers were equally disinterested in any compromise which affected their position and prosperity. Hunter was also incapable of leading or winning over difficult and obdurate people, or if this failed, having the strength of character to dominate them. Finally, he failed to fully appreciate the range of changes that had taken place during the interregnum, which overwhelmed his expectation that he would simply take over the chief jailor role where Phillip left off.

> Had the original regulations of Gov'r Phillip, as they stood when I left the colony in 1791, remain'd, with such alterations or amendments as the various existing curcumstances might have render'd necessary, I should have known at once what I had to do; but to find upon my arrival in 1795 that the whole had been abolish'd as soon as he departed, I own surprized me.[20]

Hunter could neither wind back the clock nor cope with the different and established circumstances that now prevailed. Had he been pre-warned of the real situation in New South Wales, he still would have presumed that he could have corrected the errors, but his personality, character, background and past experience would still have rendered him inadequate to handle these predicaments. The question of his competence, or lack of it, is undoubtedly part of the equation and his inadequacy manifested itself in several ways. Hunter became so engrossed and consumed by the issues of rum, trade, monopoly and personality that he lost sight of his broader leadership obligations. His letters to Portland became a litany of complaints about others, self-justification and accusations.

As the insidious economic activities of sections of the Corps became apparent to Hunter, including the sale of officers' produce to the government store, he railed to London about the attention they paid to their farms to the detriment of their professional duties. He protested often and passionately on these matters, and in one letter to Under-Secretary King dated 1 June 1797, he again 'complained of the innumerable difficultys which have somehow or other been placed in the way of my endeavours to fulfil his Majesty's commands.'[21] He also criticised the improper employment of convicts, the lack of support from senior officers and officials and his differences with John Macarthur. 'There is not a person in this colony whose opinions I hold in greater contempt.'[22] This is in stark contrast to his first impressions of him, when he wrote to Macarthur early in 1796, 'My confidence in you has been uniformly conspicuous.'[23] Also in the same letter to King he again reiterated his anxiety over rum trading and his inability to achieve reforms single-handed. 'I have not assistance sufficient; it is too much for any one man to manage in our extended state, and with our abandon'd and profligate manners and conduct to see and direct every little department.'[24] Hunter was virtually admitting defeat less than two years into his term, which could hardly have inspired confidence in him within the Colonial Office.

However, nowhere in these letters did Hunter outline any detailed proposals of how he intended to address these problems. He simply did not have or could not develop a plan to combat the abuses and evils that he repeatedly reported to Portland and King. Instead he regularly averred that he would institute the necessary reforms, but these assertions were not reinforced with remedial actions. In one letter to Portland dated 10 January 1798, Hunter again lamented on the officers' trading activities.

> Unless some mode is established for putting an effectual stop to the trading of the officers and others, and consequently to the immense prices from time to time imposed upon the articles in requisition, and the settlers are so frequently ruined, their crops mortgaged, their persons imprisoned, and their families beggared, and falling back upon the public store to prevent starving through the heavy debts they contract.[25]

He then went on to state that 'these considerations have determined me to use every effort in my power' to attack the problem, but 'to accomplish that completely will require many years, and many hands with many additional officers.'[26] Was the task really beyond any one man, or just beyond John Hunter? This question was already exercising minds in London.

Instead of proposed solutions, there were only latent pleas to London for guidance from a man whose responsibility it was to effectively manage the colony himself. Portland tired of Hunter's persistent complaints of his difficulties, particularly the despair emerging from the traffic in spirits, to the point where he pointedly informed Hunter that he had to devise remedial plans himself and engage in a course of action.

> With respect to the sale of spirits, it is certainly in your power, as well as it is your duty, to prohibit, by the most positive orders, all officers of Government, civil or military, from selling any spirituous licqors to the convicts or settlers.[27]

While Portland's none too subtle hint to Hunter to lead may have been easier said than done, given the economic and sociological power the Corps possessed, Hunter could only nibble at the edges of these practices which produced limited, even negligible results.

Hunter undoubtedly had formidable and well-entrenched foes lined up against him, but this was no reason not to at least attempt some carefully considered policies to limit their power in the common good. Vacillation only encouraged his opponents to stronger courses of action to protect their positions, including overt and covert attempts to destroy his reputation by portraying him to others as weak and corrupt. Hunter may have been weak, but he was never corrupt.

While John Macarthur may have been the principal informant against Hunter, he was not the only one. However, Macarthur certainly led the campaign, the first salvo of which was fired as early as 12 months into Hunter's administration. Macarthur (who had a fiery temperament and a devious turn of mind, who argued violently with those he disagreed with and fought three duels in the process) took it upon himself to write directly to Portland on 15 September 1796, indicating that he regretted that Hunter would not heed his advices on how to run the colony and that

> unless our present errors are corrected, more serious difficulties will yet be felt; and I hesitate not to say, further, that the interest of Government is utterly disregarded, its money idly and wantonly squandered, whilst vice and profligacy are openly countenanced.[28]

He went on to assert that government works were being neglected, the plight of free settlers was precarious, livestock was being destroyed and vice was rampant. The fact that some of the colony's predicaments were due to his own activities and to those of others, including his supporters, was not mentioned. He concluded by presenting his plan to increase the numbers of livestock.

Macarthur was at that time quite prepared to put his name to a document critical of Hunter. It is true that Portland referred this letter to Hunter, saying 'You are certainly right in thinking that the proper channel of conveyance for Captain Macarthur's representation was that of the Governor'[29], which may have prompted Macarthur to be more circumspect in the future, but he still orchestrated the attacks on Hunter.

Early in June 1797, anonymous pamphlets addressed to Hunter were left in the streets of Sydney claiming that Hunter's servants were 'carrying on a trade in spirituous liquors under the sanction of their master'[30] and a reward of 20 guineas was consequently offered by Hunter (without success) for the identification of the author. Other than impugning the governor, it is difficult to conceive Macarthur resorting to such tactics on the basis of what would he have personally gained from the accusation. On the other hand, Macarthur's periodic wars with Hunter, Balmain, Atkins, Paterson and others, combined with the vehemence of his attacks, make him a likely suspect. As Balmain himself observed, 'Mr Macarthur's propensity to turbulence and litigation has ever been conspicuous in this colony, and he has not himself scrupled to avoid his inclination to be contentious, and to undervalue the power of the civil authority.'[31]

A series of serious charges against Hunter were contained in an anonymous and extremely damaging letter to Portland which he received in January 1799, so it was probably written early in 1798. The charges essentially related to him allowing price-fixing and profiteering in grain and spirits, not restricting the continuing blow-out of the settlement's expenses and officers acting as traders. Because these charges implicated activities of the New South Wales Corps, there was little gain for Macarthur (the prime suspect as author) to raise matters in which he was a beneficiary. Did anyone else who had the education and political contacts want to see Hunter replaced? It is unlikely that senior civil officials such as Balmain or Marsden would have gone to these lengths as they had little to gain by seeing Hunter go and his pleasant disposition made him hard to dislike. Other senior Corps officers would scarcely have been the author; at least not without Macarthur's knowledge or consent. It is to be regretted that the original letter itself appears no longer to exist, as the handwriting would be of interest to compare, with that of say, Macarthur, unless it was written by another person to preserve anonymity. A likely suspect would certainly have been John Macarthur, who in early 1798 was at such a flashpoint with Hunter over control of convict labour, land grants and the spirits trade (exacerbated by Hunter's irritation over the pamphlet), that Macarthur could well have been prepared to go to any lengths to see his opponent brought down. In fact, as Governor King related in 1801, Macarthur's behaviour infuriated Hunter to the extent that, totally exasperated, Hunter challenged Macarthur to a duel, which was quite beyond his normal demeanour and temperament. 'So sensibly wounded were Gov'r Hunter's feelings previous to his leaving this Colony that he was obliged to call this perturbator to a private account, which he declined.'[32]

Another likely suspect however, could have been one of the Scottish Martyrs, Maurice Margarot or Thomas Fyshe Palmer, both of whom were bitterly resentful that Hunter would not reduce or remit their transportation sentences for sedition after proposing political freedom for Scotland in the early 1790s, but Hunter's decision in this regard had been endorsed by Portland. Margarot certainly had the erudition and capacity to draw up the offending letter, and he admitted to writing letters home outlining details of the monopolists' abuses but he was not regarded as particularly troublesome, and was described by a colleague as 'generally liked, as a quiet man, very seldom making his appearance.'[33] By contrast, Palmer 'is generally disliked, being of a litigious and troublesome disposition. His situation has most likely rendered him peevish; so say his neighbours.'[34] His biography states that he wrote letters to influential friends in England (several published anonymously) severely critical of Hunter's administration, at least one of which found its way to Portland.[35] This is most likely the letter popularly attributed to John Macarthur.

In his lengthy defence of the charges, Hunter made no attempt to identify the unnamed author, whom he called 'the dark and infamous assassin'.[36] He does however describe the person to Portland, a clue not picked up by other writers.

> He has here nothing to do: his age and his infirmities, his former situation in Society, and his respectable connections have at all times dispos'd me to render his present state of exile as easy and comfortable to him as it would admit.[37]

Hunter went on: 'The man who shall have been found inclin'd to exert his little endeavours against the Constitution and Government of his native country' and referred to the 'seditious assassin' who claimed that Hunter had thwarted his boat-building plans.[38] This description does not fit the profile of John Macarthur, but does paint a picture of Thomas Palmer, whose biography notes that he was a former Anglican clergyman, educated at Cambridge who became something of a zealous political reformer. He was 52 years of age in 1799 (Macarthur was only 33) and was confined on the voyage out to Sydney in 1794 for incitement to mutiny. A narrative outlining his sufferings was taken back to England by surgeon John White and published in 1797.[39]

During his seven-year exile in Sydney, Palmer was excused from the usual convict labours and constraints and spent his time in farming and entrepreneurial pursuits, including trading and ship building. Palmer was indeed involved in building a boat for the Norfolk Island trade and the sealing grounds in Bass Strait (and beyond), in which some voyages 'were made without Hunter's consent'.[40] Hunter's justification of the limitations imposed on boat size was his instruction not to impinge upon the East India Company's trading charter, but Palmer viewed this as interference with his commercial aspirations. Further, in a postscript to his reply to Portland, Hunter advised that 'The Military Officers have applied to me for an investigation of their conduct with respect to the charges exhibited against them in an anonimous [sic] letter already mentioned.'[41] These indicators point to Thomas Palmer as the author of the damning anonymous letter, not to John Macarthur as widely believed.

It was not this letter per se which led to Hunter's recall, as Portland had already made his mind up on the matter, but it could only have strengthened his decision. Portland's principal preoccupation was Hunter's inability to control the colony's spiralling expenses, which directly impacted upon Portland's own departmental budget which underwrote the costs of the settlement. At a time when England's war with France was consuming ever increasing time and money, the apparent free-wheeling costs of New South Wales would have been a source of embarrassment and concern to Portland and to the Treasury, to whom he had to account for his expenditure. If Hunter had been able to reduce, or at least contain costs and increase self-reliance, the other problems may have been better tolerated because they could be kept 'in-house' within Portland's portfolio. Runaway budgets involved outside political scrutiny and questions from other departments.

Portland's obsession with rising costs is evident from his repeated references to them, for example in a letter dated 31 August 1796, 'My great disapprobation at the want of economy in the expenditure of public money'[42]; and two weeks later: 'you are to resort to every practicable measure for relieving this country from the very great expenses incurred both in sending out provisions from hence and in purchasing them from other quarters.'[43] Portland wrote again on 31 August 1797 'I cannot observe without infinite surprize and regret the very heavy expenses which have been incurred.'[44] Hunter's responses to these concerns were at best vacillating and unconvincing, and accelerated Portland's declining confidence in him. 'Your Grace can scarcely suppose me responsible for the errors of a system established for the management of this colony long before it fell to my care'[45] (but Hunter had been there 20 months with no impressions made on the issue) and he then blamed Norfolk Island costs for distorting his balance sheet.[46]

His fixation on the problem rather than a solution is further evident in an eight-page, self-justifying and defensive private letter to Lord Sydney dated 30 July 1797, nearly two years into his term.

> I have found it necessary in support of my own integrity and Character, to expose in a long letter to His Grace the Duke of Portland many of the changes which had taken place since the departure of Govr. Phillip and before my arrival, in order that His Grace might see, that whatever were now the expenses of this Settlement, or from whatever cause they may have arisen, that such cause originated long before I took up the management of its concerns.[47]

Hunter's continuing incompetence and lack of decisiveness caused Portland to conclude, as early as the first quarter of 1798 (18 months before his letter of recall to Hunter), that a change was needed. A short statement appeared in *The Star* of 19 May 1798, that 'Mr King, it is finally arranged, succeeds Mr Hunter as Governor of Botany Bay.'[48] The word 'finally' would infer the matter had been under consideration for some time, so it can be presumed that Portland had begun succession plans by the end of 1797 or early 1798, but Hunter did not appear to be aware of them.

He further alienated Portland by his tardiness in carrying out his instructions. For example, on 31 August 1797, Portland proposed to Hunter that

> the individual should pay by his crops, at the market price, for the provisions, cloathing, and impliments of husbandry which he receives from the publick store for the convicts he employs, by which a great saving would accrue to the publick, and at the same time very sufficient encouragement would be held out for the cultivation of the land.[49]

While this fairly elementary advice was tendered from 12,000 miles distant, a more decisive leader would have been advising his superior of these same intentions. Hunter did not conform to these repeated instructions until 20 May 1798[50], by which time he was so bound up in the minutiae that he could not visualise a grander plan for New South Wales.

It could also be claimed that the fundamental fault behind the lacklustre leadership of the colony from 1795 to 1800 was the decision by the Colonial Office to appoint Hunter in the first place. He turned out to be ill-suited to the task, incapable of handling the economic challenges and was out-manoeuvred by his more street-wise and cunning adversaries, but this was not evident at the time of his appointment. Conversely, as has already been indicated, the true state of affairs in the settlement was not fully understood by those making the appointment. Duffy believes that 'Had King been sent out as governor five years earlier, as Phillip had recommended, the generousity of the Grose-Paterson years might have been wound back more easily.[51] But this overlooks the fact that King was not even a captain in 1794 (with only two years seniority as a commander) so this lack of ranking would have handicapped his authority; added to which he was only 37 in 1795. As it was, he too was unable to suppress the Corps' excesses during his term from 1800 to 1806, although they had become more entrenched during Hunter's time.

Hunter's inability to put down the rum traffic and trading malpractices was shown up by some of his own courses of action, which simply eroded his own endeavours. He was hardly assisting his own cause against the rum trade when he issued a public proclamation offering five gallons of spirits as a reward for the capture of a bushranger.[52] Similarly, he issued an order on 25 June 1798[53] sanctioning an agreement of Corps officers and principal civilians made on 18 June[54] to act as commercial agents for the entire colony. This could only encourage a practice to which he attributed much of the settlers' troubles, which Portland had strongly condemned, and perhaps demonstrates the muddled and besieged state of mind Hunter was in at the time. Portland must have shaken his head in bewilderment upon reading the agreement and its endorsement by Hunter, and on 5 November 1799 he expressed his surprise and fear that the officers who had denigrated the Corps by engaging in such trade, would be encouraged by such official sanction.

> I cannot but be apprehensive that that part of your Public Orders of 25th June 1798, which informs the inhabitants 'that you are assured by the Officers that they will most readily stand forward in behalf of the whole colony, and purchase from ships calling here whatever goods or comforts they may have for sale, and that every person having money to purchase may claim their proportion of such purchase without the assistance of any other agent, which will be the means of their receiving the articles at a much lower rate, and that this being the case, every person is desired to keep the possession of their own money until they are apprized by public notice that a

cargo has been brought, the Officers having undertaken the trouble of officiating as agents for the general benefit of the whole Colony', has been considered as a sanction to officers engaging in traffic, and as an apology for the proceedings which I have but too much reason to fear may be found to have disgraced his Majesty's service in the persons of several of the Officers of the New South Wales Corps.[55]

Portland here distinguished between several as opposed to 'all' of the officers; a distinction lost on later historians.

Hunter seems to have been blind to the consequences that such an order would have had in encouraging officers to engage in further trade, a practice he repeatedly censured. He attempted to defend himself by claiming that he had been duped by the officers into supporting their agreement. 'In this there appears an evident design of a confederated interest to deceive me'[56], but in so doing, he further exposed himself as being naive and unsuspecting. Portland's letter of the 5 November 1799, quoted above, concluded with the following bombshell:

> Having now made all the observations which appear to me to be necessary on the points contained in your several despatches, which are now before me, it is with very serious concern that I find myself obliged to add that I now felt myself called upon by the sense of the duty which I owe to the situation in which I have the honour to be placed to express my disapprobation of the manner in which the government of the settlement has been administered by you in so many respects— that I am commanded to signify to you the King's pleasure to return to this Kingdom by the first safe conveyance which offers itself after the arrival of Lieutenant Governor King, who is authorised by his Majesty to take upon him the government of that Settlement immediately on your departure from it.[57]

Hunter's indignant defence and rebuttal of his conduct in letters written to the Duke of Portland on 20 April 1800[58] (upon receipt of his recall) and to Under-Secretary King on 25 September 1800[59] is yet another manifestation of his inability to appreciate his own passive contribution to his woes. He was essentially in denial over his role in the colony's problems, which may have contributed to his reluctance to hand over control to King until the very last moment.

Hunter's greatest failing was his want of resolve in the face of opposition. His letters reveal a man out of his depth, but who was fundamentally an honest, upright and trusting individual. Governor King wrote to Sir Joseph Banks on 28 September 1800 (on the day Hunter handed over the administration of New South Wales to King) complaining that the previous five months since his arrival had been 'the most disagreeable and provoking part of my life'[60] because of Hunter's refusal to step down until he was ready to sail for England. 'Governor Hunter has not given up the command to me before the date of this letter. You will easily judge that the colony has not benefitted much by the interregnum of six months.'[61] But he did go on to say that

> with respect to Hunter I believe him to be what the whole colony says he is—an honest man; but the reliance he has placed on those who, to use his own words 'have tricked and deceived him in every instance' has placed every circumstance, person, and thing in such a state that much time will be lost in getting them into the path pointed out by my worthy friend Phillip.[62]

He reiterated his view of Hunter a year later in a private letter to Under-Secretary King, saying 'although made a tool of by the artful and designing friends he had in the colony, he, honest and upright as he was himself, was sadly duped and deceived by those he had about him.'[63]

The greatest proof of Hunter's somewhat pliant disposition was his continued reluctance to put into effect those instructions from London which clashed with the vested interests of the Corps officers and the principal colonists. Hunter repeatedly avoided limiting the officers to two convict servants each, despite being commanded by Whitehall to do so.

> The Governor having received instructions from his Majesty's Secretary of State relative to the number of men hitherto granted to the Officers, civil and military, and others upon their farms, he has now to inform them that two men only are to be considered as allowed at the expense of the public, and that such as they may have over that number are to be maintained and clothed at the expense of their employer.

He then qualified this by stating that employers may obtain rations and clothes from the public store by paying later with farm produce—'either grain or fresh pork.'[64] Needless to say the deferred payment system became blurred and abused, then neglected and ignored.

When King assumed power, he immediately put this order into literal effect as well as those banning private trading, especially in rum. This produced a response from the principal surgeon William Balmain and his assistant D'Arcy Wentworth, claiming that they had bought a large quantity of spirits, clothing, material and tea before they became aware of King's order. They stated that they had been engaged in open trading for some years and knew nothing of any orders prohibiting the practice, and offered to sell their stocks (14,000 gallons of rum, a few tea chests and some bale goods) to the government. They had been engaged in an extremely overt and lucrative business for some years, apparently operating either under Hunter's nose or with his tacit knowledge but not official consent, and they were indignant when King called them to account.

A further example of Hunter's inability to deal with his difficulties took place in January 1800. On the 15th of that month, Hunter wrote to Portland advising that, four days earlier, a vessel had arrived loaded with wine, spirits and general merchandise, which had been chartered by the civil and military officers 'without having signified their design to me.'[65] In his letter, Hunter advised that he initially thought to ban the landing of the cargo, especially the 9,000 gallons of spirits, but the officers pointed out to him that the rum and brandy were for the benefit of their respective farms, i.e. to pay the wages of their farm labourers. He gave way because to oppose the landing 'will be in vain on my part for the want of proper officers to execute such orders as I might see occasion to give.'[66] Hunter was virtually admitting he was powerless to halt this landing as he had insufficient backing to enforce his authority. In other words, he had effectively lost control and was unable to prevent the enormous importation of spirits, as they would have been smuggled into the settlement in spite of any orders to the contrary. By acquiescing to their demands, Hunter was conceding the veracity of the charges laid anonymously against him, but pleading in his defence that he was powerless to prevent them. The request to land the cargo came from John Macarthur, William Balmain and James Williamson, who claimed that they could control supplies and prices from being exploited by competing 'adventurers'. This flimsy excuse is in a similar vein to the self-justification offered by Elizabeth Macarthur five years earlier that the Corps was simply preventing other potential monopolists from exploiting the market—a clear case of 'the pot calling the kettle black' and confirms that by that time (1800) Hunter had lost effective authority and control of his administration.

Before King formally assumed command, he quickly came into conflict with Hunter by taking sides with those oppressed settlers whose farms were heavily mortgaged to the landed officers. He pleaded with Hunter to put a stop to 'the oppression of the infamous traders'[67] by confining these 'assassins of public liberty and destroyers of individual industry ... to a profit of one hundred per cent.'[68] In reply Hunter stated that nothing could be done and that the 'assassins' were within their legal rights. Hunter had simply run out of energy and his recall then was both justified and timely.

To his credit, Hunter did at least recognise that the only really effective means to control the trading and land domination activities of the Corps was to recall, replace or disband them. Against this however, was the cost of repatriating and replacing them plus the need to retain troops in England to fight Napoleon. In his letter to Portland of 12 November 1796, just over one year after his arrival, he had identified the problems confronting him[69] and he recommended the Corps be relieved every three to five years, but conceded that cost implications might rule this out. By May 1799, he realised that they were so entrenched that 'it will require immense labour to grub them up by the root.'[70] In fact, it took another ten years (and two more governor casualties plus a revolt in 1808) before the New South Wales Corps was finally removed and replaced with another regiment under Lachlan Macquarie in 1810, after the immediate Napoleonic threats to England had diminished.

Hunter's achievements

While elements of Hunter's performance as governor may have been inadequate, these have to be matched with other aspects of his administration, which were in fact, successful, humanitarian and forward-thinking. Hunter's concept of authority was derived from his discipline-based active naval service, but tempered with a duty of care and an entrenched sense of paternalism. This can be gleaned from the evidence of seamen under his control such as Jacob Nagle, Daniel Southwell, and his officers such as William Bradley, which indicated that Hunter was neither an autocrat nor a tyrant. He did, however, in usual naval tradition, expect total obedience and loyalty from his officers and crew, and apparently duly received it. Hunter viewed New South Wales as strategically important from a naval aspect, especially in time of war, and the consequent imperative that it be efficient, harmonious and productive.

Hunter had three distinct and separate centres of population to administer, excluding Norfolk Island, which had its own commandant, under Hunter's ultimate authority. Sydney was the largest settlement with a population of 1910 in 1796, rising to 2063 in 1800 and was the colony's naval, trading and importing centre. Parramatta was the planned civic centre with wide streets and parks. Its population grew from 814 in 1796 to 1274 in 1800, while the Hawkesbury River settlement was the western frontier populated by small farmers whose numbers increased from 383 in 1796 to 895 in 1800.[71] The total population during Hunter's term therefore rose from 3107 in 1796 up to 4232 in 1800, or by approximately 30 per cent, while the number of women actually fell from 871 in 1796 to 647 in 1800, mostly due to them leaving the colony upon the completion of their term of servitude. The other relevant statistic was that the number of convicts also fell from 2338 in 1796 down to 1558 in 1800 (while the number of free and freed people rose from 188 to 2100 over the same period) due to the slowing down in the number of convicts transported due to war considerations such as the unavailability of ships and crews, combined with the increasing number of convicts whose terms had expired. This compromised the number of convict labourers available for public projects and put some pressure on farming and food supplies.

Law and order

Hunter's first major decree as governor was to re-establish the civil magistracy in October 1795, replacing the military officials in the civil courts. The four civil magistrates appointed in their stead were Reverend Richard Johnson and surgeon William Balmain in Sydney and Reverend Samuel Marsden and Richard Atkins at Parramatta, which naturally alienated the New South Wales Corps officers.

The situation was exacerbated a few months later over the so-called Baughan affair. On 5 February 1796, four soldiers assaulted and then destroyed the house of John Baughan, an emancipated convict and a carpenter, whose complaints occasioned one of the assailants to be arrested. Hunter required Major Paterson to apprehend the soldiers and complained about the Corps' abuse of its powers, declaring that their conduct was 'the most violent and outrageous that was ever heard of by any British regiment whatever' and that 'they shall not dictate the laws and rules of the government of this settlement; they were sent here by His Majesty to support the civil power in the execution of its functions.'[72] Hunter was determined that the accused would be tried under civilian law, and not, as requested by the Corps, by court martial. John Macarthur intervened before the arrest warrants were served, and expressed the contrition of the offenders with a promise of restitution to the victim, whereupon Hunter rather weakly withdrew the warrant, causing Portland to comment later that he 'could not well imagine anything like a justifiable excuse'[73] for not bringing the soldiers to trial and punishing them severely. This incident took place only a few months into Hunter's administration and could be explained by him not wishing to alienate those upon whom he depended, so soon after taking office. Nevertheless, it was a feeble back down that would only have encouraged further transgressions and must have rung early alarm bells in London. Henceforth, the civil magistrates and the supremacy of civil law over military rule were constantly under attack during the remainder of Hunter's term. The contradiction here was that, while on the one hand Hunter was adamant that adherence to the rule of law was paramount, his very actions undermined his own aspirations and convictions, which only encouraged the Corps leaders to pursue him more vigorously.

Hunter believed that the maintenance of civil rule was not only the responsibility of the government but that the citizens also had a role to play. As well as advocating trial by jury in 1796[74], Hunter divided Sydney into four divisions, named after Banks, Nepean, King and

Maskelyne (the Astronomer Royal)—the forerunner to suburbs; the houses in each division were allocated a number and each inhabitant was registered.[75] The residents then elected annually 'three of the most decent and respectable men' in each division to act as overseers or monitors.[76] The principal duties of these overseers were to prevent robberies, reduce vagrancy and monitor appropriate observation of the Sabbath. This was perhaps the first experiment in local government and these innovations reflected Hunter's paternalistic approach and an enlightened faith in facilitating the development of those under his care. It would also have been a reaction to the hitherto unrestrained policing excesses of the New South Wales Corps.

Building policies

Like his endeavours to restore law and order, Hunter was able to successfully undertake a series of capital works projects. He also believed that, while government had a duty to plan and design, the people, too, had a part to play, especially when the project would directly benefit them.

To ensure the settlement's self-sufficiency in grain, Hunter firstly rebuilt the granaries and storehouses in Sydney and Parramatta, which he later justified to Lord Sydney.

> There was scarcely a Public Building on my arrival in this Colony but such Barracks and Stores as had been erected in the time of Governor Phillip, and they were crumbling into ruins, and were too few by far for the extended and increasing Numbers of the Colony.[77]

He then commissioned the construction of practical necessities such as schools and churches, barns, barracks, a dispensary, a blacksmith's workshop, naval buildings, a battery, fences, wharves and bridges.[78] Wherever practicable, the buildings were constructed of stone or bricks and covered with lime mortar 'to ensure their lasting at least twenty years to come.'[79]

As well as bringing the first windmill to Australia in 1795, Hunter also brought with him the first peel of bells, both of which had symbolic as well as pragmatic uses. Both represented the civilisation they had all left behind in England—the familiar sight of windmills in the countryside mechanically grinding grain while hearing the sound of church and civic bells in the villages, towns and cities. For Hunter, the bells' principal objective was not as church bells, but 'for the purpose of calling the people to and from their work, the working parties being frequently widely separated.'[80] The silence of Sydney must have reinforced the feeling of separation and nostalgia in the hearts of all its inhabitants, so the sight of a windmill and the chiming of bells would have somewhat lessened their sense of isolation. In similar vein, Hunter also brought out the first clocktower, which was erected in 1797 near the site of present day St Phillip's Church at the top of York Street in Sydney.[81] It was also a symbol of the life they had all left behind, but it too had a practical application and can be seen in Thomas Watling's 1803 painting of Sydney Cove. At 150 feet high, it also would have served as a useful surveying reference point.

Roads also slowly radiated out and improved under Hunter's plan for the colony. He decreed they should be 20 feet wide[82] and placed their construction under the supervision of the Government Surveyor, Augustus Alt. However, where possible, Hunter required that settlers living along these roads should provide some of the labour and most of the tools, as they would be the principal beneficiaries of these facilities, and the colony was generally short of both commodities. It was also a device to involve private citizens in the public good on a user-pays basis.

Hunter also required the principal officers and citizens as well as the larger landholders to assist in the construction of a new stone gaol in

1799, to replace the 1796 log prison destroyed in a storm. Citing the precedent that wealthy landowners in Britain underwrote such projects, Hunter told a meeting of these prosperous settlers that 'it is but fair therefore, that the expense of such building be defrayed by them.'[83] Although the meeting agreed to the proposal, tangible assistance was slow to appear, compelling Hunter to levy sixpence on each bushel of wheat delivered to the public store and when this was circumvented by some, he imposed a duty on imported spirits to cover the expense. Hunter's public works programme was based upon the practical requirements of the colony rather than for any self-promoting or pretentious reasons (an accusation justly levelled at Lachlan Macquarie), which Hunter summed up as being 'not mere ostentatious show; they are permanent and essential works.'[84]

Community relations

Periodic meetings with the settlers were also a key feature introduced by Hunter. His intention was threefold—to establish a rapport with the settlers (which was a reflection of his desire to relate to people around him), to bestow greater responsibility upon the community, especially in the more distant settlements where official influence was less able to be maintained and to instil an increased sense of self-reliance and personal obligation amongst the population to manage their own areas and affairs.

In February 1798, Collins recounted that

> A general muster took place on the 14th, in every district of the Colony, at which every labouring man whether free or convict, was obliged to appear. On the following morning the settlers were called over, previous to which, the Governor, who was present, informed them that he had heard of much discontent prevailing among them in consequence of certain heavy grievances which they said they laboured under. For these, as he was unacquainted with the nature of them, he was unable to

suggest a remedy; he therefore desired that they might be represented to him in writing.[85]

Collins then reported that Hunter 'gave them much good advice, and assured them that he had already from his own ideas, offered a plan to the Secretary of State for their benefit, which he hoped would in due time be attended to'[86] which represented an attempt by Hunter to govern by some measure of consensus. This was further evidenced by his entreaty two years later to the Hawkesbury settlers to play their part in curbing the power of the monopolists. 'It is the business of those who suffer from it [monopoly] to come forward and give immediate and substantiated information of such grievances and abuse, in order that it may be instantly checked.'[87]

Hunter's hands-on concern for the welfare of those under him was further demonstrated in an incident which occurred in January 1801, when he visited Parramatta. Joseph Holt, a former convict, and his wife and child met the governor who enquired after their wellbeing. He held the infant's hand and asked 'Pray madam, do you get any milk for this child?'[88] She replied that she did not know where to obtain it, whereupon Hunter spoke to the government dairy overseer, who was present, and instructed him to 'send a quart of milk to her every morning; and mind, if you neglect doing so, I will have you put out of your place.'[89] These face-to-face encounters endeared him to many settlers who respected him for so doing, their attitude epitomised by Joseph Holt, who described Hunter as 'one of the most worthy of men, and the father, and a right good father he was, to this infant colony. A perfect gentleman in his manners, he was gracious and condescending to all, without compromising his dignity, personal or official.'[90] These meetings had a mixed success as not all traders and landowners shared his vision for co-operation.

Indigenous relations, science and exploration

For all his inadequacies as governor, John Hunter did imbue an enlightened approach towards the indigenous population and the sciences, as well as encourage the exploration of Australia's south-eastern coastline. Hunter's original instructions, dated 23 June 1794, required him, inter alia, 'to endeavour by every possible means to extend your intercourse with the natives and to conciliate their affections, enjoining all our subjects to live in amity and kindness with them'[91] which was identical to that issued to Phillip seven years earlier. The enlightenment movement would have had some impact on Hunter's humane approach, as his treatment of the Aborigines indicated. Phillip's approach to the indigenous population was also benevolent, but after yet another convict had been murdered by them, his attitude uncharacteristically hardened to the point when, on one occasion towards the end of 1790, he literally sent out a head-hunting party (which was unsuccessful) in retaliation and as an example to the Aborigines.[92] Paterson was compelled to employ force to keep the Aborigines from plundering farms on the Hawkesbury River. He captured some 'to keep them until they can be made to understand that it is not in their interest to do us injuries; but that we cannot suffer our people to be inhumanely butchered'[93], at least demonstrating an appreciation of the need to communicate with them.

Hunter observed an enlightened approach by issuing an order on 12 November 1796 that

> It is his Excellency's positive injunction to the settlers and others who have firearms that they do not wantonly fire at or take the lives of any of the natives, as such an act would be considered a deliberate murder, and subject the offender to such punishment as (if proved) the law might direct to be inflicted.[94]

notwithstanding repeated attacks by Aborigines on Hawkesbury River settlers, of whom some of the latter undoubtedly were the provocateurs. Hunter's attitude was consistent with his inherently kindly disposition, whereby he attempted to preserve order in the outlying regions but also sought to protect the aboriginal population from exploitation by the newly-arrived Europeans. Hunter brought Bennelong back to Sydney on the *Reliance* in 1795, so the future governor would have had opportunities on the voyage to converse with him and obtain some understanding of their attitudes and culture, which was consistent with Hunter's enquiring mind. There are few references by Hunter to the Aborigines in his official correspondence but it can be assumed that he retained an interest in them, although probably overshadowed by his other administrative preoccupations.

His attitude towards the Irish convicts was less benevolent. Like most Protestants, he would have had reservations about Irish Catholic intentions, especially from his childhood memories of the attempted uprising by Charles Stuart in 1745. While by 1800, Irish convicts comprised only 13 per cent of the convict population, they quickly made their presence felt. Some had a genuine grievance in that when they arrived in Sydney in the early 1790s, there were no papers indicating when their sentences would expire, which Hunter admitted 'is certainly hard upon them'[95], but he could not free them until he had proper documentation. Beyond this, he regarded them as 'turbulent and worthless characters' who 'have threatened resistance to all orders, but they have not yet carried far their threats; a few of them have been punish'd.'[96] On another occasion he described them as 'so turbulent, so dissatisfyed with their situation here, so extremely insolent, refractory, and troublesome that, without the most rigid and severe treatment, it is impossible for us to receive any labour whatever from them.'[97] Fortunately for Hunter, they posed no basic threat during his term, except for their preoccupation and utter determination to escape, sometimes in bizarre circumstances such as relying upon a compass drawn on a piece of paper and believing that a utopia existed nearby where they would live in comfort and safety.

Hunter was a scientific observer in the enlightened sense of the era. His moderately competent sketching skills enabled him to draw reasonable likenesses of animals, birds and fish, many of which eventually found their way into libraries and museums in England. He used a pedometer to estimate distances walked on his inland expeditions and as a competent seaman was at ease with scientific instruments such as the sextant and logarithmic tables. He regularly sent specimens of seeds, animals and birds back to England; some to the Duke of Portland and Under-Secretary King and others to Sir Joseph Banks. It is unclear whether these gifts were motivated by scientific advancement ideals alone or whether there was an element of personal promotion involved as well. Hunter was the first to draw the wombat and the platypus and sent species of each back to England. The platypus was initially considered a hoax until the anatomist Everard Home dissected it, but it took another 30 years for its egg-laying feature to be eventually accepted.

Hunter's administrative duties (and problems) precluded him from undertaking serious exploration or travel far from Sydney, other than a few journeys along the Hawkesbury and Nepean rivers to the north-west and to the cow pastures in the south-west, each lasting only a week or two. These expeditions were primarily to ascertain the areas' suitability for agricultural expansion, as illustrated by David Collins, who recorded that in April 1797, Hunter and some gentlemen of the settlement set off from Parramatta to 'obtain some knowledge of the ground between Duck river [near Parramatta] and George's river, with respect both to its quality and quantity'[98] where they found excellent tracts of land with chains of fresh water ponds.

Although Hunter's name is prominent in the Newcastle region, (Hunter River, Hunter Valley, Hunter Street, John Hunter Hospital, etc), he did not see the river which bears his name. In 1797, Lieutenant John Shortland (who came out to Sydney with Hunter on the *Reliance*) was returning in a whaleboat from a search north to Port Stephens for convicts who escaped from Broken Bay in the *Cumberland*, then the colony's largest and best vessel. He entered and named the Hunter River and discovered easily accessible coal deposits near the shoreline. For a few years the river was also referred to as Coal River, but its original name eventually became generally accepted.

During the remaining three years of Hunter's term, small vessels came to the river to collect coal, staying for a few days only, before returning to Sydney, with the workers camping on the beach, so there was little need or reason for him to formally visit the site. However, Hunter actively encouraged this trade to the extent that the first coal export shipment from Australia was consigned to Bengal in 1799. There was no permanent settlement on the river until 1804, following the Castle Hill rebellion in March of that year. Governor King named the settlement after Newcastle-on-Tyne, the centre of extensive coal fields in the north-east of England, which was then growing in size and importance due to the industrial revolution.

Hunter, however, actively encouraged others to undertake exploration when their duties permitted, especially Bass and Flinders. With Hunter's encouragement they explored the south coast of New South Wales in the *Tom Thumb* and in 1798–99 confirmed the existence of Bass Strait and circumnavigated Tasmania in the sloop *Norfolk*. In 1797, George Bass surveyed the south-east coast around to Westernport in a whaleboat, while two unsuccessful attempts were made to scale the escarpments comprising the eastern side of the Blue Mountains. This range was not crossed for another 15 years, until in 1813 Blaxland, Lawson and Wentworth succeeded by following the high ridges rather than the valleys.

John Hunter's strengths were in some respect his weaknesses. He was kindly, unpretentious ('I am a plain man bred to the honorable and respectable profession of a seaman'[99]), trusting and honest, which unscrupulous people took advantage of, repeatedly and increasingly. He was open and approachable ('I am never innaccessable to any man in the colony'[100]) and possessed a high degree of integrity. He also had a high sense of responsibility ('I consider myself responsible for the sums drawn in my name, or by my authority.'[101]). However, his naivety encouraged others to deceive and take advantage of him. He was not a farmer and came without privilege from a narrow, sheltered, discipline-based naval environment which did not allow for dissent or disobedience. When confronted with unfamiliar circumstances, he was ill prepared and simply not able to cope.

Hunter was highly motivated ('I will persevere in my best exertions for conquering every difficulty[102] and 'I considered it my indispensible duty to give to his Majesty's minister ... the most clear, distinct, and perfect information relative to the concerns of my command'[103]) and expected others to be the same. He, unlike his successor Phillip Gidley King, was generally in excellent health, especially for his age in those times, although he did have some scares during his term as governor.

> The last summer having been excessively sultry and dry, my anxiety induced me to attempt travelling more than my strength was equal to, and I have but lately recover'd from a dangerous fever, which having fallen into my left leg, was probably the means of saving my life, but has made me a cripple for some little time to come.[104]

His lack of leadership experience ill-equipped him to plan strategically for the colony's progress, although he always believed in its ultimate success ('This is a good country and will do well.'[105]). His want of firmness contributed to the very abuses he complained of, but his lack of vision and a plan only encouraged their continuance and expansion. Yet, following his return to England in 1801 and away from the daily distractions in Sydney, he did have the clarity of thought to set out a series of recommendations to cut the costs of the colony and to improve its administration, many of which were ultimately adopted. Hunter was not fully or properly supported by his superiors because of a shortage of funds, a lack of real interest and understanding of the affairs and conditions in New South Wales, plus an obsession with a critical war with France, which at that time threatened the very security and survival of Britain.

It is perhaps useful to consider briefly whether the approaches of Hunter's immediate successors were able to overcome or overturn the activities of the monopolists. The short answer is no. Philip Gidley King (1800–06) attempted to rule by regulation but found that he too was not able to dig out entrenched activities. William Bligh (1806–08), true to his reputation, adopted a confrontational attitude and endeavoured to force Macarthur and his followers into acquiescing to his will. He only succeeded in goading the Corps officers into open rebellion, culminating in his arrest and deposition on 26 January 1808, the settlement's 20th anniversary. However, it was not until the New South Wales Corps was replaced (something which Hunter had advocated) on the arrival of Macquarie in 1810 that their economic stranglehold over the colony was finally broken.

Hunter indicated that he would have preferred more regular communications with the Colonial Office (although his letters appeared to be answered in a reasonable time frame, allowing for a 12-15 month turnaround) but he did not expand upon precisely what he meant. He claimed that regular letters 'would serve to keep the people more cheerful and contented'[106] but another factor could well have been his own sense of neglect and isolation from his superiors in London. He had no-one in Sydney that he could turn to or confide in and no valued or trusted assistants like David Collins upon whom he could rely or seek considered and dispassionate opinions or advice. He was truly on his own—a situation in which he had virtually no prior experience. When challenged by Portland on his repeated cost blow-outs and a lack of decisiveness in carrying out Portland's orders, Hunter was in uncharted waters without anyone to guide him, and tended to blame everyone or everything else but himself. It was therefore not surprising that Portland eventually ran out of patience, but somewhat surprising that he was not recalled earlier.

It can only be concluded that, overall, in spite of some successes in social policy, it was in economic matters that John Hunter was less than a competent governor, for reasons both within and beyond his control, and for which he is unfortunately best remembered.

9
The mind, the eye and the pen

While John Hunter's abilities as a seaman, administrator and leader provide a pivotal insight into his character and career path, the picture is not yet complete. There is still some light and colour to be added to the background for this portrait to be filled out. In an era without cameras, electronic communications, rapid and easy travel, when complete dependence for information and impressions rested on the written word and hand-drawn illustrations, a person's ability as a writer and artist assumed greater significance and consequence than is the case today.

Many 18th-century travellers wrote diaries of their experiences for two principal reasons: firstly as a means of noting and remembering the various incidents and impressions along the way and secondly, for potential publication upon their return for both fame and monetary reward. These could vary from the remarkable, incisive and erudite diaries of the writer James Boswell (1740–95) on his journeys to, for example, Corsica and the Hebrides[1]; or the comprehensive observations of the Deputy Judge Advocate David Collins; to the scribbled notes of the poorly educated, such as the First Fleet marine Private John Easty and the sailor on the *Sirius*, Jacob Nagle. All provided valuable but different perceptions of their subject, while many others simply wrote letters to family and friends instead. Although their accuracy, bias and interpretation are sometimes open to speculation, they nevertheless furnished vital historical reference points for scholars and readers. Some of these people would have addressed learned or interested groups back home on their travels, while all would have spoken about their adventures to family circles, but these discourses are lost to posterity.

Before the availability of photography in the mid-19th century, there was total reliance on visual impressions by hand, so any artistic abilities were a decided advantage, whether to augment diaries or as stand-alone drawings or paintings. Furthermore, in the case of a serving naval or military officer, an additional test of their abilities would be the extent to which they could 'think outside the square' or laterally approach a problem and devise solutions or innovations not reached previously. All of these attributes or skills would have been useful in a naval career such as that of John Hunter and his early sketching aptitude earned him some recognition, while the publication of his journal also assisted in raising his profile as well as his bank balance.

John Hunter's skills with the pen could well be described as workman-like rather than exceptional. While his sailing skills could be labelled excellent, his abilities as a journalist or diarist could be termed 'good' compared to David Collins' and Watkin Tench's literary abilities which would rate as 'very good'; his capacity as a sketcher of coastlines or scenes, while 'good', was outshone by his first lieutenant on the *Sirius* William Bradley and midshipman George Raper (but his charts were of a superior standard), while his drawings of animals, plants and natives were often slightly out of proportion. His talents as a designer were also in the 'useful' category, rather than brilliant or trail-blazing. These three aspects of Hunter all emanated from the same mind through the same eyes and via the same pen, and presented strong elements of similarity in their standards.

The journalist

No analysis of Hunter's capabilities would be complete without an assessment of his abilities as a diarist, given the usefulness his journal has assumed in any study of the founding of modern Australia. It should be noted at this point that the Concise Oxford Dictionary makes no distinction between the words 'diary' and 'journal', describing each as a 'daily record of events'.[2] While the two words can be interchanged, the word 'journalist' has taken on a new media-related meaning during the 20th century. Hunter had a reasonably sound schooling and he was probably better educated than most of his naval peers, many of whom would have gone to sea five years younger than when Hunter did, aged 17. He had studied the classics and at one stage was headed for the ministry, both of which would have encouraged reasonable proficiency in expression and communication.

Hunter's journal was written between early 1787, during preparations for the First Fleet's departure on 13 May of that year, and 22 April 1792 when Hunter returned to England on the *Waaksamheyd*, a period of just over five years. It was published by John Stockdale of Piccadilly on 1 January 1793. The whereabouts of the original manuscript, which would have been written by Hunter himself (as he had no secretarial assistance) is unknown, and he would have used the enforced idleness on the return voyage to complete the finishing touches to the document.

Hunter's inherently polite, measured and kindly characteristics constrained him from placing on record the stresses that he encountered during the period between 1787 and 1792. He was not vindictive by nature and his innate diplomacy overwhelmed any temptation to point-score in his journal. However, he could criticise others, especially John Macarthur, when he felt cornered or threatened.

Prior to his journal, Hunter's official writings were confined to ships' logs as sailing master and lieutenant, which were restricted to details of weather, ship's position and condition, and contained nothing of a non-technical nature. Even his narration of the near loss of the *Carysfort* is a strictly factual account of events surrounding the ship's grounding and subsequent rescue activities.

Except for the conspicuous omissions of incidents at sea which may have reflected unfavourably on Hunter's reputation, the content of Hunter's journal largely appears to be in accord with those who wrote at the same time on similar matters, for example Tench, Phillip, Collins and Bradley.

The extent to which these diarists compared notes is not known. However, Phillip's journal was 'compiled from authentic papers which have been obtained from the several [government] departments to which are added the journals of Lts. Shortland, Watts, Ball and Captain Marshall'[3] so it is not an original account by Phillip himself, unlike Tench, White, Collins and Bradley. There was undoubtedly some consultation which occasionally led to duplication and overlap, as evidenced when Hunter set down examples of the Port Jackson Aborigines' vocabulary.

> I shall add a vocabulary of the language, which I procured from Mr Collins and Governor Phillip, both of whom had been very assiduous in procuring words to compose it; and as all the doubtful words have been rejected, it may be depended upon to be correct …

To which a note has been added, 'This vocabulary was much enlarged by Captain Hunter.'[4]

A curious matter arises here, as Hunter's vocabulary amounts to just over 300 words[5]—the same number as in David Collins' diary[6]—although Collins was at the settlement five years longer than Hunter. Hunter was at Sydney Cove from 1788 to 1791 (including a lengthy period away in the *Sirius* and 11 months on Norfolk Island), while Collins' uninterrupted term there extended from 1788 to 1796. One would have therefore imagined that Collins' vocabulary would have been significantly larger. While both vocabularies are similar in extent, they are in fact only similar in content in about 50 per cent of the words, i.e. about half the words in one set do not appear in the other. This does, however, provide a total of around 450 words for readers and scholars. Where the words do coincide they are generally quite similar, although often spelt differently, but the minor variations only denote a slight distinction in spelling or aural interpretation. There is a third list, contained in the letters of Daniel Southwell, a midshipman on the *Sirius*. This brief list of 118 words does contain some references not found within the other two, and would expand the total number described to around 500. Where there are duplications, Southwell's versions are so close to the other two, e.g. hook (bur-ra), rock (ee-bah) and eye (mi), as not to warrant an additional list here (see following).[7]

While comparing the lists of Hunter and Collins, it seemed useful to determine if any of the more common words were also picked up during Cook's voyage along the eastern shoreline of Australia in 1770, to see if there were any similarities in language on different parts of the coast. The most comprehensive vocabulary was set down by Sydney Parkinson who was Joseph Banks' draughtsman on the *Endeavour*. He prepared three vocabularies in all—the others were on Tahiti and New Zealand. He remarked on the similarities between the two languages, leading him to conclude that New Zealand

> was originally peopled from Otaheite, though they are at near two thousand miles distant, and nothing but the ocean intervenes, yet what should lead two distinct people, having no communication with each other, to affix the same sounds to the same things, would be hard to account for in any other matter[8]

thus making him the first to propose a connection between the two peoples.

As the *Endeavour* spent only one week at Botany Bay (29 April to 6 May), when Parkinson was busy with his draughtsman's duties for Banks, it was not until Cook was forced to beach his ship at the Endeavour River for around six weeks to affect repairs following their near sinking on the Barrier Reef (18 June to 4 August 1770) that Parkinson had the time to write down some of the local tribe's language.[9]

Word	Hunter's Version	Collins' Version	Parkinson's North Qld. version
hook	bur-ra	bur-ra	-
yesterday	boorana	bo-ra-ne	-
hut	gon-yi	go-nie	-
black	nand	gna-na	-
white	taboa	ta-bo-a	-
rock	kibber	ice-ba	walba
swim	wadby	wad-be	mailelel
dog	tingo	dingo	cotta
hand	tamira	tam-mir-ra	mangal
foot	menoe	ma-no-e	edamal
eye	mi	mi	meul
knee	go-rook	go-rook	pongo
today	yagoona	ya-goo-na	-
egg	ca-ban	ca-bahn	-
sunrise	coing-bibo-ba	co-ing bi-bo-ba	-

The similarities between Hunter's and Collins' interpretations are quite clear; just as it is equally obvious that the North Queensland dialect, or at least the one around the Endeavour River, bears no relationship to the one some 2500 kilometres to the south. There is a distinction between Hunter's and Collins' understanding of the word 'black', but the other differences are more in emphasis. Hunter acknowledged

Collins' proficiency by saying in 1789 'Mr Collins, the judge advocate, is very assiduous in learning the language, in which he has made great progress.'[10]

While Hunter expressed an interest in others, he was equally mindful to protect his own interests by refraining from making any comment that may not have reflected favourably on himself or others, and being the professional technician that he was, he rarely allowed himself the luxury of permitting personal opinions to intrude into his text. These lapses are infrequent but they do occur. As related earlier, on 25 November 1787 when the First Fleet was south-east of Cape Town in the Indian Ocean, Phillip transferred from the *Sirius* to the *Supply* taking with him the faster transports *Alexander*, *Scarborough* and *Friendship*, in order to arrive at Botany Bay a week or two ahead of the remaining seven slower sailing vessels to prepare a site in advance of the arrival of the bulk of the convicts. This second group was under the command of Hunter in the *Sirius*. Once the fleet had split, Hunter steered a more southerly course to take better advantage of the prevailing westerly winds.

> We stood to the southward and saw no more of them. I was at this time of opinion, that we had hitherto kept in too northerly a parallel to ensure strong and lasting westerly winds, which determined me as soon as Captain Phillip had left the fleet, to steer the southward and keep in a higher latitude.[11]

This mild criticism of Phillip for steering too northerly was borne out when Hunter arrived at Botany Bay only a couple of days behind Phillip:

> the Supply had not gained more than forty hours of us, and the three transports twenty. We probably met with fresher winds than they had done, otherwise I think those ships, all sailing well, should have had much more advantage of the heavy sailing part of the convoy.[12]

Hunter was too diplomatic to point out that his sailing skills were vindicated by making better use of the westerly winds.

On 17 August 1788, Phillip ordered two boats to enter every cove in Port Jackson and count the number of canoes and natives in each to ascertain total numbers in the area. This was to be done from the water without landing. Hunter commanded one of the boats and had to decline native invitations to land, 'although I thought the counting of them from the boat was a very uncertain method of coming at their numbers.'[13] Differences such as these, albeit gentle, perhaps indicate that while Hunter had his own views on issues, this was about as far as he would venture to express any contrary opinion to those of his superior; especially as Phillip was still active and influential when the journal was published in January 1793.

A further illustration of Hunter's diplomacy can be found in his account on 7 August 1790, having been marooned on Norfolk Island for nearly five months following the loss of the *Sirius*. Hunter reported two sails being sighted, which proved to be the *Justinian* and the *Surprize* bringing provisions (and an extra 200 convicts) from Port Jackson, and he was informed that five ships had arrived in Sydney two months earlier, bringing 980 convicts and provisions for the colony. Hunter believed the delay between the arrival of the stores at Port Jackson and their despatch to Norfolk Island to be excessive,

> a delay of great length, which when it is considered that our situation, when the Governor last heard from us, was rather an alarming one. Nothing had then been saved out of the wreck of the *Sirius* [Phillip would not have known of this as the *Supply* returned to Sydney soon after the loss], so that there was no certainty that we had been able to exist. Such were the reflections which I made during a moment of anxiety, and which in a position of quiet, I do not wish to repeat.[14]

It is reasonable to assume that Hunter was biting his lip and curbing his annoyance, even anger, in his judicious and measured choice of words.

Bradley was less diplomatic. He made clear his annoyance at Phillip's seeming delay in forwarding food to Norfolk Island and the apparent lack of action on Phillip's part to repatriate the *Sirius's* crew back to Port Jackson. 'We are yet without an opportunity of being removed from Norfolk Island' and although the five ships arrived at Sydney in the beginning of June,

> in the course of the same month it was not judged necessary to send relief to the unfortunates on Norfolk Island till the 27th July and 1st August, on which days the *Justinian* and *Surprize* left Port Jackson. The reasons for their having been so long detained seems only to be known to our very <u>humane governor</u>, who no doubt must have <u>felt</u> <u>much</u> for the distressful situation of the five hundred inhabitants on Norfolk Island. If we even allow him to possess only those feelings, which a reasonable being would have for a fellow creature, it is unaccountable what could have kept him from relieving us sooner.[15]

The differences in expression are perhaps a reflection of Hunter's self-discipline, his maturity and his closeness to Phillip, contrasted to Bradley's more youthful brashness and intemperate expression, revealed by his underlining of certain words for emphasis. Bradley was 31 years old at the time; Hunter was 53.

In fairness to Phillip, it could be argued that he might have reasonably assumed that there were adequate provisions and better farming conditions to sustain the swollen population of Norfolk Island, at least that they were better off than the hungry people at Port Jackson. Furthermore, the period required to off-load stores and people would have taken some time; the food allocation, storage and distribution processes needed to be planned and implemented and then those stores earmarked for Norfolk Island would have had to be re-loaded and the ships provisioned and made ready for sea, plus a week's voyaging from Sydney Cove. He would have also had to arrange accommodation for the convicts and attend to the ever present demands of reports and letters. The anxiety and frustration expressed by Bradley are perhaps understandable but a dispassionate observer might conclude that while Phillip could perhaps have acted slightly more expeditiously, he would not have deliberately delayed or allowed apathy to hinder the passage of supplies to the Norfolk Islanders.

Hunter was also perhaps established well enough and of sufficient years to admit to deficiencies or a lack of knowledge in areas not closely allied to his career, for example agriculture. He recorded in 1788 that, with respect to the variety of plants and flowers found around the harbour, 'I am wholly unqualified to describe the different sorts which we find the woods to abound'[16] and 'I have heard it [flax plant] reckoned a good kind, but in that I must confess my ignorance'[17] and again in late 1789 when he stated 'I do not pretend to any knowledge in farming.'[18]

Occasional discrepancies can be detected in his writing which, unless tested, would pass unnoticed. For instance, before Hunter arrived at Cape Town in December 1791 on the *Waaksamheyd* from Batavia on his way to England, he lost two of his bower anchors in a storm at Table Bay on 20 November. He rode out the storm at sea and recorded in his diary that

> on the 22nd, in the evening we fetched close around Green Point at Table Bay and hoisted signal of distress, having but one small anchor left. His Majesty's ships *Providence*, the *Assistant* armed tender, and the *Pitt* transport, being in the Bay, repeated our signal with many guns, and sent all their boats; several English whalers and some Americans also sent their boats with anchors and hausers, and we were soon got into safety. I was much obliged to Captain Bligh, as well as the commanders of

all the other ships, for their exertions, without which we must again have been driven to sea.

Hunter concluded by writing: 'On the 23rd the *Providence* and *Assistant* tender left the Bay.'[19]

Prima facie the account appears credible. However, Bligh reported that 'On 6th November 1791, the two vessels anchored in Table Bay. Here they found a Dutch snow, the "Waaksamheid" having on board Captain Hunter and the remainder of the crew of HMS *Sirius*'.[20] Who arrived first and when? Hunter reported arriving on 17 November while Bligh claimed that Hunter's ship was already there on the 6th. Bradley's journal supports Hunter's version (assuming Bradley's version is independent of any external influence) that the *Providence* and *Assistant* were already at anchor.

> On Saturday 17th ... we saw an English ship of war in the road: a boat from the ship soon informed us that it was the *Providence* sloop and *Assistant* brig going to the Society Islands for the bread fruit plant. The *Providence* commanded by Captain Bligh who soon after his return to England when forced away from the *Bounty*, was made Post Captain.[21]

Not only is there some discrepancy over who arrived at Table Bay first, but there is some confusion over the dates quoted by Hunter and Bligh. Both writers cannot be correct, so who was right? In the absence of additional corroborative evidence, it can only be concluded that Hunter's version (supported by Bradley) was more likely to be accurate. Hunter's journal has not shown up other inaccuracies of this nature, so its veracity can be presumed, leaving Bligh's account as mistaken.

Tellingly, while Hunter 'was very much obliged to Captain Bligh' for his part, Bligh deprecated Hunter in a letter to Joseph Banks.

> Even on board this ship [the *Waaksamheyd*] they have been at great variance, and I may pronounce with some certainty that the present second in command of New South Wales ... is not

blessed with a moderate share of good knowledge to give much stability to the new settlement.

However, perceiving he may have been overly harsh in his assessment of another of Bank's friends and correspondents, Bligh became conciliatory, 'I think it my duty to tell everything I am acquainted with to you, and if I err by saying too much I rely on your good wishes to do it away'.[22]

Hunter was not beyond expressing constrained disapproval of King when lieutenant governor of Norfolk Island, in August 1790. Following the arrival of the *Justinian* and *Surprize* with provisions and convicts, the boats used to unload were manned by crew from the *Sirius*. On one occasion, one of the boats capsized in a heavy and treacherous surf and seven people were drowned. It was suggested that the fault lay with the midshipman in charge of the boat. However Hunter obliquely blamed King for sending him out in the first place,

> yet certain it is every officer here at this time was fully satisfied it had not been in his power to obey, owing to the outset above mentioned [i.e. the treachery of the rip] and therefore it is equally certain, the reflection upon that gentleman's conduct was highly unjuSt If there had been any act of imprudence committed at that time, it was not by the midshipman, whose duty it was to obey orders, but in sending, in that narrow and intricate passage, one boat to meet another, where they should be in each other's way, and subject, by that means (if a surf should rise at the moment) to very great danger.[23]

In other words, King should have known better than to issue such orders. Hunter then ordered that the boats not put to sea in proximity to another when there was a danger of capsizing.

Hunter's disinclination to criticise is amply demonstrated in the veiled tone of his references to the Lieutenant Governor Major Robert Ross, who was a difficult person and a thorn in the side of most of his peers, especially Phillip, Hunter and Collins. He was regarded by many of those who knew him as 'an adversarial, self-serving and peevish man with an almost obsessive pre-occupation with the status of his Corps.'[24] In order to rid himself of this troublemaker, Phillip appointed Ross to succeed King on Norfolk Island in 1790. When the *Sirius* and the *Supply* arrived at Norfolk Island in March 1790, Hunter simply recorded that on 13 March, he landed 'all the marines (including Major Ross) and a considerable number of the convicts.'[25] Bradley reported on the same operation. 'We then went around to the north side of the island and found landing practicable at low water in Cascade Bay. Landed the marines and men convicts early in the afternoon.'[26] This could be regarded as the naval or official version. Marine Lieutenant Ralph Clark, an officer under Ross, painted a quite different picture. As a subordinate of Ross, he demonstrated a sense of loyalty to his superior officer even when this superior was widely disliked. Of the landing, Clark wrote:

> I think Captain Hunter might have been more civil in sending Major Ross on shore than in the manner he did, for I think that had Major Ross been a convict he could [not] have been treated wors [sic] than he was today by Captain Hunter in the manner he was shoved out of the ship by him into a boat loaded full with cots, hamocks [sic] hoggs [sic] pigs, geese, turkeys, fouls [sic] etc., so much that he had not room for his feet and when he landed on the rock he was so much cramped that he could hardly stand—I saw on Major Ross' landing that he felt very much on the matter he was sent out of the ship, but I hope Major Ross has too much good sense to take any notice of it.[27]

Allowing for 18th-century hyperbole, Clark evidently felt that his commanding officer had been shabbily treated by Hunter. Had this been an isolated instance, it could be passed off as marine versus navy rivalry. However 11 months later, on 10 February 1791, Clark wrote to his friend Captain Campbell (a fellow marine) at Port Jackson outlining the ongoing tension between Ross and Hunter, once again being careful not to impugn Ross' character, although it can be assumed that Ross played his part in any differences with others. Such tensions, however, are almost inevitable amongst any small group of people confined in a restricted area for many months, exacerbated by inter-service rivalry and shortages of food. Once again, Hunter has tactfully omitted any reference to this feud, so it is once more necessary to read another account (Lieutenant Ralph Clark) to appreciate the nature of the difference and Hunter's reaction to it. Perhaps Hunter decided that full omission was safer than selective observations which may have inadvertently reflected badly on him. Hunter seemed keen to avoid negative publicity.

> I am exceedingly sorry to inform you that we have not lived amongst each other in that state of harmony which I flatter myself at our first arrival we should, but it has been quite the contrary—we have been constantly bickering with each other which I believed would not have happened had the Supply called here on the way to Batavia and taking Mr Bradley along with her [Bradley was obviously actively involved], which I find was to have been the case could she have made the island—if it had not been for him we should have lived as happy as the days are long. He has been the fountain I am pretty certain from whome [sic] all our hot water has flown [sic] from, for soon after the Supply's leaving this in March last, he quitted the Mess and went and messed by himself—he did all in his power to make Captain Hunter quite [sic] at the same time which he could not effect until August when that gentleman [Hunter] left the Mess also and has kept at so great a distance from Major Ross ever since as hardly to have spoke to each other (I cannot give any reasons for this strange manner of acting, except that he found that he had got all the little comforts that Major Ross had, such as tea, sugar, liquor for Major Ross's little stock which was able to save from the *Sirius* lasted him until that time for he said very little) he then went and messed with his first lieutenant which he has done ever

since—in short, every officer of the *Sirius* here has followed their Captain and first lieutenant's steps so much so that they often have breached [i.e. encountered] Major Ross without paying him the least compliment and more so the Queen's Birthday neither Captain Hunter or any of his officers waited on Major Ross to pay him the compliment in honour of the day as the King's Officer commanding in chief here—I hereby leave to mention a little circumstance to you [the bickering had clearly driven Clark into Ross' corner as a biased and vigorous advocate] to show you the generous disposition of the second Captain of His Majesty's late ship *Sirius* which is that he saved four hogsheads of wine from the wreck, three of them he said belonged to Captain K Stuart of the Navy and the other to Mr Palmer, but which last has since proved to belong to himself. [Did Hunter lie here or has he been misrepresented in the heat of the disagreement?] While he messed with Major Ross he never so much as offered a single drop of the said wine to him then or since, although he knows Major Ross had nothing but water to drink, but the moment he went and messed with his friend Mr Bradley, he began making use of it and I am told he has ever since—don't you think he is a pretty friend?[28]

Clark's language clearly indicated the intensity of feeling and the depth of the division. Was it superficial and confined to senior officers or did it permeate the ranks to become navy against the military? There are no references to the cause(s) of the enmity. Clark singled Bradley out for special reference which perhaps bears testimony to Bradley's impetuosity, but Hunter too eventually left the mess; (or was he driven out?) in effect setting up two rival camps.

There is no mention of such tensions in Hunter's journal; the nearest he comes to any reference is when learning that he was leaving the island to return to Port Jackson. He wrote:

> This information I received with joy, as our situation was now become exceedingly irksome: as we had been upon this small island eleven months, and during great part of that time,

> through various causes, had been oppressed by feelings more distressing than I can find words to express.[29]

He revealed no explanation for what the 'various causes' were, but part of his distress would have been over the loss of his ship and the impending court martial.

Bradley's account of the sojourn on Norfolk Island confines itself to recording nautical observations, descriptions of wildlife and the ever-present preoccupation with inadequate food supplies. One would not glean any hint of conflict between Ross and Hunter or the navy versus marines from statements such as those written on Friday 14 April 1790.

> A Council was held by the Lt Governor and all the commissioned officers, to take into consideration the present reduced state of the provision store and to consult upon what measures are most proper to be pursued in order to preserve life until such time as we might be relieved by some supplies arriving.[30]

And again on August 3: 'The Lt Governor assembled the council for the purpose of determining our best plan in our distressed situation to secure to ourselves the means of subsidence until we may be relieved by the arrival of some ship.'[31] No indications of any tensions here and whatever they were, Bradley kept them to himself on these occasions, as did Hunter. The only comment that could be remotely construed as mildly critical of Ross occurred in February 1791 at the time of their departure when Bradley appears to implicate Ross for the failure of the public corn crop.

> The ground is certainly capable of producing everything usually found in the same climate and although the crop of corn belonging to the Public failed the last season, there were some remarkable fine crops on the ground belonging to some of the officers who have followed the same plan as had been first adopted, which was not the case with that belonging to

government, however the whole of that failure is laid with the catterpillars.[32]

For such a confined area as Norfolk Island at that time, it would be unusual for any caterpillar infestation to be confined to one farm, although Clark did say on 28 October 1790 'I never saw anything like the Catter Pillars so thick as they are on Serjt. Smyth's corn and on the pease and beans belonging to the Government.'[33]

Jacob Nagle's account provides an additional insight.

> Through his [Ross'] tyrannicale [sic] behaviour Captain Hunter and him did not agree while on the island. He would not allow the soldiers or convicts to go a forigin [sic] and wished the Captain to prevent us likewise, but as the Governor claped [sic] sentries on the roads which led around the island, that no one could go anywhere without a pass, the Captain ordered Mr Bradley to give the seamen a pass whenever they called upon him for one.[34]

Ross' propensity for making mischief finally involved Clark himself, his supporter and advocate. In a postscript to his letter to Captain Campbell, Clark related that Ross sent on board the *Supply* some fowls and corn for Hunter's use on his passage to Port Jackson and that Hunter 'would not think of accepting the fowls and corn that Major Ross had sent on board on account of the terms which they had been for this some time past on.'[35] On learning this, Ross requested Clark to inform Hunter that

> his reasons for sending the fowls and corn on board for him was that as he Captain Hunter had accepted every little present which Major Ross had ever sent to him and knowing he had no such things of his own was his only reason for sending them—at the same time wishing to no [sic] if he had any public complaint to make against him Major Ross, or if the quarrell [sic] which seem'd to subsist between them was a private one for he wished to no [sic] on what terms if ever they should meet again they were to meet—Captain Hunter gave me for

> answer that he had no public complaint to make against Major Ross nor private quarrel with him and if ever they should meet again, he wished for nothing more than common civility as he never wished to be on the same friendly footing which they had once been—Captain Hunter and I talked over everything from the first landing on this island untill [sic] this moment—in the course of the conversation he said that he had been told that Major Ross had wrote home a complaint against him to the Admiralty (as I was certain that Major Ross had never done such a thing).[36]

Clark's faith in Ross was rewarded by a scathing reply from Campbell in Sydney dated 6 August 1791.

> I am not as angry as I am vexed with you for entertaining so despicable an opinion of both yourself and me as Major Ross informs me you do ... I would not possibly have alluded to any more than Major Ross himself had said to me of some of the young people of the *Sirius* [including Bradley?] and what Captain Hunter said of the same people ... I was no longer surprized at what Major Ross had said.[37]

It is reasonable to conclude that Ross was indeed a vexatious person and that Hunter constrained himself in not placing on record the pressures that undoubtedly existed on Norfolk Island from March 1790 to February 1791.

In reviewing Hunter's capacity as a journalist, it is important to ascertain how it was received by his peers. A few months after the journal's publication early in 1793, there appeared in the May-August edition of *The British Critic* an eight-page review of Hunter's work.[38] (This was not the first account published—of the more important works, Phillip's was published in 1789, White's in 1790 and Tench's also in 1793.) The introduction revealed it was available from the publishers, Stockdale, for £1.11.6. After summarising the journal's contents and quoting extracts, the reviewer commended Hunter on his seamanship.

> It is proper, and indeed an act of Justice, to remark, that the care with which the observations for the longitude have been made, and the Tables for the Winds and Weather kept, throughout this work, entitle the author of this Journal to the highest praise, and cannot fail of being highly acceptable and useful to all future navigators in the same track. His voyage [to Cape Town] is accurately described; it was painfully tedious and laborious, and alike evinces his seamanship, resolution and persevering care to accomplish successfully the object of his mission—

and again, 'The instructive communications of this able navigator ...'[39] However, Hunter does not escape criticism.

> The volume commences with the Journal of Captain Hunter, some parts of which might, perhaps, without any detriment to the publication, have been omitted, as they contain a formal and minute description of many places and circumstances, already and sufficiently known from the work of Governor Phillip. Some anecdotes are, however, related, and some facts made known, which will make compensation to the reader, being not without their portion of amusement.[40]

The critique finishes on a mixed note, commenting on Hunter's language deficiencies but commending him for his insights and revelations.

> We repeat our acknowledgement for this publication, which, though the language has not been sufficiently attended to, has illustrated much that was obscure, has effectively removed much doubt and apprehension concerning the condition of our unfortunate countrymen at so remote a distance, and at the same time, exhibits a most respectable miscellany of instruction and amusement of all tastes and propensities.[41]

Hunter's grammar and syntax may have let him down on occasions, but he made no pretention to exceptional literary skill and his prose was not noticeably different to that of Bradley, Clark, Tench or King.

Collins' literary abilities were possibly superior to the others, but he was Phillip's secretary and judge advocate so he would have had a solid grasp of the language. Before going to sea, Hunter's inclinations were musical and artistic rather than those of a student of letters and classics. His education was more comprehensive than most other officers of his time which confers some validity on the criticism and which, with more care, may have been avoided.

Hunter's own copy of the printed work resides in the Mitchell Library[42] and contains no marginal notes or additional references, other than some latitude and longitude markings. Why did he publish it in the first place? There could have been four motivations. He wanted to capitalise on the popularity of travel literature in late 18th century England. The income would be useful as he was of limited means. The book may have helped his career prospects. By publishing quickly, Hunter produced an almost contemporary review, relating events to the close of 1791 at the start of 1793, a difference of about one year. This would add to the work's currency and relevancy, as well as popularity. It is reasonable to speculate that Hunter did satisfy each of these objectives. The book was popular and sold well and it may have helped him to secure the role of Phillip's successor.

On balance, Hunter was a capable journalist. It was largely though not always accurate. He admitted to ignorance in certain areas which enhanced his credibility and he wrote in a reasonably readable manner. His expression and prose were clear and while his grammar may have had some deficiencies, it does not detract from our understanding of his writings. His style was uncomplicated and reflected the basic, down-to-earth nature of the man. There are some notable (and presumably deliberate) omissions concerning potentially negative issues such as his feud with Major Ross, the two ship near-losses and finally the wreck of the *Sirius* while under his command. Overall, Hunter emerges as a mostly reliable journalist.

The sketcher

Hunter's ability with his pen (or quill) was recognised and acknowledged. He developed a skill for drawing which, by his early 20s, was sufficient for the biographical memoir to record that by 1760 (when Hunter was 23) he 'became tolerably expert in drawing views, either on land or water.'[43] All midshipmen were encouraged or taught to draw as part of their training to record, chart or map coastal features, reefs or islands and while all may have received this basic training, their natural abilities with the pen would have then sorted out those who were average or better. Eleven years later in 1771, Hunter, then the sailing master of the frigate *Carysfort* in the West Indies, was reported to have climbed to the masthead dressed as a common seaman, from which

> he made drawings of everything to be seen [in Havana harbour] from that station, which drawings he afterwards presented to Sir H. Palliser, then Comptroller of the Navy, who during his life-time duly appreciated Mr Hunter's talents.[44]

Hunter had also made charts and plans of coasts and harbours during the American War of Independence and during his time in the Indian Ocean on the *Intrepid* in 1773–74; all of which would suggest that his drawing abilities were above average.

The comment of Surgeon John White, 'Captain Hunter has a pretty turn for drawing', was made as the First Fleet rounded southern Tasmania in January 1788 and would tend to confirm Hunter's abilities, as he went on to say:

> ... which will enable him, no doubt, to give such a description of this coast as will do credit to himself, and be of singular advantage, as well as to those whose lot it may be to visit, hereafter, this extensive coast, as to navigation at large.[45]

Manning Clark took a more realistic view, stating that 'he drew with competence, not with distinction.'[46] Nevertheless, Hunter's plan of Port

Jackson was used by ships entering and leaving the harbour for the next 34 years, not being superseded until 1822, when a more complete survey was conducted and published by John Septimus Roe.

What is meant by 'sketching' and how is it being interpreted for these purposes? The subject is broken down into three categories—mapping, flora and fauna and people—each being examined separately, to determine how adept Hunter was in each of these fields.

(i) Mapping

Maritime mapping falls into three different categories—charts, plans and sketches—which Dr Tom Perry described as follows: 'Charts were usually small-scale depictions of coastlines, while plans were larger-scale maps of bays, harbours and islands'[47] which were usually drawn to a scale. Sketches, eye-sketches and eye-draughts were less rigorous in their geometry and were often accompanied by 'views' which highlighted landmarks to assist mariners in identifying coastal features to confirm their positions, or depicted a site or a particular location. Taking Hunter's journal as an example, facing page 110 is a 'chart of the Coast between Botany Bay and Broken Bay surveyed in 1788 and 89 by Captain John Hunter'[48]; opposite page 260 is a 'Plan' of Norfolk Island drawn by William Bradley[49], while against page 112 is a 'view' of Rose Hill 'drawn by E. Dayes from a sketch by J. Hunter.'[50] Beside page 70 of 'The Voyage of Governor Phillip to Botany Bay' is a 'Sketch of Sydney Cove, Port Jackson' completed in July 1788 with the acknowledgement 'The Coastline by W. Dawes; the soundings by Captain Hunter.'[51] This is a vertical depiction of the settlement showing hills, buildings and the Tank Stream. Perry erroneously described this as 'Hunter's Map of Sydney Cove'[52], whereas it was Marine Lieutenant William Dawes who effectively drew the sketch and incorporated Hunter's soundings of the Cove into it.

In view of the fact that there were no professional artists, draughtsmen or surveyors accompanying the First Fleet, perhaps one of the lesser reasons Howe chose Hunter to be second captain of the *Sirius* was his abilities with the pen. There were two other officers on the *Sirius* who were also creditable sketchers, First Lieutenant William Bradley, and Midshipman George Raper. Bradley's journal *A Voyage to New South Wales* contains 22 charts and plans and 29 views and sketches, but many of the charts are copies made of surveys conducted with Hunter while on the *Sirius* in New South Wales and Norfolk Island and on the *Waaksamheyd*. George Raper[53] was an accomplished draughtsman (rather than artist) who, like Hunter and Bradley, had come up through the nautical school of drawing. It should be noted that, in the days before mechanical copying and reproduction, it was commonplace to exchange drawings and notes and to make multiple copies, but with so many people making copies, the original authorship could become blurred or lost, making it difficult to assign undated and unsigned drawings to a particular draughtsman, unless there were distinctions in style or original handwritten commentary to assist.

An outstanding example of muddied authorship surrounds the well-known earliest view of Sydney Cove dated 20 August 1788. In Hunter's journal, the view is captioned 'view of the Settlement on Sydney Cove, Port Jackson, 20th August 1788 Drawn by E Dayes from a sketch by J. Hunter.'[54] An almost identical view appears in Bradley's journal beside page 84, entitled 'Sydney Cove, Port Jackson 1788—Wm Bradley.'[55] While there are subtle differences in detail, they are essentially the same picture. It is more likely that Bradley copied his view from Hunter's original sketch or even from the drawings by Edward Dayes from Hunter's original, in view of the amount of copying Bradley undertook. It would also appear that Bradley made multiple copies of his version, as the words 'Sydney Cove, Port Jackson 1788—W Bradley' are written differently (but in the same hand) and to the left of centre in the one used by John Cobley as the frontpiece for his *Sydney Cove 1788*[56] to that contained in Bradley's journal, where the caption is centred and a finer pen has been used. There are also some almost imperceptible differences in detail in the copies. For instance, the large shed above the bowsprit of the *Sirius* in Cobley's rendition has clearly defined windows, whereas they are indistinct at best in Bradley's journal and Bradley has a flag flying from the stern of the *Sirius,* which is absent in Hunter's depiction. While Hunter's sketch is most likely the original, there is still some confusion among recent historians. For example, in Russel Ward's *Finding Australia* the Hunter version is included[57] whereas in John Currey's *David Collins A Colonial Life* the Bradley version is shown, with the caption 'Sydney Cove 1788, by Lieutenant William Bradley of the *Sirius*.'[58]

The quality of Hunter's mapping expertise can be demonstrated by reference to his chart of Botany Bay, Port Jackson and Broken Bay, together with the connecting coasts and soundings surveyed in 1788 and 1789[59], while the examples of his 'views' of the coastline between Botany Bay and Port Jackson[60] provide an indication of his ability to reproduce the appearance of the coastal cliffs and openings pertinent to the needs of mariners sailing north towards the heads of Port Jackson. A further example is that part of the southern coast of Tasmania at South West Cape where eastbound ships from Cape Town usually made their landfall between Cape South and the Maatsuyker Group of islands.[61] By comparing these views with the coast which lay half a mile or more away, ships' captains could confirm their own positions.

The largest collection of Hunter's charts, comprising 16 manuscripts, is located at the Hydrographic Department at Taunton in the United Kingdom. These include charts sent to England by Phillip in 1790 and others made in New South Wales and on the *Waaksamheyd*, marked 'Rec'd with Captain Hunter's Narrative 24th April 1792.' Although the *Waaksamheyd* arrived in Portsmouth on 22 April and Hunter's court martial for the loss of the *Sirius* was held four days later, it can be presumed that the reference to 'Narrative' inferred Hunter's draft of the forthcoming publication of his Journal, rather than the statement he prepared to be used at the court martial, but this is not certain.

One method of distinguishing drawings by Hunter as opposed to Bradley and Raper is by their style. Most of the nine charts with views produced by Hunter on the *Waaksamheyd* are depicted at a greater distance from the land than those drawn by the other two. There is more sky and sea in Hunter's drawings and little close detail. Hunter's treatment of the sea is more representational than real, unlike the sea and surf impressions of Bradley and Raper, which are more complete but somewhat wooden or stilted. Bradley had limited aptitude in representing human figures, so his distant drawings showed them as stick figures.[62] Both Bradley[63] and Raper[64] produced at least two drawings of the wreck of the *Sirius* probably because of the need to use them in support of their case at the subsequent court martial. Comparing these two perspectives however, provides a useful vehicle to distinguish between their styles—Raper uses a finer, stronger pen with more definitive colours, while Bradley's water colours are softer but with a greater sense of action and movement. Hunter's use of colour was also more limited than the other two. On balance, Hunter's skill as a draughtsman of nautical drawings, maps and sketches is clearly above average as the following examples, and those in his journal and in *The Art of the First Fleet*, demonstrate. As Manning Clark remarked, he may not have been distinguished, but he was certainly competent.

(ii) Flora and Fauna

Hunter's abilities and limitations as a sketcher of flora and fauna are vividly apparent from an examination of his sketchbook, now in the possession of the National Library of Australia.[65] It contains 100 coloured paintings of birds, plants, flowers and marine life, one kangaroo and five depictions of native people. Hunter's use of colour is far bolder than in his nautical drawings, but their accuracy in relation to proportion, size and detail leave something to be desired.

This can be explained, however, by the fact that he had not been required to paint or draw natural history subjects previously and would not have received any training in this field. Hunter's depiction of a kangaroo bordered on the misshapen but no more so than those drawn by others and depicted in Phillip's *Voyage*[66] or White's *Journal*.[67]

Figure 18. Two views by Hunter of the coastline near South West Cape, Tasmania.

Figure 19. Engraving from a sketch by John Hunter of Sydney Cove, 20th August 1788. Courtesy of the Royal Australian Historical Society.

Figure 20. William Bradley's version; probably copied from Hunter's original sketch. Mitchell Library, State Library of NSW.

Hunter's version of a platypus is also out of proportion with its tiny feet overshadowed by a large body[68], but a number of English artists appeared to have had difficulty in drawing the correct shape of these new and strange animals. Some of his plant colours are not accurate, e.g. the 'boronia' should be a bright pink colour, not the maroon shade that Hunter used. While perhaps scientifically interested, Hunter was not scientifically trained and was in no position to bestow botanical or species names and tended to give the animals and birds their aboriginal names; for instance, all the parrots (whether cockatoos, rosellas or lorikeets) were called by their generic name 'go-ril', or he simply utilised a European word, e.g. fish or gave it its European name when it resembled a known variety, such as snapper.

That the paintings in the sketchbook are actually by Hunter, even though only two of the 100 (Numbers 88 and 100) are signed by him, is beyond reasonable doubt, given their similarity in style and consistency of depiction and colouring. Andrew Sayers has concluded that Hunter used a box containing only eight basic colours—two greens, two browns, crimson, yellow, blue and black. 'Even using these diluted as washes or in combination, he was only able to produce a limited range of colours'[69], which would assist not only in identifying those drawings done by Hunter, but also in evaluating or allowing for the accuracy of his illustrations, i.e. any painting with colours outside Hunter's range could be discounted as one of his. The inaccuracies in the colouring of many of his birds and flowers are a reflection of these limited colour options—his colours of the sweetlip emperor are brighter than those found on this species of fish, while his wrens lack the greyness to be found on their wings. The tail feathers are also far too short. Hunter's style was also a useful identifying indicator. His depiction of the sulphur-crested cockatoo shows a thinner yellow comb than actually exists and the feathers are long and thin instead of the smaller number of broader feathers shown. The same characteristics are evident in his version of the crimson rosella. Hunter did not pretend to any great anatomical expertise, as his painting of a whaler shark indicates. Its top tailfin is disproportionately long and it should only have five gill slits behind its mouth, rather than the six portrayed by Hunter.

While care needs to be exercised in imposing 21st-century photographic and copying standards on 18th-century artists who were attempting to represent flora and fauna previously unknown and quite strange to them, the artistic value of Hunter's drawings is of considerable interest when assessing early efforts to come to grips with these novelties. Modern readers can at least appreciate how these various extraordinary species appeared to the early colonists and how they provided a distinct service in supporting the observers' written descriptions of them. While they may not be anatomically correct in every sense or always in proportion, they are a useful insight into what the first European settlers saw.

(iii) People

It is unfortunate that none of the early artists was able to capture the physical characteristics of the Aboriginal people they encountered. One of Hunter's attempts is included in the following illustrations. This initialled drawing is of a New South Wales' man, but Aborigines of central New South Wales had straight hair (or at least wavy) rather than frizzy, while the neck length is unusually long (but reflecting the style of portraiture at that time, when many Europeans were portrayed with low 'triangular' shoulders and abnormally long necks). The chest is much fuller than the slightly built people of the region at that time and the nose is also slighter than the broader, flatter nose typical of these people. It is possible that Hunter drew this picture much later (it is not dated) relying on memory and employing some artistic licence in the process. These general observations can also be noted in his drawing of a man from the Lord Howe's Group of Islands in the

Solomon Islands[70] completed in 1791 during his return voyage on the *Waaksamheyd*.

Hunter's artistic skills lay principally in the field in which he was well trained and reached a high standard—nautical charts, plans and sketches. His efforts beyond this were less notable, but nevertheless to a competent standard, and while perhaps not of the quality of Raper or Thomas Watling later, he was undoubtedly better than most of his contemporaries in New South Wales, and he was prepared to make the attempt. He had no pretensions to greatness in this regard, as two extracts from his journal reveal:

> There are a great variety of birds in this country; all those of the parrot tribe, such as the macaw, cockatoo, lorey, green parrot, and parroquets of different kinds and sizes, are cloathed with the most beautiful plumage that can be conceived; it would require the pencil of an able limner to give a stranger an idea of them, for it is impossible by words to describe them,[71]

and

> the vast variety of beautiful plants and flowers, which are to be found in this country, may hereafter afford much entertainment to the curious in the science of Botany; but I am wholly unqualified to describe the different sorts with which we find the woods to abound.[72]

The remarks indicate that Hunter thought himself no 'able limner' and was under no illusion as to his artistic expertise. But this begs two questions: was this the reason why so many of his paintings were unsigned, and did he undertake the task because he was a relatively better artist than most of his colleagues and simply attempted to depict the flora and fauna to assist scientists in England to describe, name and record these discoveries? Alternatively, but less likely, Hunter may have merely painted his impressions principally for his own enjoyment and edification, for he was a man of many interests, including natural history, which was then a significant arm of the Enlightenment.

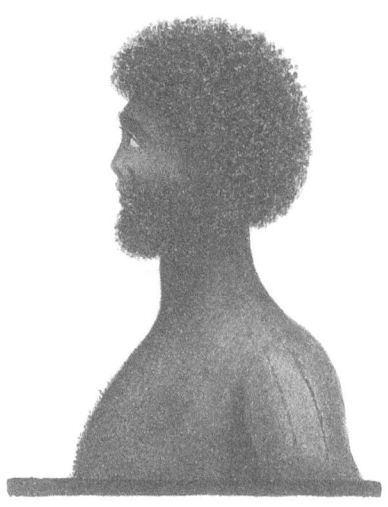

Figure 21. 'Man of New South Wales', drawing no.88, from John Calaby (ed) 1989, *The Hunter Sketchbook*, Canberra, National Library of Australia, page 210.

Figure 22. 'Large Blue Shark', drawing no.74, from *The Hunter Sketchbook*, 182.

Figure 23. 'Kang-oo-roo', drawing no.60, from *The Hunter Sketchbook*, 254.

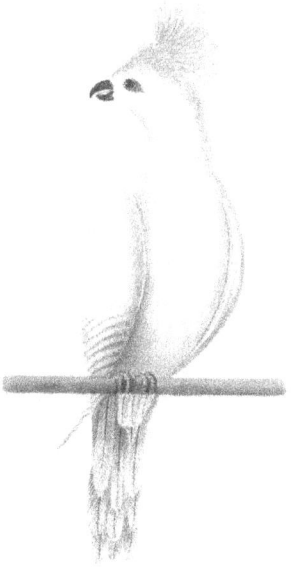

Figure 24. 'Gar-a-way' or sulphur crested cockatoo', drawing no.37, from *The Hunter Sketchbook*, 108.

He also may have been motivated to use the paintings to retain and expand the interest and support of people like Joseph Banks, whose influence was far-reaching, and which could be of benefit to Hunter.

John Hunter could be described as an amateur naturalist, for he did send samples of animals and plants back to England for examination and recording, some of which he also sent to Joseph Banks, for perhaps similar reasons as the paintings. Others he sent to learned societies such as The Literary and Philosophical Society of Newcastle-upon-Tyne, of which he was made an honorary member just before leaving for New South Wales in 1795. He also probably realised that once a flower, shrub or animal had been properly named and described, his supporting illustrations would make way for more accurate depictions by scientific experts and professional artists. Nevertheless, for whatever purpose, his paintings did perform a useful service and are a valuable record. They could be regarded as at least competent, and perhaps even as reasonably good for an interested amateur, and would have undoubtedly assisted to enhance Hunter's own image.

The designer

John Hunter exhibited a practical approach to physical or mechanical problems and an ability to devise lateral solutions. Four examples will be cited to demonstrate Hunter's pragmatism and his capacity to think outside the square.

The first testifies to Hunter's early ability to improvise. Soon after Hunter was promoted to midshipman on the *Centaur* in 1756 when aged 19, the biographical memoir reported that

> His situation now gave him more frequent opportunities of following up his favourite studies of mathematics and drawing, and we find him employing himself in constructing an instrument for measuring inaccessible heights, for he could not

afford to purchase a quadrant, and amusing himself in trying its truth, by ascertaining the length of the ship's masts above the deck, and in proving its correctness by real measurement.[73]

While no description of his height-measuring implement is known to exist, it can be presumed that it was either a home-made quadrant or a right-angled triangular device with scaled notches using trigonometry to calculate the heights. That he had the interest (as well as the impecunious necessity) and innovation to design the instrument and apply his mathematics, demonstrates a practical mind, a willingness to solve problems, sufficient arithmetical skills to work through the necessary calculations and the ability to design and construct a measuring device.

The second illustration reflects Hunter's capacity to not only identify and solve a problem, but to also formulate a design to put the solution into effect—in this instance an 'unsinkable life-boat'.

In *The Naval Chronicle* for 1811 is a letter from a Tim Weatherside.

> Mr Editor,
> It is now 40 years ago, since my friend, Admiral John Hunter, late governor of New South Wales, and then a midshipman at Virginia, in the Launceston [i.e. when Hunter was in his early 30s] under Captain Gell (with his brother, a lieutenant of the same ship) tried the following plan, with great success. The Admiral, I remember gave it to Sir R. Bickerton, to submit to the Admiralty Board, in order to shew with what ease, every boat in the King's service might be converted into a life-boat.
>
> The following is the answer which Admiral Hunter received from the Board, dated November 1, 1808; and, as no further notice has been taken of this hint at least that I ever heard of, or, if there has, in order that my friend may receive the merit he deserves, of having been the original inventor of the plan, I request the insertion of the enclosed in your useful Chronicle.[74]

The acknowledgement to Hunter from the Admiralty read as follows.

> Sir,
> In reply to your letter of the 17th ult. relative to fitting boats with air trunks, to prevent their sinking, in case of being struck by a sea etc. I am commanded by My Lords Commissioners of the Admiralty, to acquaint you, that they are sensible of your zeal for the public service, in transmitting your ideas with respect to these boats.
> I am Sir, Your most obedient humble servant
> (Signed:) J. Barrow

Hunter's concept involved a series of air trunks which were

> nothing more than four planks of pine, well plained at the edges, so as to make them fit so close, that when nailed together, with a piece of tar'd paper between them, no air can escape, nor water be admitted.[75]

Each end was to be closed in a similar manner, with the length of the 'trunk' either a standard size to fit most boats or made particularly to measure. These air trunks (or tanks) would be fitted along the inside of each side of the boat and another down the middle to fit under the seats. Hunter stated that he tried the experiment in 1768 and 1769 and found that it answered his 'expectations most fully'.[76] His theory was that if the boat was swamped for any reason, the trunks would act as ballast tanks and keep the boat afloat for it to be clung onto or bailed out. He stressed the need for the trunks to be near the top of the sides; for if they were too low and the boat capsized, the tanks could hinder the re-righting of the boat.

While Hunter's theory had much to commend it, he was endeavouring to convince an ultra-conservative body of men that took 30 years to accept the cure for scurvy, and the Lord Commissioners' non-committal reply to Hunter indicated a distinct lack of interest or enthusiasm in the idea. Hunter's design was not only deceptively simple in concept, it was also confronted with physical as well as bureaucratic complications and it did have some drawbacks. The size of these trunks or tanks would have reduced the carrying capacity of the boat as they needed to be sufficiently large to provide adequate flotational capacity using uncompressed air. They would have also considerably added to the boat's weight. How long these trunks would have remained water-tight (or air-tight) is problematical, given the propensity of pine to warp. The lack of any internal air pressure would have reduced the flotational potential of the boxes, but there were neither pumps then capable of inserting air under sufficient pressure nor valves to maintain the pressure as the pumps were withdrawn. The fact that the idea was not seriously pursued until such pumps and valves were available and synthetic pressurised air tanks were devised in the 20th century is a further indicator that his design, while sound in principle, was not then practicable due to lack of materials and pumps. The only material available to Hunter that would have helped him to turn boats into lifeboats was cork. Lining the boats with cork may have assisted, but cork was not then available in commercial quantities large enough to make this option viable.

Hunter was ahead of his times with this design, as well as encountering a wall of bureaucracy inherently resistant to change. Nevertheless, the mere fact that he thought of the idea, tested it and found it to work in theory as well as in limited practice, demonstrates his breadth of interests.

A third instance exemplifies Hunter's enquiring mind in creating a spring-based support for a ship's chronometer to reduce its accuracy being affected by hard jolts in rough weather. Following the near-loss of the *Sirius* off south-eastern Tasmania near Tasman's Head in March 1789, Hunter noted that their time-keeper (for determining longitude) was in error, and mused on the probability that the cause was the buffeting it received during the wild motions of the ship, including a momentary grounding, as it strove to escape being wrecked on the coast.

> There was every reason to think, that the violent agitation of the ship during that time, was the cause of that change in the watch, and which I own I was not at all surprised at, but think it highly probable, as the watch lay in a box upon soft cushions, and that box screwed down to a place securely and firmly fixed for that purpose.[77]

Having identified a reason behind the watch's inaccuracy, Hunter went on to speculate on a system to overcome the problem.

> I cannot help thinking but that so very valuable a piece of watch-work (for I do really think, from the experience I have had of it, that a superior piece of work was never made) would be better fixed upon a small horizontal table, made on purpose, and well secured; and under the box which contains the watch, a kind of spiral spring or worm, which, with every jerk or pitch of the ship, would yield a little with the weight of the watch, and thereby take off much of that shock which must in some degree affect its going.[78]

Hunter envisaged a concept which would cushion and reduce the motion of the watch, especially against sharp bumps, which could affect its delicate movements. In the book *Longitude* which examines the development of William Harrison's chronometers to measure longitude with a high degree of exactitude, there is a photo of one of Harrison's timekeepers on a cushion in a box which would have been similar to the one used by Hunter on the *Sirius*.[79] To observe its complexity and fine delicacy is to understand the need for a cushioning device. Hunter's practical mind had conjured up a solution which unfortunately had practical limitations in the size and tensile strength of the springs, and the problem was ultimately solved by the use of gimbals, a series of rings and pivots which protected and kept compasses, barometers and chronometers horizontal at sea. Many mariners must have puzzled over this problem, but Hunter at least took the additional step of proposing an answer to it, even if the ultimate outcome was based upon different principles to his.

Hunter's practical mind is again in evidence after arriving back at Port Jackson on 9 May 1789, when he contemplated the possibility that Tasmania was separated from the mainland by a large strait of water.

> In passing between the islands of Schooten and Furneux and Point Hicks ... there has been no land seen, and from our having felt an easterly set of current, when the wind was from that quarter (north-west) we had an uncommon large sea, there is reason thence to believe, that there is in that space either a very deep gulf or straight, which may separate Van Diemen's Land from New Holland.[80]

This demonstrates that Hunter could propose conclusions to issues that others may have merely contemplated, as it was he who commissioned Bass's whaleboat expedition to the Victorian coastline and the subsequent voyage of the *Norfolk* which circumnavigated Tasmania and proved the existence of a large strait of water separating it from the mainland.

Finally, Hunter's lateral thinking abilities are again demonstrated by an ingenious and logical plan that was simply ahead of its time. Later in the same edition of *The Naval Chronicle* which contained Hunter's design for lifeboats, there is another contribution by him; this time a proposal to reduce the impact of the recoil of heavy guns at sea, especially when the ship was operating in rough weather.[81] The often violent recoil of larger ships' guns, particularly the 18- and 32-pound cannon, posed significant safety threats to gun crews, comprising six or seven men per gun. This could be exacerbated if the ship was rolling in a heavy sea. Not only was there danger in being in the path of a recoiling cannon, there was also the uncertainty of the cannon twisting or turning when suddenly halted by the ropes designed to check the recoil. Occasionally, the intensity of the recoil could pull out the rings securing the recoil ropes, all of which could result in injury to gun crews as well as causing time delays in repositioning the cannon before being able to reload it.

Hunter's plan was to drill two holes in the deck below the gun port and to insert a roller in each hole, through which a rope was passed; one end connected to a front corner of the cannon and the other hanging down to the deck below, at the end of which was tied heavy weights such as lead or pig-iron. The principle was that the recoil of the gun would be slowed and contracted by the upwards drag of the weights towards the holes in the deck. Similarly, when the gun had been reloaded, the weights would facilitate running the gun forward through the gunport. Furthermore, these ropes and weights would assist in securing the guns during bad weather.

The description was accompanied by three diagrams depicting the rope and weights' placement before and after firing as well as a vertical plan showing the placement of the ropes and the holes in the deck. Hunter's conceptualisation appeared to be soundly based and practical, but there is no evidence that the idea was ever seriously considered or pursued by the admiralty. It is probable that a steady flow of suggestions, both feasible and impractical, were continually being put before naval authorities (who were generally resistant to change) however, the fact that Hunter's idea was considered suitable for inclusion in an esteemed naval publication would imply that it was judged by some as worthy of further investigation.

The plan was simple, almost self-evident and easily implemented; in which case, why would it have not been pursued further? Perhaps the risk-ratio to gun crews was not thought high enough or the concept was not politically fashionable. The Napoleonic naval war had been won at Trafalgar in 1805, so it is possible that the issue was not sufficiently critical or of adequate strategic importance six years later. It was not until the mid-19th century that the problems of cannon recoil were solved with retractable gun barrels. Whatever the reason, the idea had intrinsic merit, but like Hunter's other designs, it was too early and not quite good enough to break through the curtain of official complacency. It did however, demonstrate the fertile mind of the designer.

John Hunter did indeed have an active mind, with sufficient literary and artistic ability to be able to effectively convert his thoughts onto paper. His writings, drawings and ideas were generally above average and each facet would have reinforced his technical reputation. The publication of his journal early in 1793 may have facilitated his appointment as Phillip's successor later that year, while his sketches and drawings would undoubtedly have been appreciated by the various (potentially influential) recipients in England. On balance they probably had only a minor, rather than significant, impact on his career, but they would have favourably influenced his standing as a practical naval officer. At least, while they may have marginally enhanced his technical reputation, they certainly did him no harm and do help to fill out the picture of John Hunter as it relates to his abilities. He can safely be described as a competent communicator, artist and designer.

10
Restored and respected

When Hunter returned to England from New South Wales on 24 May 1801, with his reputation in some disarray, he was determined to restore his name. However, following his patron Earl Howe's death two years earlier, he was again without direct influence. Repeated attempts to see the Duke of Portland were rebuffed and there is no evidence to demonstrate that his friends were able or willing to intercede on his behalf. However, by persistent and dogged determination, Hunter's efforts were effective in rehabilitating himself in the face of seemingly powerful impediments and indifference and he was able to reinstate both his name and his standing.

The Duke of Portland was colonial secretary for seven years from 1794, and it was not until he was succeeded by Lord Hobart in August 1801 that Hunter had any chance to re-establish his image. There were three principal reasons behind this gradual return to favour. Firstly, with his approaches to Portland being rebuffed or ignored, Hunter commenced writing to others of influence seeking vindication. Following Portland's departure, Hunter wrote to Lord Hobart in June 1802 soliciting a pension for his past services as governor.[1] Hobart sought Portland's views on this submission two months later[2], which Portland responded to in October of that year, signifying that Hunter was entitled to some financial acknowledgement 'although not to the same extent as Adm'l Phillip'[3] and recommended an annual allowance of £300.

Interestingly, in the New South Wales Civil Establishment Estimates drawn up on 1 May 1802, there appear two entries: one for £500 being an 'Allowance to Governor Phillip in consideration of his meritorious services' and another for £300 for an 'Allowance to Governor Hunter'[4], which would imply that this sum had already been budgeted some months prior to Hobart and Portland formally deciding the matter. Hobart was advised of the decision on 15 October 1802[5], and Hunter was duly informed the following month. Henceforth, the New South Wales Civil Establishment Estimates included the £300 for Hunter (until his death), but entitled 'Allowance to Governor Hunter in consideration of his long Services'[6] whereas Phillip's entitlement was for 'meritorious services', implying a distinction made between Phillip's and Hunter's contribution as governor. Portland at least was prepared to offer some recognition of Hunter's service in New South Wales, which considerably augmented the £100 per annum he was receiving as a post captain on half-pay.

Under Hobart's administration as colonial secretary, there appeared to be a relaxing of attitude towards Hunter. On 20 March 1802, Under-Secretary King wrote to Hunter seeking his opinion on the timing and frequency of sending convict ships to the colony and what cargoes (timber, coal, wool, flax, tobacco etc.) could be used as back-loading to England. Hunter replied in detail two days later[7], outlining the various potential industries in New South Wales and the excellent quality of local timber for ship-building and repairs. In December 1802, Hunter's views were again sought; this time by Secretary Evan Nepean who enquired as to the best type of vessel to be sent to Sydney for local transportation requirements. He was beginning to be perceived as a local expert on matters relating to New South Wales.

The second reason for his gradual rehabilitation was two publications which appeared soon after Hunter's return. The first was the article on Hunter that was contained in *The Naval Chronicle* of July-December

1801, which had a wide circulation and the piece on Hunter read more like a panegyric into which Hunter himself clearly had a substantial input. It could only have reinforced and enhanced his image as a naval officer.

The second publication was a 74-page document entitled *Governor Hunter's Remarks on the causes of the Colonial Expense of the Establishment of New South Wales and Hints for the Reduction of such Expenses and for Reforming the Prevailing Abuses.*[8] Hunter underwrote the cost of the booklet which was intended to identify the colony's problems as he perceived them and to outline his remedies for their eradication or correction. It was very much a bold and blatant attempt to vindicate himself via the printed word when personal explanations were denied him. It dealt with issues such as prices, dispersion of convict labour, public worship, private trade, Norfolk Island expenses, the appointment of magistrates and juries, coinage and currency, the provision and regulation of spirits and the evils of monopoly. It highlighted Hunter's difficulties, while his recommendations, written away from the immediate pressures of office, comprise a cogent and logical set of proposals which could have only benefitted the colony. The booklet was undoubtedly read by senior staff at the Colonial Office, if not by Portland and Hobart themselves. Hunter's *Remarks* encapsulated all he wanted to say to Portland and it was an imaginative strategy to get his message across to colonial policy makers. Its length and detail would suggest it was probably drafted during the long voyage home on the *Buffalo* (before Hunter had been snubbed by Portland), as he would have been still smarting at the brusque method of his recall and eager to put his case as strongly as possible.

The third reason for the revival of his fortunes was the fact that Governor King experienced many of the same problems that beset his predecessor and he too was largely unsuccessful in imposing his remedies. The New South Wales Corps officers continued to dominate trade and remained active in farming and the sale of spirits. While the colony continued to slowly prosper, it soon became apparent to both King and Hobart (and later Camden who succeeded Hobart in May 1804) that the Corps-based challenges that Hunter faced were almost intractable and that King was experiencing similar difficulties as those outlined by Hunter in his *Remarks*. There was a slow realisation percolating through the Colonial Office that the essence of the problem lay with John Macarthur and sections of the New South Wales Corps rather than the governor of the day, which tended to at least partly exonerate Hunter. Ongoing complaints about Macarthur's behaviour continued during King's six-year term of office[9], but King himself was not without his critics.[10]

At least King was relieved at his own request because of increasing ill-health (gout)[11] which may have partly contributed to his inability to deal adequately with Macarthur. Unlike Hunter, he left with the best wishes of Viscount Castlereagh who wrote 'to express His Majesty's entire approbation of the conduct you have manifested in the important charge committed to you, and his satisfaction at the improvement which the colony has received under your superintendence.'[12] Although King was also not successful in curbing the excesses of Macarthur and his colleagues, he would have learnt from Hunter's mistakes regarding issues such as cost controls and convict labour allocation, thus containing the expenditure anxieties of the Colonial Secretariat. In any event, the continuing saga of events in New South Wales after 1800 added weight to Hunter's self-revival campaign and probably accelerated his rehabilitation. It can therefore be claimed that, while other circumstances also contributed, Hunter's efforts to redeem himself were quite successful.

His reputation now on the road to recovery, Hunter was also successful (albeit aided by patronage) in being appointed captain of

HMS *Venerable* in August 1804 as part of the Channel Fleet, but he lost the ship three months later. This was his last sea-going appointment, which concluded an active naval career of 50 years. However, it did not prevent Hunter from seeking further employment, even though he was now 67 years of age. It is worthy of note that Portland told Hobart in 1802 that he 'had it in contemplation to appoint him [Hunter] to the Government of the Bermudas (a situation for which he was peculiarly qualified by his professional talents and experience)'[13], but the proposal did not proceed. This was the same man who three years earlier had recalled Hunter because of his incompetence in financial management and his failure to control the militia. It is of some interest to speculate on this apparent change of heart (no reason is given) and whether Hunter would have been more successful in a second term as governor. As he was then still protesting his innocence to the aspersions cast on his competence, it is unlikely he would have been able to materially modify his modus operandi at that stage of his life.

While Hunter was not a vindictive person by nature, he certainly mellowed with time, enabling him to reconcile with former colonial antagonists such as Macarthur and George Johnston. John Macarthur's third son James, wrote to Judge Therry saying,

> I well remember that from 1810–14, while a boy at school near London, I repeatedly accompanied my father to see Governor Hunter, with whom he parted on perfectly friendly terms, as he [Macarthur] did with Governor King and his family, and with General Grose and Colonel Paterson.[14]

In July 1804, just before joining the *Venerable*, Hunter gave evidence to a Privy Council Enquiry into sheep breeding in New South Wales at which Macarthur was a key witness. Hunter was asked whether he knew of Macarthur and his sheep breeding activities. Hunter replied:

> I do. He has the largest stock of sheep in that country, and has been very industrious in improving his flock and the breed of cattle, and with care and attention I am of the opinion that a

> great quantity of fine wool may be produced. I have no doubt that any offer he can make will be worth attending to.[15]

It would seem that Hunter was not one to bear grudges.

Hunter's last naval appointment was again the outcome of some vigorous lobbying on his part. Still seeking an active occupation, he petitioned the Admiralty to become a paymaster at one of the principal ports, and on 21 May 1805 (six months after losing the *Venerable*) he was appointed captain superintending 'the payment of HM ships at Portsmouth'[16], a position he held until promoted to rear admiral in October 1807. Although in his late 60s, Hunter most likely secured this position through persistence, his ability to relocate to Portsmouth, his long experience plus influential friends.

Although financially able to retire, Hunter's restless energy, his continuing good health and lack of direct family responsibilities saw him also active in a variety of different interests. He joined the Literary and Philosophical Society of Newcastle-upon-Tyne before leaving for Sydney in 1795 and sent specimens of a platypus and wombat to it from New South Wales. By 1815 he was an honorary member.[17] He attended meetings of the Royal Society presided over by Sir Joseph Banks as well as the Naval Charitable Society. In 1803 he bought a three-storey house in Leith, built of grey stone with seven or eight rooms plus entertaining and amenities areas, which still stands today. He bequeathed it to his widowed sister and stayed there with them on his subsequent visits to Leith. He presumably became a freemason, as amongst some of his possessions auctioned in Melbourne in 1924 were: 'two fine Masonic ornaments—Star of the Order of St John of Jerusalem and another Masonic order—both of these orders formerly belonged to Captain John Hunter.'[18]

Hunter was still keen to undertake some further form of active duty, preferably relating to New South Wales, because of his recognised

Figure 25. Hunter's house in Leith. Photograph courtesy of the author.

expertise and his unabated interest in its progress. In February 1805, he advised Sir Charles Middleton (who was one of the Lords Commissioners of the Admiralty and became First Lord of the Admiralty in the following May) on the possibilities of flax production in the colony.[19] In 1808, aged 70 and then a Rear Admiral of the Blue,

Hunter volunteered for active service 'wherever or in whatever way their Lordships shall consider my endeavours likely to be beneficial to the public service. I have never been indulg'd in an inactive life: I am therefore the more particularly desirous of some employment.'[20] More specifically, he wrote two letters to the Earl of Galloway on 20 May and 5 November 1808, discussing the problems in 'that unfortunate and ill-managed Colony.'[21] Hunter evidently had maintained a close watch on the deteriorating state of affairs in Sydney as Governor Bligh attempted to confront the monopolists, indicated by his remarks concerning 'the intelligence lately receiv'd from our unfortunate Colony in New South Wales; and which I have learnt from those who have their correspondents there.'[22]

Hunter's observations revealed a close understanding of the problems confronting the colony, and he now displayed a progressive and enlightened approach to their solution—'the continual dread and daily examples of punishment is not the best means of reforming bad characters, from too great a frequency they become familiar and lose their effect.'[23] He continued, 'Our Courts of Law in that Country, of which I have often serv'd as a Member, it is now time to Revise and change to something more like those of this Country'[24], i.e. civil courts with trial by jury, and 'Let the Government be strict, but Just; a Tyrannic Government will never be Just and Men from Violence and cruel treatment may be driven to acts of desperation.'[25] These remarks reinforce the impression of Hunter's essentially humanitarian outlook and complement the proposals for reform contained in his *Remarks* published six years earlier. Once he was away from the immediate pressures and suffocations of government, Hunter was able to clearly perceive and enunciate a progressive vision for New South Wales.

He then proposed to the earl that a Commission of Inquiry be established to travel to New South Wales and examine all facets of the colony's management, and that 'I am ready and willing to become a member of the Commission for investigating and bringing into some kind of order, the Confess'd and complicated Concerns of New South Wales, and its dependent Settlements, in this business I think I cou'd be useful, I desire no other Authority there.'[26] He then offered some reassurance that he was up to the task, 'Your Lordship supposes my health to be good by my offering to go out again; I thank God I am in perfect health, and am both willing and able to undertake any Service in my power to that Settlement.'[27] He reiterated his belief to Galloway in the future of the colony and that he had no vested interest in either the proposal or the settlement, 'I cannot well be suspected of interesting myself so frequently as I have done for the advantage of that Settlement, from motives of self interest' and 'I do not now (nor never did) possess, one single foot of ground in it, or any of its dependencies.'[28] The proposal was never taken up, but does reflect Hunter's eagerness to retain an interest in (and some influence over) the colony's fortunes. It was also an extension of his need to consolidate his return to favour.

There are two additional points worth noting at this juncture. Firstly, while Hunter's (and Phillip's) Commission and Instructions[29] did not specifically forbid them from granting land to themselves, there is no evidence that either ever contemplated acquiring real estate for their own purposes, nor is there any record of Governor King granting land to himself. Other senior officials, such as surgeon John White and Reverend Richard Johnson, did accept gifts of land in recognition of their years of service, and Rex Rienits claimed that David Collins never 'sought or received a single acre'.[30] This is incorrect, since in Collins' papers there is a copy of a grant of 100 acres at Mort Bay, Balmain, and he later obtained a further 100 acres on the Hawkesbury River.[31]

Secondly, in relation to Hunter's suggestion for a Commission of Inquiry, it was not until ten years later, in 1818, that the government resolved to send a Commissioner of Inquiry, the lawyer John Thomas Bigge (1780–1843), to New South Wales to examine the effectiveness of transportation in response to criticisms of Governor Macquarie's emancipist and public works' policies. This led, inter alia, to the establishment of limited constitutional government and some legal reforms (foreshadowed by Hunter) but not trial by jury. It also precipitated Macquarie's resignation.[32]

Hunter's rehabilitation was largely brought about by his own incessant and persistent attempts to cultivate a network of influential contacts, especially following the death of his patron in 1799. The list of his correspondents and contacts almost reads like a who's who of British VIPs; for example Lord Sydney, Lord Pelham, Lord Howe, William Pitt the Younger, Earl of Galloway, Sir Joseph Banks, Sir Charles Middleton, Duke of Portland, Lord Hobart, Secretary Sullivan and Secretary Pole. That he was successful in his restoration attempts is a reflection of his energy and dedication. He made himself available to give evidence or opinions on matters relating to New South Wales, such as the 1804 Privy Council Enquiry into the value of New South Wales to grow fine wool and at the court martial of Lieutenant-Colonel George Johnston on 31 May 1811 for mutiny over the deposing of Governor Bligh three years earlier. In his evidence, he related that he had known Johnston for about 25 years and that he was 'as perfect as any man I ever knew' and that he was 'a most zealous, active officer'.[33] As alluded to earlier, this testimony would indicate that Hunter was then favourably disposed towards Johnston, notwithstanding his former association with Macarthur and the New South Wales Corps, and that he was somewhat sympathetic to his position vis-a-vis Bligh and his 'crash through or crash' approach. Johnston was ultimately found guilty but he was only cashiered from the army (perhaps indicating a partial indictment of Bligh's tactics) and returned to Sydney where he became a successful farmer, a member of the establishment and died in 1823. The following year,

1812, Hunter (as well as Bligh) was one of the witnesses called to give evidence to a Select Committee of the House of Commons on transportation to New South Wales.[34] The inquiry was principally on convict shipboard death rates, but also on the broader aspects of life in the penal colony, such as the need for a police force and an advisory Legislative Council, both of which became realities soon after Hunter's death in 1821.

Hunter's final promotions, to that of Rear Admiral of the White on 2 October 1807, Vice Admiral of the Blue on 31 July 1810, Vice Admiral of the White on 4 December 1813 and finally Vice Admiral of the Red on 4 June 1814, were less based on competence and more on the survival of the fittest. The Royal Navy in Hunter's time was never short of admirals, especially in peacetime, although few ever hoisted their flag on active service. Until 1864, the navy was roughly divided into three squadrons—red, white and blue—each containing, in descending order of seniority, admirals, vice admirals and rear admirals. Each group of admirals had a quota. For instance there were 24 Rear Admirals of the Blue, and the number was replenished when vacancies arose through death or promotion. As admirals were generally older men, the mortality rate was quite high, thus ensuring regular intakes to restore the allocated quota. While longevity was a key factor, a person's service record could also be taken into consideration, so that for Hunter to be eventually appointed a vice admiral of the red would infer that his rehabilitation was complete. For the retired list, there was little real differentiation between the colours, although there was additional kudos in being of the red over the white or the blue. On active service however, the senior squadron was always red, and an admiral of the red was in fact the Admiral of the Fleet and in overall command, with an Admiral of the White being senior to an Admiral of the Blue squadron.[35] When Phillip died in 1814, he had just been appointed an Admiral of the Blue, while Bligh was a Vice Admiral of the Blue when he died three years later.

Hunter, aged 83, drew up his will on 9 March 1821, just four days prior to his death, which would presume that he had a premonition that the end was near, but the exact cause of his demise is not known. In his will, he stated that he had £11,000 pounds in consolidated bank annuities plus his material possessions which, considering that he had not invested in real estate (other than the house in Leith) or speculated in other ventures, would have largely accumulated from his naval income. This represented a substantial amount in those days, although since he had no immediate family to support during his adult life, he would have had few direct expenses during the many years he spent on active naval service and, from his early background, would have been thrifty in his lifestyle and sensitive to the need for financial security.

He divided the cash amongst his nephews and nieces and to some of their offspring and he bequeathed the title of his house in Leith to the unmarried daughters of his late widowed sister, Janet Maule, as described earlier. He decreed that his gold chronometer clocks, watches, books, charts and instruments be sold and the proceeds added to the residue of his estate, which would imply that these became widely scattered. There is no reference to any letters held by him, so it is presumed that they too were distributed amongst his extended family or even destroyed. In any event, there is no extant evidence of their existence, in spite of efforts to locate them by distant descendants such as William Griffiths who wrote some family notes on Hunter and his relatives in 1948[36], and whose wife had inherited the portrait of Hunter now located in the National Library in Canberra. The distribution of Hunter's assets confirms the close attachment he retained with his family during his lifetime, which seemed to be reciprocated, as witnessed by the decision of Eliza Grant to inter his body into the Grant family vault at St John's Church, Hackney in London. Eliza Grant was the daughter of Hunter's nephew Captain William Kent, who with his family (including the two-year-old Eliza) went to New South Wales with Hunter in 1795 and lived with him in Government House, with Mrs Kent acting as first lady. In his will, Hunter left Eliza Grant £550.

Curiously, some of Hunter's possessions found their way to Melbourne, for on Tuesday 25 November 1924, there was an auction in the rooms of W.J. Butcher & Son, 124 Queen Street of 'The Admiral John Hunter Collection'[37], which included (as well as the Masonic items already referred to) Hunter's verde watch and chain, two buffalo horns made into cups, a button from the coat of William Pitt the Younger (which Pitt gave to Hunter), a pair of old silver spectacle mounts (indicating that Hunter needed glasses in his later years), a naval uniform, books, a pair of Sheffield plate candlesticks, a small mahogany box made of wood from the Spanish Armada, an old 'Aboriginal tomahawk', old coins and an old silver snuff box. However, eight years later on Thursday 9 June 1932, there was another auction of 'The valuable, old and rare Admiral John Hunter Collection', this time by Leonard Joel of 362 Little Collins Street, Melbourne[38] (neither auction notice mentions the year, but by process of calendar elimination, the years can be identified) for some of the items listed in the earlier catalogue, including two Turner paintings, Hunter's Bible, the small mahogany box, the buffalo horns, Pitt's coat button and the spectacle mounts.

The first auction was by order of the Trustees of the late James Moore Kelly and the following day (26 November 1924), an article appeared in the *Argus* entitled 'Admiral Hunter Antiques. Sale Not Effected'. This report stated that under the terms of Kelly's will,

> the collection is to be preserved in its entirety—not to be broken up among individual purchasers ... Negotiations were entered into with public libraries and museums in Australia with a view to the purchase of the collection in order that it might be preserved to the nation, but so far these negotiations have been unsuccessful.[39]

The identity of James Moore Kelly is a mystery. The Victorian Index to Deaths has no entry for James Moore Kelly, while a conversation with the Registrar of Births, Deaths and Marriages in Melbourne confirmed there was no death for a person of that name in Victoria around that time.[40] A search of all probate files held at the Public Record Office, North Melbourne, under James and Jas Kelly between 1913 and 1924 also proved negative. Perhaps he died interstate or even overseas.

The negotiations referred to above were evidently unsuccessful, as the second auction in 1932 was also for John Hunter's effects, but this time belonging to 'the late Miss Alan Kelly, James Moore Kelly and Commander John Moore'.[41] The 'Miss Alan Kelly' was actually Miss Elizabeth Allen Kelly, a cameo cutter and wax modeller[42] who worked in Melbourne and then in London before returning to Victoria where she died a spinster in East Melbourne in 1928, aged 85 years.[43] The death certificate records her parents as Charlotte and Jonathan Kelly. The English Census entry for 1871 gives the mother's full name as 'Charlotte Moore Kelly'[44], indicating a relationship between James Moore Kelly and Elizabeth Allen Kelly—perhaps brother and sister or uncle and niece. A likely scenario is that Hunter's possessions were originally purchased by a member of the Moore or Kelly family in England and passed down through their connections to Melbourne where they were ultimately inherited by Miss E.A. Kelly. The result of the second auction was not reported in the press and discussions with Mr Joel in September 2005 revealed that their records did not extend back to 1932, so the whereabouts of the collection is currently unknown.

In the front of Hunter's copy of the original edition of his journal published by John Stockdale in 1795, and now held at the Mitchell Library, there appears a coat of arms purporting to be Hunter's crest. Above the shield is a greyhound, over which is the motto 'Vigilantia Robur Voluptas', which translates into vigilance, strength and enjoyment. However, there is no record as to where it originated or when it was designed. Elsewhere in the Mitchell Library (ML Doc.383) is a note which reads:

> W.R.C. Lawrence, a relation of the Hunter family, stated in a letter to the Mitchell Librarian 3rd April 1963 (418/1963) that the coat of arms in Hunter's Journal 'is not a registered coat of arms. It would appear that Hunter either drew it up himself, or had someone draw it for him, possibly with the view of having the arms registered with the Court of the Lord Lyon, Edinburgh. However, recent research and enquiries from the Lyon Court show that the arms of this particular design were never registered'.

Presumably the arms were created after Hunter returned from New South Wales in 1792 and before he left for Sydney in 1795. It is an interesting insight into Hunter's quest for status and respectability and could also help to explain his need to restore his reputation following his dismissal in 1800.

The aim of this book was to examine the character and the competence of John Hunter as a seaman, captain, governor, leader, draftsman and journalist. It was not intended to exhaustively describe Hunter's life, as just another narrative, but rather to concentrate upon whether he deserved the responsibilities conferred upon him and how well he discharged them. The biographical works to date are somewhat superficial in nature and there was an analytical void on John Hunter which this book has attempted to fill.

Like most people, Hunter's life contained a mixture of successes and disappointments. It is hazardous to generalise that a person's life was either a success or a failure, because most lives are a blend of highs, mediums and lows. It is only within the context of a particular issue that individuals can fairly be described as competent, adequate or incompetent, and most will display elements of all three characteristics during their lifetime. While Lord Nelson, Winston Churchill and

Douglas MacArthur could be described as great and successful leaders, other aspects of their lives were less so. Life is a blend of contrasts which makes it difficult to judge people in a general sense in black and white terms. John Hunter is no exception.

Figure 26. Hunter's Coat of Arms.

While Hunter may have lost two ships, failed to curb the traffic in spirits and the excesses of Macarthur and his colleagues in New South Wales, it cannot be claimed on balance that he was incompetent. In some respects it can be contended that his life was a triumph over the twin adversities of the lack of influence or patronage when most needed and his ill-preparedness to effectively govern the colony in New South Wales. He did his best to heed the advice of Sir Joseph Banks in the midst of his troubles with those in Sydney seeking to bring him down. 'Persevere however, my good sir, in the manly, honest and open conduct you have hitherto held, and you must in time prevail.'[45] Not only does this reveal Banks' appreciation of Hunter's character, but the words were prophetic since Hunter's recommendations for the colony's reform contained in his *Remarks* ultimately formed part of the gradual development of measures and policies designed to ameliorate conditions in the settlement, both for its people and its economy. In fact, he can be credited with setting in motion the forces that enabled Macquarie to steer the fortunes of New South Wales into a more positive and productive direction.

His proficiency can be called into question over his handling of the ships under his direct command as well as some aspects of his governorship, but his friendliness, honesty, integrity, morality and openness did much in compensation. His technical abilities in nautical terms were of the highest order, while his enquiring mind and his mapping and charting skills were also of a high standard. His Leith background and the time spent before the mast endowed him with a common touch, while his ambitions and his character enabled him to establish friendships with those in high places. It is possible to envisage the man as being as much at home with those in the fo'c'sle as with those in the great cabin or in a sophisticated sitting room. People of all classes can relate to a person with an open face.

The fact that the Duke of Portland was considering appointing Hunter as governor of Bermuda and supporting his request for a pension, after ostensibly refusing to receive him upon his return from Sydney, is more likely a reflection of Portland's quirky nature than of Hunter's character and approach. His troubles as governor were more revealing of his personality than he would have liked or was even prepared to admit, and demonstrated his inability to cope with pressures beyond his immediate experience and abilities to control. He was an excellent naval technician even under trying circumstances at sea, but was both unused and unable to deal with strategic issues.

Figure 27. Bust of John Hunter, located near the waterfront at Leith. Photograph courtesy of the author.

Was Hunter promoted beyond his levels of competence? For his promotion to captain the answer is probably yes, but this was as much an outcome of the lack of suitable training and experience as opposed to an innate inability to lead. Had Hunter been commissioned ten or even 15 years before he finally was, this would have given him more extensive and valuable independent command time which would have better equipped him as a leader. His early promotions to midshipman, master's mate, master, lieutenant and then commander were undoubtedly merit-based, whereas his appointments as captain and governor were founded more on patronage than sheer ability. His promotions to admiral were essentially a function of longevity with his service record playing a secondary role. It could also be fairly claimed that perhaps he lacked the hardness required of a good leader, but against that, his genuineness made him a good and reliable friend. His North American experiences showed him to be brave under fire while his strong and enduring family ties revealed him to be caring and considerate.

As suggested at the outset, many Australians have heard of John Hunter, but few know anything of him. Other than Hunter Street in Sydney and Newcastle, the Hunter River and Hunter Valley in New South Wales, Hunter Park in Balmoral, Sydney, the Hunter Island group off the North West coast of Tasmania, the Hunter Range in New South Wales, the Sydney suburb Hunter's Hill and the John Hunter Hospital in Newcastle, there is little evidence of his achievements or contributions. In physical terms, there are no full-size statues of John Hunter, but there are three busts. One was unveiled by the Governor of New South Wales, Rear Admiral Peter Sinclair at Hunter Park, Balmoral on 29 August 1993 and another at Elizabeth Park, Scone on 26 March 1994 by the Hon George Souris, the New South Wales Minister for Land and Water Conservation. The third is by the waterfront at Leith, which was unveiled on Friday 26 August 1994 by the Australian High Commissioner and the Lord Provost of

Edinburgh, and was a gift to the Scottish people from the Scottish Australian Heritage Council.[46] There is therefore not a lot to remember him by, so if this book can add something to an understanding of John Hunter and his times, its objectives will have been accomplished.

Hunter died on 13 March 1821 in London and the following day *The Times* ran an obituary, which concluded:

> His mild conciliatory manners endeared him to all classes of society in his government and to his indefatigable exertions may be attributed in a great measure the rising prosperity of that Settlement. A kind and affectionate relative, a sincere and warm friend, a generous and liberal benefactor to the poor, for such was the natural benevolence of his heart that he never saw a fellow creature in distress without relieving him to the utmost extent of his abilities; in short, his character may be summed up by remarking he was one of the noblest works of God—an honest man.[47]

An epitaph to be envied.

Notes

Chapter 1

[1] Malcolm Ellis, *John Macarthur* (Sydney: Angus & Robertson, 1955).
[2] Michael Duffy, *Man of Honour—John Macarthur* (Sydney: Macmillan, 2003).
[3] F.M. Bladen 'Notes on the life of John Hunter' *Journal and Proceedings. The Australian Historical Society* Part III 1901, 27.
[4] Frederick Watson (ed) *Historical Records of Australia* Vol. 1. Hunter (Sydney; Government Printer, 1914) v–xx.
[5] C.M.H. Clark, *A History of Australia* Vol. 2 (Carlton, Vic.: Melbourne University Press, 1962), 144.
[6] Ibid., 145.
[7] James Auchmuty, *John Hunter* (Melbourne: Oxford University Press, 1968), 30.
[8] John Bach (ed) *John Hunter: An Historical Journal of Events at Sydney and at Sea 1787–92* (Sydney: Angus & Robertson, 1968), xvi.
[9] Michael Duffy, *Man of Honour*.
[10] Barbara Tuchman, 'Biography as a Prism of History', Gates S. B. (ed) *Biography as High Adventure* (Boston: University of Massachusetts Press, 1986), 94.
[11] James Anderson, 'The Methodology of Psychological Biography: *Journal of Interdisciplinary History*, 11:3 (Winter, 1981) 456.
[12] L. Stephen & S. Lee (eds.) *The Dictionary of National Biography* Vol X (London: Oxford University Press, 1960) 294.
[13] B. Murphy (ed) *Dictionary of Australian History* (Sydney: McGraw Hill, 1982) 145.
[14] C.M.H. Clark, *A History of Australia*, Vol 1 (Carlton, Vic.: Melbourne University Press, 1962) 142.
[15] Biographical Memoir of Captain John Hunter, *The Naval Chronicle* Vol VI July–December 1801, 349.
[16] R.W. Barnes, Litt. B. Thesis, 'David Collins Coloniser', 1978, Univerity of New England, 98.

[17] F.M. Bladen (ed) *HRNSW* Vol. 3 (Sydney: Govt Printer, 1895) xxi.
[18] Frederick Watson (ed) *HRA*, Series 1 Vol. 2 (Sydney: Gullick, 1914) v.
[19] Church of Jesus Christ of Latter Day Saints. Christenings 1737–1739 South Leith, Midlothian, Scotland. Microfilm No. 1067771.
[20] Edinburgh Commissary Court: 26 March 1756 'William Hunter Tayler Burges of Edingh'.
[21] George Drummond who was Commissioner of Excise, appears as one of the guardians or godparents on the baptismal certificate of Hunter's sister, Janet, born 5 January 1739. Christenings 1737–1739, South Leith, Midlothian, Scotland. Microfilm No. 1067771.
[22] Church of Jesus Christ of Latter Day Saints: Old Parish Registers of Scotland. William, Sarah and George Hunter appear in the baptismal registers of Edinburgh Parish Church Christenings, see Film Nos. 1066666 and 1066667; John and Janet appear in the baptismal registers in the South Leith Parish Christenings, see Film No. 1067771; Agnes, James, Margaret and Archibald Hunter appear in the baptismal registers in the North Leith Parish Christenings, see Film No. 1067766. The baptismal record for Mary Hunter, an elder sister of John Hunter, seems not to have survived. Mary married Henry Kent and their son served in New South Wales whilst John Hunter was Governor. John Hunter's Will confirms the relationship. Also see Family Tree in the Appendix.
[23] B.R. Blaze, *Great Scot* (Melbourne: Limited Edition, Private Circulation, 1975) 1.
[24] Biographical Memoir of Captain John Hunter, 349.
[25] Biographical Memoir of Captain John Hunter, 351.
[26] Ibid., 355.
[27] Ibid., 356.
[28] The Southwell Papers, F.M. Bladen (ed) *HRNSW* Vol. 2, 1793–95 (Sydney: Government Printer, 1893) 706.
[29] Lisa Pickard, *Dr Johnson's London* (London: Weidenfeld & Nicolson, 2000) 156.
[30] Lisa Pickard, *Restoration London* (London: Weidenfeld & Nicolson, 1997) 77.
[31] Lisa Pickard, *Dr Johnson's London*, 156.

Chapter 2

[1] Percy Scholes, *The Oxford Companion to Music* (London: Oxford University Press, 1980) 141.
[2] Biographical Memoir of Captain John Hunter, 350.

[3] P. Serle (ed) *Dictionary of Australian Biography* Vol. 1 (Sydney: Angus & Robertson, 1949) 464. [The Edinburgh University Archivist, Arnott Wilson, emailed the writer on 13 September 2004: 'I checked our matriculation records which revealed a couple of references to a John Hunter in the 1740s, perhaps too early? [Yes]. I didn't pick up any for the 1750s at all, and the next JH's do not appear till the 1760s.']
[4] Biographical Memoir of Captain John Hunter, 350.
[5] Bonwick Transcripts, ML Vol. 3, A2000-3, 666-70.
[6] Biographical Memoir of Lt. William Hunter of Greenwich Hospital, *The Naval Chronicle* Vol. XIII January-June 1805 (London: Gold, 1805) 1-45.
[7] Biographical Memoir of Lt. William Hunter, 2.
[8] Ibid., 11.
[9] Ibid., 31.
[10] Ibid.
[11] Biographical Memoir of Captain John Hunter, 354.
[12] Biographical Memoir of Lt. William Hunter, 33.
[13] Biographical Memoir of Captain John Hunter, 354.
[14] Biographical Memoir of Lt. William Hunter, 34.
[15] Biographical Memoir of Lt. William Hunter, 45.
[16] Bonwick Transcripts, ML Vol. 3, A2000-3, 666-70.
[17] Ibid.
[18] John Hunter, *An Historical Journal of Events at Sydney and at Sea 1787-92* (Sydney: Angus & Robertson, 1968) 96.
[19] Ibid., 97-98.
[20] Ibid., 98.
[21] Carlton Hayes, *Modern Europe to 1870* (New York: Macmillan, 1967) 377-78.
[22] Mary Johnson to Henry Fricker, 21 December 1796, ML zml Mss 6722, Mircofilm 4036.
[23] Phillip to Sydney, 1 November 1786, ML Add. 290.
[24] The Southwell Papers, *HRNSW* Vol. 2, 1793-95, 684 and 778.

Chapter 3

[1] Biographical Memoir of Captain John Hunter, 367.
[2] Michael Lewis, *A Social History of the Navy 1793-1815* (London: Allen & Unwin, 1960) 162.

³ *The Naval Chronicle*, 351.
⁴ Ibid., 352.
⁵ Harold Perkins, *The Origins of Modern English Society 1780-1880* (London: Routledge and Kegou Paul, 1969) 45.
⁶ Christopher Hibbert, *Nelson A Personal History* (London: Viking, 1994) 414-15.
⁷ Michael Lewis, *A Social History of the Navy*, 225.
⁸ Christopher Hibbert, Nelson *A Personal History*, 122.
⁹ Michael Lewis, *A Social History of the Navy*, 202-27.
¹⁰ Harold Perkins, *The Origins of Modern English Society*, 46.
¹¹ *The Naval Chronicle* 353-54.
¹² Alan Villiers, *Captain Cook, The Seamen's Seaman* (London: Hodder and Stoughton, 1967) 22.
¹³ Michael Lewis, *A Social History of the Navy*, 294.
¹⁴ *The Naval Chronicle*, 355.
¹⁵ National Maritime Museum, Greenwich Ref. No. PAD 5476.
¹⁶ Steve Pope, *Hornblower's Navy (*London: Orion) 32-34.
¹⁷ *The Naval Chronicle*, 355.
¹⁸ Ibid., 355-56.
¹⁹ PRO London, ADM 1/5305.
²⁰ PRO London, ADM 52/1186.
²¹ It is a matter of curious speculation why Hunter's exertions would cause a blood vessel in his lung to rupture, causing him to cough up copious quantities of blood. Hard work alone would not normally have resulted in that manifestation after the event; perhaps Hunter had a mild form of tuberculosis which was exacerbated by the activities, but the fact that he remained active and apparently healthy for the next 50 years is yet another tribute to his constitution and determination. Whatever the cause, Hunter appeared to recover completely.
²² PRO London, ADM. 1/5305.
²³ N.A.M. Rodgers, *The Insatiable Earl: A Life of John Montagu, Fourth Earl of Sandwich 1718-1792* (London: Harper Collins, 1993) 308.
²⁴ Sir John Barrow, *The Life of Richard, Earl Howe KG* (London: John Murray, 1838) 117.
²⁵ Ibid.
²⁶ *The Naval Chronicle*, 358.
²⁷ Ibid., 359.

[28] Ibid.
[29] Ibid., 358.
[30] Ibid., 360.
[31] Howe Papers, Huntington Library as quoted by Arthur Hoyle, *The Life of John Hunter*, 24.
[32] *The Naval Chronicle*, 360.
[33] Ibid., 361.

Chapter 4

[1] Carlton Hayes, *Modern Europe to 1870* (New York: Macmillan, 1967) 469.
[2] National Maritime Museum, Greenwich, ADM/L/V63.
[3] Steve Pope, *Hornblower's Navy*, 59.
[4] *John Hunter, An Historical Journal of Events at Sydney and at Sea 1787-1792* (Sydney: Angus & Robertson, 1968) 28.
[5] Ibid., 63.
[6] Stephen Bown, *Scurvy*, 9.
[7] John Hunter, *Journal*, 68.
[8] William Bradley, *A Voyage to New South Wales* (Sydney: Ure Smith, 1969) 147.
[9] John Hunter, *Journal*, 68.
[10] Ibid., 69.
[11] Ibid., 69–70.
[12] Nance Irvine (ed) *The Sirius Letters*, (Sydney: Fairfax Library, 1988) 100–02.
[13] John Hunter, *Journal*, 78.
[14] Charles Bateson, *The Convict Ships 1787-1868* (Sydney: Reed, 1974) 116.
[15] John White, *Journal of a Voyage to New South Wales* (Sydney: Angus & Robertson, 1962) 244.
[16] Watkin Tench, *Sydney's First Four Years* (Sydney: Angus & Robertson, 1961) 32.
[17] David Collins, *An Account of the English Colony in New South Wales* Vol. 1 (Sydney: Reed, 1975) 1.
[18] *An Officer, An Authentic and Interesting Narrative of the late Expedition to Botany Bay* (Aberdeen: Alexander Kieth, 1789) 20.
[19] J.C. Beaglehole, *The Journals of Captain James Cook*, Vol 1 (Cambridge: Hakluyt Society, 1968) 589–600.
[20] J.C. Dann (ed) *The Nagle Journal* (New York: Weidenfeld & Nicholson, 1988) 131.

[21] The Southwell Papers, *HRNSW* Vol. 2 (Sydney: Govt Printer, 1893) 726.
[22] Southwell Papers, *HRNSW* Vol. 2, 726–27.
[23] John Hunter, *Journal*, 146.
[24] Watkin Tench, *Sydney's First Four Years*, 218.
[25] John Hunter, *Journal*, 146.
[26] B.R. Blaze, *Great Scot* (Melbourne: Printed for Private Circulation, 1975) 68.
[27] John Easty, *A Voyage from England to Botany Bay 1787–1793* (Sydney: Angus & Robertson, 1965) 26.
[28] William Bradley, Voyage, 247.
[29] John Hunter, *Journal*, 148.
[30] J.C. Beaglehole, *The Journals of Captain James Cook* Vol. 11 Cambridge: Hakluyt Society, 1961) 556.
[31] Hunter to Secretary Stephens, 23 April 1792, *HRNSW* Vol. 1 Part 2, 617.
[32] John Hunter, *Journal*, 154.
[33] Southwell Papers, *HRNSW* Vol. 2, 727.
[34] William Bradley, *Voyage*, 256.
[35] Ibid., 158.
[36] Southwell Papers, *HRNSW* Vol. 2, 728.
[37] Ibid.
[38] William Bradley, *Voyage*, 260–61.
[39] Southwell Papers, *HRNSW* Vol. 2, 729.
[40] John Hunter, *Journal*, 171.
[41] J.C. Dann (ed) *The Nagle Journal*, 138–39.
[42] Southwell Papers, *HRNSW* Vol. 2, 730.
[43] J.C. Dann (ed) *The Nagle Journal*, 140.
[44] John Hunter, *Journal*, 173.
[45] Arthur Hoyle, *The Life of John Hunter*, 85.
[46] Miriam Estensen, *Matthew Flinders* (Sydney: Allen & Unwin, 2002) 42.

Chapter 5

[1] J.C. Beaglehole, *The Journals of Captain James Cook* Vol. 1 (Cambridge: Hakluyt, 1968) 378.
[2] Ibid., 379.
[3] J.C. Beaglehole, *The Endeavour Journal of Joseph Banks* Vol. 11 (Sydney: Angus & Robertson, 1963) 106.

[4] John Hunter, *An Historical Journal of Events at Sydney and at Sea 1787-92* (Sydney: Angus & Robertson, 1970) 27.
[5] William Bradley, *A Voyage to New South Wales* Vol. 1 (Sydney: Ure Smith, 1969) 64.
[6] James Auchmuty (ed) *The Voyage of Governor Phillip to Botany Bay* (Sydney: Angus & Robertson, 1970) 27.
[7] Paul Fidlon & R.J. Ryan (eds) *The Journal of Philip Gidley King 1787-1790* (Sydney: Griffin Press, 1980) 36.
[8] Derek Neville, *Blackburn's Isle* (Lavenham: Dalton, 1975) 130.
[9] Nance Irvine (ed) *The Sirius Letters* (Sydney: Fairfax, 1988) 73.
[10] George Worgan, *Journal of a First Fleet Surgeon* (Sydney: Library of Australian History, 1978) 7.
[11] David Collins, *An Account of the English Colony in New South Wales* Vol. 1 (Sydney: Reed, 1975) 4-5.
[12] Watkin Tench, *Sydney's First Four Years* (Sydney: Angus & Robertson, 1961) 38.
[13] The Southwell Papers, *HRNSW* Vol. 2 (Sydney: Govt. Printer, 1893) 666.
[14] Waterhouse Family Papers 1782-1819, ML Mss 6544, CY 3970.
[15] *Sirius'* Log 1786-1790 Captain J. Hunter, La Trobe Library, AJCP 6925,5328, 6.
[16] Charlotte's Log 1786-88, Captain T. Gilbert, La Trobe Library, AJCP 5777, 4375.
[17] Friendship's Log 1786-89, Captain F. Walton, La Trobe Library, AJCP 5777, 4376.
[18] Lady Penrhyn's Log 1786-88, Captain W. Sever, La Trobe Library, AJCP 5777, 4376.
[19] John White, *Journal of a Voyage to New South Wales* (Sydney: Angus & Robertson, 1962) 112.
[20] Paul Fidlon & R.J. Ryan (eds) *The Journal and Letters of Lt. Ralph Clark* (Sydney: Library of Australian History, 1981) 93.
[21] Paul Fidlon & R.J. Ryan (eds), *The Journal of Arthur Bowes Smyth* (Sydney: Australian Documents Library, 1979) 64.
[22] The Southwell Papers, *HRNSW* Vol. 2, 666.
[23] Charlotte's Log 1786-88, AJCP 5777, 4375.
[24] John White, *Journal*, 105.
[25] The British Critic, May-August 1793. ML 991/B, 81-2.
[26] John Hunter, *Journal*, 83.
[27] John Hunter, *Journal*, 82.

[28] Newton Fowell, *The Sirius Letters*, 110.
[29] Ibid.
[30] William Bradley, *Voyage to New South Wales*, Vol 1, 156.
[31] The Southwell Papers, *HRNSW* Vol. 2, 708.
[32] Newton Fowell, *The Sirius Letters*, 110-11.
[33] William Bradley, *Voyage to New South Wales* Vol. 1, 158-59.
[34] J. Dann (ed) *The Nagle Journal* (New York: Weidenfeld & Nicholson, 1988) 108.
[35] Ibid., 107.
[36] John Hunter, *Journal*, 118.
[37] William Bradley, *Voyage to New South Wales* Vol. 1, 189.
[38] Newton Fowell, *The Sirius Letters*, 117.
[39] The Southwell Papers, *HRNSW* Vol. 2, 705.
[40] David Collins, *An Account* Vol. 1, 80.
[41] Watkin Tench, *Sydney's First Four Years*, 163.
[42] Letters of David Blackburn, ML Mss 6937/1/1-5, CY4084.
[43] J. Dann (ed) *The Nagle Journal*, 118.
[44] *The Journal and Letters of Lt. Ralph Clark*, 117.
[45] John Hunter, *Journal*, 62.
[46] Newton Fowell, *The Sirius Letters*, 118.
[47] John Hunter, *Journal*, 120.
[48] Ibid., 412.
[49] Ibid.
[50] William Bradley, *Voyage to New South Wales* Vol. 1, 193-94.
[51] E. McHugh, *Shipwrecks* (Melbourne: Viking, 2003) 73.
[52] Newton Fowell, *The Sirius Letters*, 14.
[53] J. Dann (ed) *The Nagle Journal*, 110.
[54] The Southwell Papers, *HRNSW* Vol. 2, 705.
[55] Letters of David Blackburn, ML Mss 6937/1/1-5, CY4084.
[56] *The Journal and Letters of Lt. Ralph Clark*, 121.
[57] Paul Fidlon & R.J. Ryan (eds), *The Journal of Phillip Gidley King 1787-90* (Sydney: Australian Documents Library, 1980) 343.
[58] J. Dann (ed) *The Nagle Journal*, 118-19.
[59] Hunter to Secretary Stephens, 23 April 1792, La Trobe Library, AJCP 3272.

[60] Stephens to Hunter, 24 April 1792, *HRNSW* Vol. 1, Part 2 (Sydney: Government Printer, 1892) 618.
[61] Steve Pope, *Hornblower's Navy* (London: Orion, 1998) 77.
[62] Ibid.
[63] *Sirius* Court Martial, La Trobe Library, AJCP 6925/5329, 1791–92.
[64] Ibid.
[65] Ibid.
[66] Ibid.
[67] William Bradley, *Voyage to New South Wales* Vol. 1, 193–94.
[68] J. Dann (ed) *The Nagle Journal*, 118.
[69] Ibid.
[70] Ibid.
[71] Ibid.
[72] Ibid.
[73] Ibid.
[74] George Mackaness, *The Life of Vice Admiral William Bligh* Vol. 1 (Sydney: Angus & Robertson, 1931) 186–88.
[75] HMS Venerable's Muster Rolls. PRO, ADM 36/15534.
[76] Minutes of the Court Martial of Captain John Hunter, 10 December 1804 for the loss of HMS Venerable. PRO ADM 1/5367.
[77] Extract from Avis's Birmingham Gazette, 3 December 1804, ML, BT Box 12, 44–46.
[78] Bonwick Transcripts, ML Vol. 3, A 2000–3, 701.
[79] Bonwick Transcripts, ML, Madras Courier 1/5/1805, A 2000–3, 679–83.
[80] Gerald E. Boyle, *Loss of HMS Venerable in Torbay* (Torquay: Iredale & Son, 1913).
[81] Arthur Hoyle, *The Life of John Hunter* (Canberra: Mulini Press, 2001) 166.
[82] Minutes of John Hunter's Court Martial for the loss of the Venerable, 10 December 1804, PRO ADM 1/5367, 3.
[83] Ibid., 6.
[84] Ibid.
[85] Ibid., 22.
[86] Bonwick Transcripts, ML Vol. 3, A2000–3, 701.

Chapter 6

[1] John Hunter, *An Historical Journal of Events at Sydney and at Sea 1787–1792* (Sydney: Angus & Robertson, 1968) 93.

² William Bradley, A *Voyage to New South Wales* 1786–1792 (Sydney: Ure Smith, 1969) 162.
³ *Historical Records of New South Wales* Vol. 2 (Sydney: Government Printer, 1893) 377.
⁴ David Collins, *An Account of the English Colony in New South Wales* Vol. 1, (Sydney: Reed, 1975) 53.
⁵ Hunter, *Journal*, 272.
⁶ Ibid., 270.
⁷ *HRA* Vol. 1, Part 1, Phillip to Sydney, 12 February 1790, 145.
⁸ Ibid., 159.
⁹ Sibella Macarthur Onslow (ed) *Some Early Records of the Macarthurs of Camden* (Sydney: Angus & Robertson, 1914) 33.
¹⁰ William Charles Wentworth, *Descriptions of the Colony of New South Wales* (London: Whittaker, 1819) 44.
¹¹ John White, Journal of a *Voyage to New South Wales* (Sydney: Angus & Robertson, 1962) 18–19.
¹² Watkin Tench, *Sydney's First Four Years* (Sydney: Angus & Robertson, 1961) 146.
¹³ Ibid., 153.
¹⁴ Noel Butlin, *Our Original Aggression* (Sydney: George Allen & Unwin, 1983).
¹⁵ *The Age*, Saturday Extra, 7 January 1984.
¹⁶ *New South Wales Medical Gazette* Vol. 1, 1870–71 (Sydney: Gibbs, Shallard & Co., 1871).
¹⁷ James Bonwick, *First Twenty Years in Australia* (Sydney: Robertson, 1882) 180–81.
¹⁸ J.H.L. Cumpston, *The History of Small-Pox in Australia* (Melbourne: Government Printer, 1914).
¹⁹ Ibid., 2.
²⁰ Ibid.
²¹ Ibid.
²² Ibid., 1.
²³ Ibid.
²⁴ Butlin, *Our Original Aggression*, 18.
²⁵ Ibid., 17.
²⁶ Ibid., 25.
²⁷ Ibid., 20.

28 Ibid., 21.
29 Ibid., 21.
30 P.H. Curson, *Times of crisis: epidemics in Sydney, 1788-1900* (Sydney: Sydney University Press, 1985) 47.
31 Ibid.
32 John Goldsmid, *The Deadly Legacy* (Sydney: University of New South Wales Press, 1988) 30.
33 Ibid., 30.
34 Ibid., 31.
35 J. Hardy and Alan Frost, *Studies from Terra Australis to Australia* (Canberra: Australian Academy of the Humanities, 1989) 145.
36 Alan Frost, *Botany Bay Mirages* (Melbourne: Melbourne University Press, 1994) 209.
37 Hardy and Frost, *Studies*, 146.
38 Ibid., 149.
39 Frost, *Botany Bay Mirages*, 192.
40 Ibid., 198.
41 Hunter, *Journal*, 51-2.
42 Frost, *Botany Bay Mirages*, 201.
43 Collins, *Account* Vol. 2, 53, 496; Tench, *First Four Years,* 149.
44 Hunter, *Journal,* 93.
45 Frost, *Botany Bay Mirages*, 203.
46 H. Brainerd, S. Morgan and M. Chatton, eds. *Current Diagnosis and Treatment* (California: Lange, 1968) 741-42.
47 Frost, *Botany Bay Mirages,* 193.
48 Newton Fowell, *The Sirius Letters* (Sydney: Fairfax, 1988) 113.
49 Frost, *Botany Bay Mirages, 206-09.*
50 Judy Campbell, *Invisible Invaders* (Carlton, Vic.: Melbourne University Press, 2002) reviewed by *The Age* 13 October 2003.
51 Ibid., 104.
52 Ibid., 87.

Chapter 7

1 C.M.H. Clark, *A History of Australia* Vol. 1 (Carlton, Vic.: Melbourne University Press, 1968) 142.

[2] John Ritchie, *The Wentworths* (Carlton, Vic.: Melbourne University Press, 1997) 74.
[3] A.G.L. Shaw in *A New History of Australia*, Frank Cowley (ed) (Melbourne: Heinemann, 1974) 25.
[4] Russel Ward, *Finding Australia* (Melbourne: Heinemann, 1987) 229.
[5] Walter Murdoch, *The Making of Australia* (Melbourne: Whitcombe & Tombs, 1917) 67.
[6] C.M.H. Clark, *A History of Australia* Vol. 1, 144.
[7] R. Knight and A. Frost (eds) *The Journal of Daniel Paine 1794-1797* (Sydney: Library of Australian History, 1983) 35.
[8] *Historical Records of Australia Series 1* Vol. 1, Phillip to Sydney, 15 April 1790 (Sydney: Government Printer, 1914) 171.
[9] *HRA*, 1, i, Grenville to Phillip, 19 February 1791, 225.
[10] *HRA*, 1, i, Phillip to Grenville, 25 March 1791, 262.
[11] John White, *Journal of a Voyage to New South Wales* (Sydney: Angus & Robertson, 1962) 140.
[12] *HRA*, 1, i, Phillip to Grenville, 21 November 1791, 313.
[13] *Historical Records of New South Wales* Vol. 2 1793-1795, Curtis to Nepean, 8 October 1793 (Sydney: Government Printer, 1893) 67.
[14] *HRNSW*, 2, Hunter to Dundas, 14 October 1793, 73.
[15] *HRNSW*, 2, Howe to Chatham, 15 October 1793, 74.
[16] *HRNSW*, 2, Phillip to Dundas, 26 October, 1793, 75.
[17] *HRA* 1, i, Hunter's Commission, 6 February 1794, 513-19.
[18] *HRA* 1, i, Phillip's Commission, 2 April 1787, 1-8.
[19] Gazetteer, London 30 December 1793, Bonwick Transcripts, ML Vol. 3, 2000-3, 671.
[20] See note 18.
[21] *HRA*, 1, i, Dundas to Grose, 15 February 1794, 464.
[22] *HRNSW*, 2, Hunter's Instructions, 23 June 1794, 227-34.
[23] Hunter to Stephens, 29 July 1794, ML, AJCP, ADM 1, PRO 3272.
[24] *HRNSW*, 2, Grose to Dundas, 30 May 1793, 29; 12 October 1793, 69; 29 April 1794, 207.
[25] *HRNSW*, 2, Grose to Dundas, 9 January 1793, 3.
[26] *HRNSW* 2, Grose to Dundas, 12 October 1793, 69.
[27] *HRNSW* 2, Grose to Dundas, 29 April 1794, 208.
[28] Ibid., 210.

[29] *HRA* 1, i, Paterson to Dundas, 15 June 1795, 500.
[30] Sibella Macarthur Onslow, *Some Early Records of the Macarthurs of Camden* (Sydney: Angus & Robertson, 1914) 46.
[31] *HRNSW*, 3, Hunter to Portland, 15 November 1799, 745.
[32] Bentham Papers Vol. V11, 1799–1802, British Library, Add. 33–543, f.36.
[33] Ibid.
[34] Brian Fletcher, 'The Development of Small Scale Farming in New South Wales under Governor Hunter', Journal, *RAHS* Vol. 50, Pt 1, June 1964, 4.
[35] *HRNSW* 3, Hunter to Portland, 10 August 1796, 65.
[36] H.C. Foster, *Journal RAHS* Vol. 60, Pt 2, June 1974, 84.
[37] *Governor Hunter's Remarks on the Causes of the Colonial Expense and Hints for the Reduction of Such Expense and for the Reforming of the Prevailing Abuses* (London: Gornell, 1802) 16.
[38] Ibid., 32.
[39] Alan Shaw, 'The New South Wales Corps', *Journal RAHS* Vol. 47, Pt 2, June 1961, 129.
[40] C.M.H. Clark, *A Short History of Australia* (New York: Mentor Books, 1963) 30.
[41] Herbert Evatt, *Rum Rebellion* (Sydney: Angus & Robertson, 1938) 17.
[42] Walter Murdoch, *The Making of Australia*, 63.
[43] Sibella Macarthur Onslow (ed) *Some Early Records of the Macarthurs of Camden*, 51.
[44] Valerie Ross (ed) *The Everingham Letterbook* (Wamberal, NSW: Anvil Press, 1985) 44–5.
[45] Ibid., 43.
[46] Phillip Lisle, 'Rum Beginnings' *Journal RAHS* Vol. 9, Pt 1, June 2005, 21.
[47] *HRA* 1, ii, Settlers' Statement to Hunter, 19 February 1798, 136–140.
[48] John Hunter, *An Historical Journal 1787–1792* (Sydney: Angus & Robertson, 1968) 94.
[49] *HRA* 1, i, Grose to Dundas, 9 January 1793, 414.
[50] R.J. Ryan (ed) *Land Grants 1788–1809* (Sydney: Australian Documents Library, 1974) Book No. 65, 15 September 1796.
[51] Alan Frost, *Convicts and Empire* (Melbourne: Oxford University Press, 1980) 161. G. Abbott and N. Nairn, *Economic History of Australia 1788–1821* (Carlton, Vic.: Melbourne University Press 1969) 96. C.M.H. Clark, *A History of Australia* Vol. 1 (Carlton, Vic.: Melbourne University Press 1968) 132–33.

[52] *HRA* 1, i, Governor Phillip's Instructions, 25 April 1789, 14.
[53] *HRA* 1, i, Return of Lands Granted, 5 November 1791, 279–82.
[54] *HRA* 1, i, Grenville to Phillip, 20 August 1789, 125.
[55] Brian Fletcher, 'The Development of Small Scale Farming in New South Wales under Governor Hunter', *Journal RAHS* Vol. 50, Pt 1, June 1964, 1.
[56] John Fisher, *The Australians* (London: Hale, 1968) 45.
[57] *HRA* 1, i, Dundas to Phillip, 14 July 1792, 365.
[58] *HRA* 1, i, Phillip to Sydney, 13 February 1790, 157.
[59] Valerie Ross (ed) *The Everingham Letterbook*, 36–7.
[60] *HRA* 1, i, Return of Land Grants, 31 December 1792 to 1 April 1793, 438.
[61] Ibid.
[62] David Collins, *An Account*, 225–26.
[63] P. J. Ryan, Land Grants 1788–1809 Book Nos. 583 and 593.
[64] *HRA* 1, i, Hunter to Portland, 25 September 1800, 566.
[65] *HRA* 1, i, Introduction by F. Watson, xxvi.
[66] *HRA* 1, i, Macarthur to Portland, 15 September 1796, 90.
[67] David Collins, *An Account*, 266–27.
[68] James Bonwick, *First Twenty Years of Australia* (Sydney: Angus & Robertson, 1882) 176.
[69] Ibid.
[70] *HRNSW* 3, Hunter to Portland, 1 September 1796, 99.
[71] C.M.H. Clark, Select Documents, 141.

Chapter 8

[1] *HRNSW* iii, 171, Hunter to Portland, 12 November, 1796.
[2] John Cobley, *Sydney Cove 1795–1800* (Sydney: Angus & Robertson, 1986) 457
[3] 2. *HRA* 1, i, Hunter to Portland, 11 September 1795, (Sydney: Gullick, 1914) 528.
[4] 3. *HRA* 1, i, Hunter to Portland, 25 October, 1795, 533.
[5] Ibid.
[6] *HRA* 1, i, Hunter to Portland, 25 October, 1795, 534.
[7] *HRNSW* 3, Macarthur to Hunter, 24 February, 1796 (Sydney: Potter, 1895) 28.
[8] *HRA* 1, i, Hunter to Portland, 12 November, 1796, 666–674; *HRNSW* 3, Hunter to Portland, 12 November, 1796, 174–177.
[9] *HRA* 1, ii, General Orders 22 March 1796, 690; 18 June 1796, 693; 11 July 1796, 694.
[10] *HRA* 1, i, Hunter to Portland, 12 November, 1796, 670.

[11] *HRA* 1, i, Hunter to Portland, 12 November, 1796, 669.
[12] *HRNSW* 3, John Black letter 8 September, 1798, 730.
[13] *HRNSW* 2, letter quoted in Dublin Chronicle, 3 March, 1792, 778.
[14] *HRNSW* 2, Daniel Southwell to his mother, Sydney, 5 May 1788, 682.
[15] *HRNSW* 3, Marsden to Hunter, 25 July 1798, 442.
[16] Neil Macintosh, *Richard Johnson* (Sydney: Library of Australian History, 1978) 88–89.
[17] R. Knight and A. Frost (eds) *The Journal of Daniel Paine*, 1794–1797, 34.
[18] *HRNSW* 3, Hunter to Portland, 21 February, 1799, 548.
[19] *HRA* 1, i, Hunter to Portland, 21 February, 1799, 244.
[20] *HRNSW* 3, Hunter to Under-Secretary King, 1 June 1797, 212.
[21] *HRNSW* 3, Hunter to King, 1 June 1797, 209.
[22] Ibid., 211.
[23] *HRNSW* 3, Hunter to Macarthur, 26 February, 1796, 27.
[24] *HRNSW* 3, Hunter to King, 1 June 1797, 212.
[25] *HRNSW* 3, Hunter to Portland, 10 January 1798, 346–47.
[26] Ibid.
[27] *HRNSW* 3, Portland to Hunter, 18 September 1798, 490.
[28] *HRNSW* 3, Hunter to Portland, 15 September 1796, 133.
[29] *HRNSW* 3, Portland to Hunter, 30 August 1797, 293.
[30] *HRNSW* 3, Government and General Order, 21 June 1797, 231.
[31] *HRNSW* 3, Memorandum, 7 March 1796, 20.
[32] *HRA* 1, iii, King to Under-Secretary King, 8 November 1801, 322.
[33] *HRNSW* 3, letter by John Black, 31 October 1798, 730.
[34] Ibid.
[35] *Australian Dictionary of Biography* Vol. 2 (Carlton, Vic.: Melbourne University Press 1967) 312.
[36] *HRNSW* 3, Hunter to Portland, 15 November 1799, 742.
[37] Ibid.
[38] Ibid.
[39] *Australian Dictionary of Biography* Vol. 2, 312.
[40] Ibid.
[41] *HRNSW* 3, Hunter to Portland, 15 November 1799, 748.
[42] *HRNSW* 3, Portland to Hunter, 31 August 1796, 91.

[43] *HRNSW* 3, Portland to Hunter, September 1796, 96.
[44] *HRNSW* 3, Portland to Hunter, 31 August 1797, 294.
[45] *HRNSW* 3, Hunter to Portland, 25 May 1798, 386.
[46] *HRNSW* 3, Hunter to Portland, 25 May 1798, 388.
[47] Hunter to Sydney, 30 July 1797, ML Sydney Collection MS Q354.
[48] *HRNSW* 3, 19 May 1798, 384.
[49] *HRNSW* 3, Portland to Hunter, 31 August 1797, 295.
[50] *HRNSW* 3, Government and General Order, 20 May 1798, 384.
[51] Michael Duffy, *Man of Honour John Macarthur*, 171.
[52] Walter Murdoch, *The Making of Australia*, 67.
[53] *HRNSW* 3, Government and General Order, 25 June 1798, 408.
[54] *HRNSW* 3, Agreement between Officers and Others, 18 June 1798, 405.
[55] *HRNSW* 3, Portland to Hunter, 5 November 1799, 737.
[56] *HRNSW* 3, Hunter to Portland, 15 November 1799, 744.
[57] *HRNSW* 3, Portland to Hunter, 5 November 1799, 738.
[58] *HRNSW* 4, Hunter to Portland, 20 April 1800, 73–4.
[59] *HRNSW* 4, Hunter to King, 25 September 1800, 149–51.
[60] *HRNSW* 4, King to Banks, 28 September 1800, 205.
[61] Ibid.
[62] Ibid.
[63] *HRNSW* 4, King to King, 8 November 1801, 613.
[64] *HRNSW* 3, Government and General Order, 20 May 1798, 384–85.
[65] *HRA* 1, ii, Hunter to Portland, 15 January 1800, 436–7.
[66] Ibid.
[67] *HRA* 1, ii, King to Hunter, 26 June 1800, 167.
[68] *HRA* 1, ii, King to Hunter, 24 June 1800, 166.
[69] *HRA* 1, i, Hunter to Portland, 12 November 1796, 666–74.
[70] Bentham Papers Vol. V11, 1799–1802, British Library, Add. 33–543, f.36.
[71] These figures are compiled from Population Returns in HR NSW 3, 92–93; 684, 749 and HRNSW 4, 213–14. They are slightly up on John Cobley's figures quoted earlier, which were taken the previous year.
[72] *HRNSW* 3, Hunter to Paterson, 7 February 1796, 17.
[73] *HRNSW* 3, Portland to Hunter, 31 August 1797, 294.
[74] *HRNSW* 3, Hunter to Portland, 26 August 1796, 87–8.

[75] *HRNSW* 3, Government and General Order, 9 November 1796, 165.
[76] Ibid.
[77] Hunter to Lord Sydney, 1 June 1799, ML MSQ 522.
[78] *HRNSW* 4, Hunter to Portland, 25 September 1800, 151–56.
[79] *HRNSW* 3, Hunter to Portland, 12 November 1796, 176.
[80] John Hunter, Memorandum, 'Articles which will be much wanted at the Settlement of New South Wales', 6 February 1794, PRO 6.7.
[81] Herman Morton, *The Early Australian Architects and their Work* (Sydney: Angus & Robertson, 1970) 22.
[82] *HRNSW* 3, Government and General Order, 11 January 1797, 188, 412.
[83] *HRNSW* 3, Hunter to Portland, 10 July 1799, 694–5.
[84] Hunter to Lord Sydney, 1 June 1799, ML, MSQ 522–3.
[85] David Collins, *An Account of the English Colony in New South Wales* Vol. 11, 66.
[86] Ibid.
[87] *HRNSW* 4, Hunter to Hawkesbury River Settlers, 8 February 1800, 31.
[88] T. Crofton-Croker, *Memoirs of Joseph Holt* Vol. 11 (London: Colburn, 1838) 83.
[89] Ibid.
[90] T. Crofton-Croker, *Memoirs of Joseph Holt* Vol. 11, 85.
[91] *HRA* 1, i, Governor Hunter's Instructions, 23 June 1794, 522.
[92] Inga Clendinnen, *Dancing with Strangers* (Melbourne: Text, 2003) 172–81.
[93] *HRA* 1, i, Paterson to Dundas, 15 June 1795, 499.
[94] *HRA* 1, i, Government and General Orders, 12 November 1796, 689.
[95] *HRA* 1, i, Hunter to Portland, 12 November 1796, 674.
[96] Ibid.
[97] Alan Atkinson, *The Europeans in Australia: A History* Vol. 1 (Carlton, Vic.: Melbourne University Press 1997) 248.
[98] David Collins *An Account of the English Colony in New South Wales*,Vol 11, 23–4.
[99] *HRA* 1, i, Hunter to Portland, 5 January 1800, 429.
[100] *HRNSW* 3, Hunter to Portland, 30 April 1799, 661.
[101] *HRA* 1, ii, Hunter to Portland, 15 November 1799, 747.
[102] Bentham Papers Vol. V11, 1799–1802, British Library. Add 33.543, f.36.
[103] *HRNSW* 3, Hunter to Portland, 10 June 1797, 215.
[104] *HRA* 1, ii, Hunter to Under-Secretary King, 1 June 1797, 12.
[105] Bentham Papers Vol. V11, 1799–1802, British Library. Add 33.543, f36.
[106] *HRNSW* 3, Hunter to Portland, 1 May 1799, 667.

Chapter 9

[1] James Boswell, *Account of Corsica* (Glasgow: Foulis and Dilly, 1768); *Journal of a Tour to the Hebrides* (London: Baldwin and Dilly, 1785).

[2] H.W. Fowler (ed) *The Concise Oxford Dictionary* (London: Oxford University Press, 1949) 316, 616.

[3] James Auchmuty (ed) *The Voyage of Governor Phillip to Botany Bay*, (Sydney, Angus & Robertson, 1970) XV.

[4] John Hunter, *An Historical Journal of Events at Sydney and at Sea* (Sydney: Angus & Robertson, 1968) 270.

[5] Ibid., 270–74.

[6] David Collins, *An Account of the English Colony in New South Wales* Vol. 1 (Sydney: Reed, 1975) 507–13.

[7] The Southwell Papers, *HRNSW* Vol. 2 (Sydney: Govt. Printer, 1893) 697–699.

[8] Sydney Parkinson, *A Journal of Voyage to the South Seas* (Adelaide: Libraries Board of South Australia, 1972) 51–65.

[9] Ibid., 145–52.

[10] Hunter, *Journal*, 269.

[11] Ibid., 22.

[12] Ibid., 28.

[13] Ibid., 56.

[14] Ibid., 128.

[15] William Bradley, A *Voyage to New South Wales* (Sydney: Ure Smith, 1969) 208–9.

[16] Hunter, *Journal*, 49.

[17] Ibid.

[18] Ibid., 137.

[19] Ibid., 190–91.

[20] George Mackaness, *The Life of Vice Admiral William Bligh* Vol. 1 (Sydney: Angus & Robertson, 1931) 318.

[21] Bradley, Voyage, 296–7.

[22] Mackaness, *Life of Admiral Bligh* Vol. 1, 319.

[23] Hunter, *Journal*, 131.

[24] John Currey, *David Collins A Colonial Life* (Carlton, Vic.: Melbourne University Press 2000) 59.

[25] Hunter, *Journal*, 119.

[26] Bradley, *Voyage*, 191.
[27] Ralph Clark, *Journal and Letters of Lt. Ralph Clark* (Sydney: Library of Australian History, 1981) 120.
[28] Clark, *Journal*, 287–8.
[29] Hunter, *Journal*, 131.
[30] Bradley, *Voyage*, 202.
[31] Ibid., 206.
[32] Ibid., 223.
[33] Clark, *Journal*, 166.
[34] John Dunn (ed) *The Nagle Journal* (New York: Weidenfeld and Nicolson, 1988) 127.
[35] Clark, *Journal*, 291.
[36] Ibid.
[37] Ibid., 294.
[38] *The British Critic* Vol 1, May–August 1793, 79–87.
[39] Ibid., 82.
[40] Ibid., 79.
[41] Ibid., 87.
[42] Mitchell Library, Sydney, Ref. 991/B.
[43] Biographical Memoir of Captain John Hunter, *The Naval Chronicle* Vol. V1, July–December 1801, 353.
[44] Ibid., 355.
[45] John White, *Journal of a Voyage to New South Wales* (Sydney: Angus & Robertson, 1962) 105.
[46] C.M.H. Clark, *A History of Australia* Vol. 1 (Carlton, Vic.: Melbourne University Press, 1968) 142.
[47] Ibid., 70.
[48] Hunter, *Journal*, 110.
[49] Ibid., 260.
[50] Ibid., 112.
[51] Auchmuty, *Voyage*, 70.
[52] T.M. Perry, *The Discovery of Australia* (Melbourne: Nelson, 1982) 71–72.
[53] K.A. Hindwood, 'George Raper: An Artist of the First Fleet, *Journal RAHS* Vol 50 Pt 1 June 1964, 32–57.
[54] Hunter, *Journal*, 96.
[55] Bradley, *Voyage*, 84.

[56] John Cobley, *Sydney Cove 1788* (Sydney: Hodder and Stoughton, 1963).
[57] Russel Ward, *Finding Australia* (Melbourne: Heineman, 1987) 195.
[58] Currey, *David Collins*, 47.
[59] Hunter, *Journal*, 110.
[60] Smith & Wheeler, *Art*, 80–81.
[61] Ibid., 102–3.
[62] Bradley, *Voyage*, 182, 260, 276.
[63] Ibid., 194–5.
[64] Smith & Wheeler, *Art*, 121.
[65] John Calaby (ed) *The Hunter Sketchbook* (Canberra: National Library of Australia, 1989).
[66] Auchmuty, *Voyage*, 59.
[67] White, *Journal*, 163.
[68] Collins, *Account*, 45.
[69] Calaby, *Hunter Sketchbook*, 22.
[70] Hunter, *Journal*, 113.
[71] Ibid., 48.
[72] Ibid., 49.
[73] Biographical Memoir of Captain John Hunter, 352.
[74] *The Naval Chronicle* Vol. XXV, July–December 1811 (London: Gold, 1811) 144, ML 359.05/N.
[75] Ibid.
[76] Ibid., 145.
[77] Hunter, *Journal*, 85.
[78] Ibid.
[79] Dava Sobel and William Andrews, *Longitude* (London: Fourth Estate, 1998) 171.
[80] Hunter, *Journal*, 86.
[81] Plan for Checking the Violence of the Recoil of our heavy Naval Artillery when engaged on the weather side, with a fresh gale. *The Naval Chronicle* Vol. XXV, July–December 1811, 296–299.

Chapter 10

[1] *HRNSW* 4, Hunter to Hobart, 7 June 1802, 786.
[2] *HRNSW* 4, Hobart to Portland, 24 August 1802, 821.
[3] *HRNSW* 4, Portland to Hobart, 3 October, 1802, 847.

[4] *HRA* 1, iii Under-Secretary Sullivan to Governor King, 1 May 1802, 485.
[5] *HRNSW* 4, Addington to Hobart, 15 October, 1802, 854.
[6] for example, *HRA* 1, v, Under-Secretary Cooke to Governor King, 20 March 1805, 298.
[7] *HRNSW* 4, Hunter to King, 22 March 1802, 728–733.
[8] *Governor Hunter's Remarks on the Causes of the Colonial Expense of the Establishment of New South Wales* (London: Gosnell, 1802).
[9] *HRNSW* 5, Adjutant-General Calvert to Under-Secretary Sullivan, 31 January 1803, 11;
HRNSW 5, Macarthur to Sullivan, 20 September 1804, 465;
HRNSW 5, Colley to Banks, 7 July 1808, 685.
[10] *HRNSW* 5, King to Paterson, 25 January 1803, 10;
HRNSW 5, Banks to King, 29 August 1804, 460;
HRNSW 6, Mann to Castlereagh, 26 May 1806, 76;
HRNSW 6, Surgeon Luttrell to Sullivan, 8 October 1807, 296;
HRNSW 6, Blaxland to Under-Secretary Chapman, 15 October 1807, 303.
[11] *HRNSW* 5, King to Banks, December 1804, 530.
[12] *HRNSW* 5, Castlereagh to King, 20 November 1805, 735.
[13] *HRNSW* 4, Portland to Hobart, 3 October 1802, 847.
[14] Sibella Macarthur Onslow (ed) *Some Early Records of the Macarthurs of Camden* (Sydney: Angus & Robertson, 1914) 57.
[15] *HRNSW* 5, Sheepbreeding Enquiry Transcript, 11 July 1804, 393.
[16] Bonwick Transcripts, ML, 696.
[17] George Townsend Fox, *Synopsis of the Newcastle Museum* (Newcastle: Hodgson, 1827) 248–250.
[18] W. J. Butcher & Son, *Auction Catalogue*, 25 November 1924, ML 708/H.
[19] *HRNSW* 5, Hunter to Middleton, 22 February 1805, 560.
[20] *HRNSW* 6, Hunter to Secretary Pole, 7 February 1808, 412.
[21] Hunter to Galloway, ML Mss 164, CY 3613.
[22] Ibid.
[23] Ibid.
[24] Ibid.
[25] Ibid.
[26] Ibid.
[27] Ibid.

[28] Ibid.
[29] *HRA* 1 i, 1-16 and 513-527.
[30] Rex Rienits, *David Collins* (Melbourne: Oxford University Press, 1969) 13.
[31] Collins Papers, ML Vol 4, 19; *HRNSW* 4, Collins to Sullivan 27 December 1802, 926.
[32] John Ritchie, *Lachlan Macquarie* (Carlton, Vic.: Melbourne University Press, 1988) 194-96, 200-03.
[33] Proceedings of a General Court Martial held at Chelsea Hospital, 7 May to 5 June 1811 for the Trial of Lt. Col. Geo Johnston on a charge of Mutiny (London: Sherwood, Nealy & Jones, 1811) 367.
[34] George Mackaness, *The Life of Vice Admiral William Bligh* Vol. 11, 335.
[35] Richard O'Neill (ed) *Patrick O'Brien's Navy* (London: Salamander, 2003) 44.
[36] William Arthur Griffiths, *Some Notes on the family of Admiral John Hunter* (Private Circulation, 1948) ML A3102.
[37] W.J. Butcher & Son, *Catalogue*, 25 November 1924, ML 708H.
[38] Leonard Joel, *Catalogue*, Thursday 9 June 1932, ML 645H.
[39] *Argus*, Wednesday, 26 November 1924, 7.
[40] Conversation with Registry staff member, 15 September 2005.
[41] *Leonard Joel Catalogue*, Thursday 9 June 1932, ML 645H.
[42] *London Art Journal* (reprinted in the Sydney Mail, 8 January 1870) 4.
[43] Registry of Births, Deaths and Marriages. Death Certificate No. 6653, Elizabeth Allen Kelly, died 11 May 1928.
[44] English Census returns 1871 for District of Strand. No. 10 Portugal Street in the parish of St Clement Danes, Westminster: 'Charlotte Moore Kelly "Head" 46 years; Elizabeth Kelly, daughter, unmarried, 26 years, Sculptor, born Ballyscullion, Ireland.'
[45] J.H. Marden, *Sir Joseph Banks* (Sydney: Gullick, 1909) 190.
[46] *The Evening News*, Edinburgh, 26 August 1994.
[47] *The Times*, 14 March 1821, Bonwick Transcripts, ML Vol. 3, A2000-3, p.704.

APPENDIX 1

JOHN HUNTER'S FAMILY TREE

William Hunter married 28th March, 1697 **Sarah Thomson**
Edinburgh Parish, daughter of Andrew Thomson,
Edinburgh, Scotland (Tailor and Burgess of Edinburgh)

Children:

- **Alexander Hunter** born 6/2/1698 Edinburgh
- **William Hunter** christened 14/9/1701 Edinburgh, died infancy
- **William Hunter** christened 14/12/1703 Edinburgh, married Helen Drummond only dau. of J. Drummond
- **James Hunter** born 15/12/1704 Edinburgh
- **Margaret Hunter** christened 21/12/1705 Edinburgh
- **John Hunter** christened 17/4/1709 Edinburgh, died infancy
- **John Hunter** christened 3/10/1711 Edinburgh
- **Sarah Hunter** born 27/11/1712 Edinburgh
- **Elizabeth Hunter** born 15/10/1714 christened 16/10/1714 Edinburgh
- **Mary Hunter** born 10/2/1716 christened 12/2/1716 Edinburgh
- **Robert Hunter** christened 9/6/1717 Edinburgh

Children of William Hunter and Helen Drummond:

- **William Hunter** born 7/5/1730 christened 13/5/1730 died 17/2/1810 Issue: daughters
- **Sarah Hunter** born 19/3/1733 christened 20/3/1733
- **George Hunter** born 5/2/1735 christened 10/2/1735
- **Mary Hunter** born circa 1736 married Henry Kent Issue
- **John Hunter** born 29/8/1737 christened 1/9/1737 died 13/3/1821 No Issue
- **Janet Hunter** born 5/1/1739 christened 16/1/1739 died pre 1821 married Dr Charles Maule Issue
- **Agnes Hunter** christened 28/10/1740
- **James Hunter** christened 19/12/1741 died pre 1821 Issue: daughters
- **Margaret Hunter** christened 13/5/1743
- **Archibald Hunter** christened 8/10/1744

308

Appendix 2
John Hunter's statement of the loss of the *Sirius*

On the 6th of March everything being embark'd, I sailed from Port Jackson. On the 19th in the morning by a slant from S.E. I was enabled to get in with the land again. The *Supply* had parted Company the preceeding night which was squally with strong gales.

In Standing in for the land as I found we could fetch the Windward part of the island, I steer'd in for Sydney Bay, which is that part on which the Settlement is formed, and is the only part of the island on which provisions or stores of any weight can be landed, as we drew near we discover'd the *Supply* close in under the land and the boats passing between her and shore—The signal was at this time flying upon the island, signifying, that longboats or any other boats might land without any danger from the Surf.

The very great difficulty and danger which does, I may venture to say, almost continually attend the landing upon any part of this island, made me exceedingly anxious to avail myself of this very favourable signal and to get some part of the provision landed I consider'd that I had put on shore, two hundred and seventy people in addition to one hundred and thirty before upon the island; I also knew that the Provision Store there, was in so very Exhausted a state, that with the numbers now to be fed from it, altho' short allowance had taken place, it could support them but a very short time; and the Natural Resources of the Island, if it could be said to have any, were such as were of too precarious a Nature to hope any relief from; No provision, stores or necessaries belonging to those I had landed, had I yet been able to put on shore—I dreaded the loss of one favourable Moment, so great was the probability of meeting bad weather at this season of the year which might force me from the island for some considerable time and it was further probable that upon my recovering it again, an immediate opportunity might not happen for my landing anything for the relief of its inhabitants. These considerations with the observations I had made in sailing around this island, and looking into all Bays on it, that whatever direction the wind blows from, if it blows strong, there is no access to any part of the shore without imminent danger, so great is the surf all round, occasion'd by the narrow limits of the island. Had I been blown from the island for any considerable length of time, it might have been attended with very distressing consequences to those upon it; to prevent which as much as in my power. This day appearing by signal from the shore to be a favourable one in the passage of the surf thro' which the boats had to pass to the landing place. I stood in as far as I judged safe, and brought the Ship too with her head off shore in the S.E. or windward part of the Bay. Got the boats out, loaded and sent them in. The Supply was at this time close in and to leeward of the Sirius, as soon as the boats were despatched or rather before the second boat quitted the Ship, observing that she fell part to leeward, and settled in upon the shore, the Maintopsail was fill'd, the Fore and Main Tacks were got on board, mizen and Maintopsails set whilst sail was making the wind Southar'd two or three points, the Supply had also made Sail, and Lieut Ball waved with his hatt towards a surf which enter'd from the NW point of the Bay, and which he suppos'd, as we were strangers here we might not be acquainted with. He was ahead of us, but could not weather this reef, He tack'd and as he stood towards us, I expressed my doubt of his being able to pass to windward of us, but at this Critical instance, when the Situation of both ships was such that neither could afford to give away a single point without the utmost risk, the wind veer'd still more to the Southward upon us, as we fell off, We consequently upon the other tack came up and pass'd close athwart our weather bow, Mr Ball then told me that he thought we were both too near in, I answer'd that I thought so too and intended working further out, and in that intention, I thought the East'ly tide which was suppos'd to be made some time would enable us with ease to get off: But in this favourable tide which I had observ'd since my arrival here, had been very regular on both sides of the island, we were much disappointed, and instead of which we had a strong Westerly Set or Current the whole of that day—I stood on with a hope of being able to Weather this Reef off the NW point of the Bay, but on finding that we were not assisted by any Easterly tide, but that we drop'd fast into the Bay, I continued to stand upon this, as it was the most favourable tack, as far as possible without imminent danger, and then order'd the ship in Stays, She came up almost head to wind, but was there baffled by the wind in unsteady flaws, at the unfortunate moment of her having lost her headway, she fell off again, I then took the trumpet from the Master, and advised him to get the driver clear for setting upon the other tack. I hauled the after sails to prevent the ship as much as possible from gathering head way in war'ing.

She pay'd short round on her Hull, but altho she went round in as little room as any ship could, yet being disappointed in stays in this particular situation and the ground consequently lost by that accident, I consider as the original and principal cause of our misfortune.

We got the tacks on board on the Starboard tack, let the first reef out of the Mizentopsail and set the driver, that there might be no defficiency of after sail—I should have mentioned that before we got in with the Land, there was so much wind, that we had been under close-reeft topsails, but that the ship might be more under command in the Bay, a reef had been let out of each top sail as we stood in; Being now haul'd to the wind upon the other tack, on which we lay little better than parallel to the shore, I ordered axes by one of the bower anchors—there had been a man at the lead since our first entering the Bay. The wind had now got so far to the Southward that it blew nearly dead into the Bay and upon the Shore, finding after a short time upon this tack, that we still wear'd the Shore and had shoal'd the water to 5 fathoms, I put the ship in stays. She again disappointed me and on looking over the side, I observ'd that she was going very fast astern, having all her sails aback, I order'd the anchor to be cutt away and all the haulyards tacks and sheets to be let fly, that they might not prevent the anchor from holding, but before the Cable could be brought to check her, she struck violently upon some sharp rocks which went immediately through her bottom.

Here I must observe that the ship's striking where she did was rather unexpected by me, for I had never understood that the water was so very choal at such a Distance from the surf on the Shore, so very imperfect had the information been which we had from time to time receiv'd of this place—

[Extracted from *Sirius* Court Martial, La Trobe Library, AJCP 6925/5329, 1791–92]

Bibliography

Primary Material Sources

Sydney
Mitchell Library:
Banks Papers. Brabourne Collection Vol. 4, A78-3.
Bonwick Transcripts Vol. 3 A 2000-3.
Hunter Papers. Mss 164 CY 3613, MSQ 522, MSQ 354 and MSQ 647.
David Blackburn letters Mss 6937/1/1-5, CY 4084.
Avis's *Birmingham Gazette* 3 December 1804 BT Box 12.
Phillip to Sydney, 1 November 1786, Add. 290.
Mrs Richard Johnson's Letters, zml. Mss 67222, Microfilm 4036.
Kent Family Papers.
Wentworth Family Papers.
W. J. Butcher & Son Catalogue 25 November 1924 ML 708/11.
Leonard Joel Catalogue 9 June 1932 ML 645H.
Henry Waterhouse Papers 1786-1811 Mss 6544, Microfilm CY 3970.
The British Critic May-August 1793, ML 991/B.

Melbourne
La Trobe Library:
Sirius' Log 1786-1790, Captain John Hunter. AJCP 6925.5328.
Charlotte's Log 1786-1788, Captain T. Gilbert. AJCP 5777.4375.
Friendship's Log 1786-1789, Captain F. Walters AJCP 5777.4376.
Lady Penrhyn's Log 1786-1788, Captain W. Sever AJCP 5777.4376.
Hunter's *Sirius* Court Martial, AJCP 6925.5329.

Church of Jesus Christ of Latter Day Saints, Heidelberg:
Genealogical Records - Church of Scotland Christenings/Baptisms:
Microfilm Nos. 1066666 Edinburgh Parish 1706-1732; 1066667

Edinburgh Parish 1732–1739; 1067771 South Leith, Midlothian; 1067774 South Leith, Midlothian; 1067766 North Leith, Midlothian.

Canberra
National Library of Australia:
Hunter's Drawings.
Hunter's Portrait.

United Kingdom
Public Record Office, Kew:
Caryfort's Pilots Court Martial, Adm. 1/5305.
HMS *Venerable's* Muster Rolls, Adm. 36/15534.
Hunter's *Venerable* Court Martial, Adm. 1/5367.
Hunter's Letters Adm. 1/3272

National Maritime Museum, Greenwich:
Print of HMS *Carysfort* PAD 5476.
Painting of HMS *Venerable* PAH 0741.
Victory's Masters' Logs, 1780–1786 ADM/L/V63.

British Library:
Gazetteer London, 30 December 1793.
Bentham Papers Vol.VII 1799–1802, Add. 33.543, f.36.

Edinburgh Central Library:
Births, South Leith 1687–1784 Microfilm OPR 692/2/5.

Published Primary Sources

An Officer. *An Authentic and Interesting Narrative of the late Expedition to Botany Bay*, Aberdeen: Kieth, 1789.
Auchmuty, J. (ed). *The Voyage of Governor Phillip to Botany Bay,* Sydney: Angus & Robertson, 1970.
Beaglehole, J. C. (ed). *The Journals of Captain James Cook, Vol I. The Voyage of the Endeavour,* Cambridge: Hakluyt Society, 1968.

Beaglehole, J. C. (ed). *The Journals of Captain James Cook, Vol II. The Voyage of the Resolution and Adventure 1772–1775*, Cambridge: Hakluyt Society, 1961.

Beaglehole, J. C. (ed). *The Endeavour Journal of Joseph Banks*, Sydney: Angus & Robertson, 1963.

Bladen, F. M. (ed). *Historical Records of New South Wales, Vols 1–6*, Sydney: Gullick, 1897.

Boswell, James. *Account of Corsica,* Glasgow: Foulis and Dilly, 1768.

Boswell, James. *Journal of a Tour to the Hebrides,* London: Baldwin and Dilly, 1785.

Bradley, William. *A Voyage to New South Wales*, Sydney: Ure Smith, 1969.

Clark, C. M. H. *Select Documents in Australian History, Vol I*, Sydney: Angus & Robertson, 1950.

Clark, C. M. H. *Sources of Australian History*, London: Oxford University Press, 1963.

Collins, David. *An Account of the English Colony in New South Wales, Vols 1 & 2*, Sydney: Reed, 1975.

Crofton-Croker, T. *Memoirs of Joseph Holt, Vols 1 & 2*, London: Colburn, 1838.

Dann, John (ed). *The Nagle Journal*, New York: Weidenfeld & Nicolson, 1988.

Dawson, W. R. (ed). *The Banks Letters*, London: British Museum, 1958.

Easty, John. *Memorandum of Transactions of a Voyage from England to Botany Bay 1787–1793*, Sydney: Angus & Robertson, 1965.

Fildon, P. G. & Ryan, R. J. (eds). *The Journal and Letters of Lt. Ralph Clark*, Adelaide: Griffin, 1981.

Fildon, P. G. & Ryan, R. J. (eds). *The Journal of Arthur Bowes Smyth*, Adelaide: Griffin, 1979.

Fildon, P. G. & Ryan, R. J. (eds). *The Journal of Phillip Gidley King*, Adelaide: Griffin, 1980.

Fowell, Newton (Irvine, Nance ed). *The Sirius Letters*, Sydney: Fairfax, 1988.

Hunter, John (Back, J. ed). *An Historical Journal of Events at Sydney and at Sea*, Sydney: Angus & Robertson, 1968.

Hunter, John. *Remarks on the Causes of Colonial Expenses and Hints for the Reduction of such Expenses*, London: Gosnell, 1802.
Knight, R. & Frost, A. (eds). *The Journal of Daniel Paine 1794-1797*, Sydney: Library of Australian History, 1983.
Macarthur-Onslow, Sibella. *Some Early Records of the Macarthurs of Camden*, Sydney: Angus & Robertson, 1914.
Neville, Derek. *Blackburn's Isle*, Suffolk: Lavenham, 1975.
Parkinson, Sydney. *A Journal of a Voyage to the South Seas*, Adelaide: Libraries Board of South Australia, 1972.
Ritchie, John (ed). *A Charge of Mutiny against Lt. Col. George Johnston 1808*, Canberra: National Library, 1988.
Ross, Valerie (ed). *The Everingham Letterbook*, Sydney: Anvil, 1985.
Scott, James. *Remarks on a Passage to Botany Bay 1787-1792*, Sydney: Angus & Robertson, 1963.
Tench, Watkin. *Sydney's First Four Years*, Sydney: Angus & Robertson, 1961.
The Naval Chronicle Vol VI July-December 1801, London: Bunney, 1801.
The Naval Chronicle Vol XIII January-June 1805, London: Gold, 1805.
The Naval Chronicle Vol XXV July-December 1811, London: Gold, 1811.
Watson, F. (ed). *Historical Records of Australia Vols 1-5*, Sydney: Commonwealth Library Committee, 1915.
Wentworth, William Charles *Descriptions of the Colony of New South Wales 1819*, Adelaide: Griffin, 1978.
White, John. *Journal of a Voyage to New South Wales*, Sydney: Angus & Robertson, 1962.
Worgan, George. *Journal of a First Fleet Surgeon*, Sydney: Library of Australian History, 1978.

Secondary References

Abbott, G. J. & Nairn, N. B. *Economic Growth of Australia 1788-1821*, Melbourne: Melbourne University Press, 1969.
Atkinson, Alan. *The Europeans in Australia: A History, Vol 1*, Melbourne: Melbourne University Press, 1997.

Barrow, J. *Life of Richard, Earl Howe K.G.*, London: John Murray, 1838.
Bassett, Marnie. *The Governor's Lady*, London: Oxford University Press, 1940.
Bateson, Charles. *The Convict Ships*, Sydney: Reed, 1974.
Blazé, B. R. *Great Scot*, Limited Edition, Private Circulation, 1975.
Bonwick, James. *Curious Facts of Old Colonial Life*, London: Sampson Low, 1870.
Bonwick James. *First Twenty Years in Australia*, London: Sampson Low, 1882.
Bowden, Keith. *George Bass*, Melbourne: Oxford University Press, 1952.
Bown, Stephen. *Scurvy*, Melbourne: Penguin, 2003.
Caloby, John (ed). *The Hunter Sketchbook*, Canberra: National Library of Australia, 1989.
Cameron, Hector. *Sir Joseph Banks*, Sydney: Angus & Robertson, 1966.
Clark, C. M. H. *A Short History of Australia*, London: Heinemann, 1969.
Clark, C. M. H. *A History of Australia Vol 1*, Melbourne: Melbourne University Press, 1968.
Clendinnen, Inga. *Dancing with Strangers*, Melbourne: Text, 2003.
Cobley, John. *Sydney Cove 1788*, Sydney: Hodder & Stoughton, 1963.
Cobley, John. *Sydney Cove 1795–1800*, Sydney: Angus & Robertson, 1986.
Crowley, Frank. *A New History of Australia*, Melbourne: Heinemann, 1974.
Currey, John. *David Collins: A Colonial Life*, Melbourne: Melbourne University Press, 2000.
Davison, Graeme, Hirst J & MacIntyre S. (eds). *The Oxford Companion to Australian History*, Melbourne: Oxford University Press, 2001.
Dening, Greg. *Mr Bligh's Bad Language*, Cambridge: Cambridge University Press, 1992.
Duffy, Michael. *John Macarthur, Man of Honour*, Sydney: Macmillan, 2003.
Eldershaw, M. Barnard. *Phillip of Australia*, Sydney: Angus & Robertson, 1972.
Ellis, Malcolm. *Francis Greenway, His Life and Times*, Sydney: Angus & Robertson, 1949.
Ellis, Malcolm. *Lachlan Macquarie*, Sydney: Angus & Robertson, 1965.
Ellis, Malcolm. *John Macarthur*, Sydney: Angus & Robertson, 1973.
Estensen, Miriam. *The Life of Matthew Flinders*, Sydney: Allen & Unwin, 2002.
Evatt, Herbert. *Rum Rebellion*, Sydney: Angus & Robertson, 1944.

Fisher, John. *The Australians*, London: Hale, 1968.
Fletcher, Brian. *Ralph Darling, A Governor Maligned*, Melbourne: Oxford University Press, 1984.
Fowler, Richard. *The Furneaux Group*, Canberra: Roebuck, 1980.
Fox, G. T. *Synopsis of the Newcastle Museum*, Newcastle: Hodgson, 1827.
Frost, Alan. *Convicts and Empire*, Melbourne: Oxford University Press, 1980.
Frost, Alan. *Arthur Phillip, 1738-1814: His Voyaging*, Melbourne: Oxford University Press, 1987.
Goodwin, A. (ed). *The New Cambridge Modern History Vol VIII*, London: Cambridge University Press, 1965.
Griffiths, William A. *Some Notes on the Family of Admiral John Hunter*, Private Circulation, 1948.
Hayes, Carlton. *Modern Europe to 1870*, New York: Macmillan, 1967.
Henderson, Graeme & Stanbury, Myra. *The Sirius*, Sydney: Collins, 1988.
Hibbert, Christopher. *Nelson A Personal History*, London: Viking, 1994.
Hoyle, Arthur. *Life of John Hunter*, Canberra: Mulini Press, 2001.
Hughes, Robert. *The Fatal Shore*, London: Collins Harvill, 1987.
Ingleton, Geoffrey. *Charting a Continent*, Sydney: Angus & Robertson, 1944.
Joy, William. *The Exiles*, Sydney: Shakespeare Head, 1972.
Macintosh, Neil. *Richard Johnson* Sydney: Library of Australian History, 1978.
Macintyre, Stuart. *A Concise History of Australia*, Cambridge: Cambridge University Press, 1999.
Mackaness, George. *The Life of Vice-Admiral William Bligh Vols 1 & 2*, Sydney: Angus & Robertson, 1931.
McHugh, E. *Shipwrecks*, Melbourne: Viking, 2003.
McIntyre, Kenneth. *The Rebello Transcripts*, London: Souvenir Press, 1984.
Maloney, John. *History of Australia*, Melbourne: Viking, 1987.
Marden, J. H. *Sir Joseph Banks*, Sydney: Gullick, 1909.
Martell, G. & Twitcher J. *A Life of the Fourth Earl of Sandwich 1718-1792*, London: Jonathon Cape, 1962.
Murdoch, Walter. *The Making of Australia*, Melbourne: Whitcombe & Tombs, 1914.

Newman, G. (ed). *Britain in the Hanovarian Age 1714-1837*, New York: Garland, 1997.
Perkins, Harold. *The Origin of Modern English Society 1780-1880*, London: Routledge & Kegan Paul, 1969.
Perry, Tom. *Australia's First Frontier*, Melbourne: Melbourne University Press, 1963.
Perry, Tom. *The Discovery of Australia*, Melbourne: Nelson, 1982.
Perry, Tom & Prescott D. *A Guide to Maps of Australia in Books Published 1780-1830*, Canberra: ANU Press, 1996.
Pickard, Liza. *Restoration London*, London: Weidenfeld & Nicolson, 1997.
Pickard, Liza. *Dr. Johnson's London*, London: Weidenfeld & Nicolson, 2000.
Ritchie, John. *The Wentworths*, Melbourne: Melbourne University Press, 1997.
Rodgers, N. A. M. *The Insatiable Earl: A Life of John Montague, Fourth Earl of Sandwich 1718-1792*, London: Harper Collins, 1993.
Ryan, R. J. (ed). *Land Grants 1788-1809*, Sydney: Australian Documents Library, 1974.
Scott, Ernest (ed). *The Cambridge History of the British Empire Vol VII, Part 1*, Cambridge: Oxford University Press, 1933.
Scott, Ernest. *A Short History of Australia*, Melbourne: Oxford University Press, 1950.
Scott, Ernest. *The Life of Matthew Flinders*, Sydney: Angus & Robertson, 2001.
Shann, Edward. *An Economic History of Australia*, Cambridge: Cambridge University Press, 1938.
Smith, B. & Wheeler, A. (eds). *The Art of the First Fleet*, Melbourne: Melbourne University Press, 1988.
Taylor, Peter. *Australia: The First Twelve Years*, Sydney: Allen & Unwin, 1982.
Trevelyan, George. *History of England*, London: Longmans, 1952.
Valentin, F. *Voyages and Adventures of La Perouse*, Honolulu: University of Hawaii Press, 1969.
Villiers, Alan. *Captain Cook: The Seaman's Seaman*, London: Hodder & Stoughton, 1967.
Ward, Russell. *Finding Australia*, Melbourne: Heinemann, 1987.

Wilson, C. *Australia – The Creation of a Nation*, New Jersey: Barnes & Noble, 1987.
Yarwood, Alexander. *Samuel Marsden*, Melbourne: Melbourne University Press, 1977.

Journals and Articles

Anon. Review of Journal of Captain John Hunter 1793. *The British Critic* May–August 1793, Article xxi.
Allars, Kenneth 'Richard Dore Re-examined'. *JRAHS Vol.50, Pt. 2* (July 1964).
Atkinson, Alan. 'The First Plans for Governing New South Wales 1786-7'. *Australian Historical Studies, Vol.24, No.94* (April 1990).
Auchmuty, J. J. 'The Background to the Early Australian Governors'. *Historical Studies, Vol.61, No.23* (November 1954).
Bladen, F. M. 'Notes on the Life of John Hunter'. *JAHS Vol.1, No.3* (1901).
Fletcher, Brian. 'The Development of Small Scale Farming in New South Wales under Governor Hunter'. *JRAHS Vol.50, Pt 1* (June 1964).
Fletcher, Brian 'Government Farming and Grazing in New South Wales 1788–1810'. *JRAHS Vol.59, Pt 3* (September 1973).
Gibbons, P. 'The Administration of Governor Hunter'. *JRAHS Vol.26, Pt 5* (1940).
Hindwood, K. A. 'George Raper: An Artist of the First Fleet'. *JRAHS Vol.50, Pt 1* (June 1964).
Lisle, Phillip 'Rum Beginnings'. *JRAHS Vol.91, Pt 1* (June 2005).
Mear, Craig. 'The origin of the smallpox outbreak in Sydney in 1789' JRAHS Vol.94, Pt 1 (June 2008).
Perry, Tom. 'The Spread of Rural Settlement in New South Wales 1788-1826'. *Historical Studies Australia and New Zealand Vol. 6, No.24* (May 1955).
Parsons, T. G. 'The Social Comparison of the Men of the New South Wales Corps'. *JRAHS Vol.50, Pt 4* (October 1964).
Parsons, T. G. 'Was John Boston's Pig a Political Martyr?' *JRAHS Vol.71, Pt 3* (December 1985).

Roe, Michael. 'New Light on George Bass'. *JRAHS Vol.72, Pt 4* (April 1987).
Shaw, A.G.L. 'The New South Wales Corps'. *JRAHS Vol.47, Pt 2* (June 1961).
Wood, George. 'Governor Hunter'. *JRAHS Vol.14, Pt 6* (1928).

Reference Sources

Colledge, J. J. *Ships of the Royal Navy.* London: Greenhill.
Gillen, Mollie. *The Founders of Australia: A Biographical Dictionary of the First Fleet,* Sydney: Library of Australian History, 1989.
Heathcote, T. A. *The British Admirals of the Fleet 1734-1795,* Barnsley: Cooper, 2002.
Lee. S. (ed). *National Dictionary of Biography,* London: South Elebin, 1981.
Lewis, Michael. *A Social History of the Navy 1793-1815,* London: Allen & Unwin, 1960.
Murphy, B. (ed). *Dictionary of Australian History,* Sydney: McGraw Hill, 1982.
O'Neill, Richard (ed). *Patrick O'Brien's Navy,* Philadelphia: Running Press, 2003.
Pike, Douglas (ed). *The Australian Dictionary of Biography Vols 1 & 2,* Melbourne: Melbourne University Press, 1966.
Pope, Steve. *Hornblower's Navy,* London: Orion, 1998.
Rodger, N. A. M. *The Wooden World: An Anatomy of the Georgian Navy,* London: Collins, 1986.
Serle, Percival (ed). *Dictionary of Australian Biography Vol 1,* Sydney: Angus & Robertson, 1949.
Scholes, Percy. *The Oxford Companion to Music,* London: Oxford University Press, 1980.
Sobel, Dava & Andrews, William. *Longitude,* London: Fourth Estate, 1998.
Stephan, L. & Lee, S (eds). *The Dictionary of National Biography,* London: Oxford University Press, 1960.
Thompson, L. (ed). *Dictionary of Nautical Terms,* New York: Facts on File, 1984.

Scotland
Brown P. Hume. *History of Scotland Vol III*, Cambridge: Cambridge University Press, 1911.
Chitnis, Anand. *The Scottish Enlightenment*, London: Crown Helm, 1976.
Ferguson, W. *Scotland - 1769 to the Present*, Edinburgh: Oliver & Boyd, 1968.
Fry, Michael. *Patronage and Principle: A Political History of Modern Scotland*, Aberdeen: Aberdeen University Press, 1987.
Gibb, Andrew. *Scottish Empire*, London: Maclehouse & Company, 1937.
Grave, S. A. *The Scottish History of Common Sense*, Oxford: Clarendon Press, 1960.
Mackenzie, A. *Scotland in Modern Times 1720-1939*, London: Chambers, 1941.
Robertson, John. *The Scottish Enlightenment and the Militia Issue*, Edinburgh: John Donald, 1985.
Sher, Richard & Smitten, Jeffrey (eds). *Scotland and America in the Age of Enlightenment*, Edinburgh: Edinburgh University Press, 1990.
Trevor-Roper, Hugh. 'The Scottish Enlightenment' *Blackwoods Magazine Vol.322, No.1945* (November 1977).
Youngson, A. J. *The Making of Classical Edinburgh1750-1840*, Edinburgh: Edinburgh University Press, 1966.

Index

Aberdeen University, 24, 28, 45
Atkins, Richard, 201, 213
Atlantic (transport), 78, 103, 170
Auchmuty, Professor James, 5
Bach, John, 5, 128
Ball, Lt Henry, 80, 89, 126, 129–133, 139, 149, 229, 310
Balmain, William, 87, 168, 183, 195, 197, 201–202, 210–211, 213, 274
Banks, Sir Joseph, 10, 21, 27, 47, 108, 110, 140, 209, 214, 221, 230, 231, 236, 258, 271, 275, 282
Barnard, Eldershaw M, 7
Bass, George, 10, 36, 107, 204, 222, 263
Batavia, 89, 93, 98, 101–103, 152, 163, 235, 239
Baughan, John, 213
Bennett, Dr George, 16, 156
Bentham, Sir Samuel, 47, 177
Berry Head, 142–145
Berwick, HMS, 52, 75–77, 142
Bigge, Thomas, 275

biography, xi, 7, 8, 32, 203
Blackburn, David, 110, 123, 131
Blaze, B R, 6, 12
Bligh, William, 2, 10, 30, 44, 64, 107, 139, 191, 224, 235–237, 273–276
Bonnie Prince Charlie, 25, 43
Bonwick, James, 142, 156
Boswell, James, 7, 226
Botany Bay, ix, 19, 82, 87, 109–114, 149, 153, 158, 161, 163, 206, 231–232, 247, 249
Bounty, HMS, 106, 139, 236
Bradley, Lt William, 47, 84, 93, 95, 98, 109, 118, 119, 123, 129–132, 138–140, 152, 212, 227, 229, 234–244, 247–252
Brest, 141, 142
Brown, Capt William, 39, 57–58
Bruny Island, 116
Buffalo, HMS, 51, 104, 105, 145, 268
Burney, Dr Charles, 27, 45
Burney, James, 27
Butcher, W J & Son, 278

Camden, 19, 269
Campbell, Judy, 164
Cape Town, 19, 83–85, 93, 115–116, 121, 151, 232, 235, 244, 249
Carysfort, HMS, ix, 39, 51, 52, 65–69, 71, 75, 125, 229, 246
Cascade Bay, 126, 131, 238
Centaur, HMS, 39, 52, 57–58, 258
Charlotte, HMS (transport), 87, 93, 103, 111–114, 145, 170, 279
Clark, Lt Ralph, 111, 123, 124, 131, 238, 239
Clark, Manning, 5, 10, 166, 246, 250
Coat of Arms, 279–281
Cobley, John, 248
Collingwood, Vice-Admiral Cuthbert, 146
Collins, David, 2, 3, 11, 36, 88, 91, 110, 123, 152, 162, 174, 197, 217–218, 221, 224–231, 237, 245, 249, 274, 278
Colonial Office, 3, 89, 166, 172, 192, 199, 206, 224, 268, 269
Cook, Capt James, 17, 27, 30, 46, 64, 71, 78, 88, 94, 107–108, 140, 154–159, 163, 230–231

Cornwallis, Admiral Sir William, 141–143
Cranson, Capt James, 39
Cumpston, J H L, 157–159, 162
Curson, P H, 159, 162
Curtis, Capt Roger, 74, 103, 105, 136, 170–171
Dampier, Sir William, 155, 158–159, 163
Deas, Midshipman Frederick, 144, 149
Dore, Richard, 197
Drummond, George, 12, 30
Drummond, Helen, 11, 12
Drummond, John, 12
Duffy, Michael, 3, 7, 206
Dundas, Henry, 171–175, 186, 188
Durell, Admiral, 33
Eagle, HMS, 52, 70, 71, 73
Earl St Vincent, 69
Easty, John, 92, 226
Edinburgh, 4, 10, 12, 22–32, 40–45, 280, 285
Edwards, Capt John, 106
Ellis, Malcolm, 3, 7
Endeavour, HMB, 55, 88, 89, 93, 96, 108, 157, 163, 230, 231
Enlightenment, 41, 42, 255
epaulettes, 15

Evatt, Herbert, 180
Everingham, Matthew, 182, 187
Firth of Forth, 24
Fletcher, Brian, 179, 185
Flinders, Matthew, 3, 10, 36, 104, 107, 222
Florida, 39, 65, 66
Foudroyant, HMS, 52, 69
Fowell, Lt Newton, 85, 110, 118, 119, 123, 126, 130, 152, 163
Friendship (transport), 87, 111, 112, 232
Frost, Alan, 7, 160–165
Galloway, Earl of, 273–275
George III, 20, 78, 103, 171
Glasgow, 23, 24, 42
Glorious First of June, 70, 103
Goldsmid, John, 159, 162
Goliath, HMS, 145
Grampus, HMS, 13, 39, 52, 53, 56
Grant, Eliza, 36, 37, 277
Great Britain, 19, 22, 46
Grenville, Lord, 169, 170, 185–186
Grose, Major Francis, 168, 172–175, 180, 183–189, 194, 196, 206, 270
Harrison, William, 262
Havana, 65, 246

Hawke, Admiral, 61
Hawkesbury River, 155, 175, 185, 193, 213, 218–221, 274
Hay, Capt William, 39, 65–71
Hayes, Carlton, 41
Hill, Capt William, 186, 222, 247, 284
Hobart, Lord, 11, 266–270, 275
Holt, Joseph, 218
Howe, Lord, 33, 39, 47, 60, 70–81, 103–105, 140, 170, 171, 173, 248, 254, 266, 275
Hoyle, Arthur, 6, 146
Hughes, Robert, 161
Hunter River, 10, 221, 284
Hunter Valley, 10, 221, 284
Hunter, John
 and NSW, 166, 171–172, 193, 213–217, 268, 273
 birth date, 10, 11
 character, 3, 166
 court martials, 68, 134, 136–139, 146
 diplomacy, 96, 98, 101
 drawing skills, 65, 66, 227, 246, 247, 250, 253
 early life with Uncle Robert, 13, 26
 early maritime experience, 12
 first appointment as post captain, 81

influences on his career, 31, 33, 39
injuries, 17, 18
interest in joining the clergy, 13, 28, 43
lack of leadership, 5, 199, 205, 206, 207, 209, 210, 223
longevity, 19
maritime incidents, 106, 107, 109, 111, 114–116, 118, 120, 121, 123
musical ability, 13, 27
navy as a career choice, 29
personal relationships, 45, 46, 47
physical characteristics, 17, 40, 54
portraits, 14–20
recall from governorship, 51, 166, 169, 179, 180, 204, 209, 211, 225, 268
seamanship, 47, 50, 51, 63, 66, 75, 83, 105, 149, 282
Impeteux, HMS, 144, 146
Intrepid, HMS, 39, 52, 69, 71, 83, 84, 246
Irish convicts, 195, 220
Joel, Leonard (auctioneer), 278, 279
Johnson, Rev Richard, 27, 44, 173, 197, 213, 274

Johnston, George, 183, 188, 270, 275
Kelly, Elizabeth Allen, 279
Kelly, James Moore, 278, 279
Kent, HMS, 34–36, 52, 189, 278
Kent, William, 35, 36, 189, 277
King, Phillip Gidley, 2, 78, 132, 169, 171, 223, 224
La Perouse, Jean de, 107, 113, 157
Lady Penrhyn (transport), 87, 111, 112
Launceston, 33, 52, 64, 259
Leith, 10, 12, 22–28, 32, 34, 37, 40–43, 46, 271–272, 277, 282–284
Lizard, HM Sloop, 26
Lord North, 73, 74, 78
Lynn (see also King's Lynn), 13, 26, 28–30, 40, 53
Macarthur, Elizabeth, 154, 175, 181, 211
Macarthur, John, viii, 2, 3, 7, 10, 45, 48, 154, 168, 175, 180–183, 188–197, 199–204, 211, 214, 224, 228, 269–270, 275, 281
Macquarie, Lachlan, 2, 7, 10, 183, 212, 217, 224, 275, 282
Manly, 19, 36
Margarot, Maurice, 203

Marquis de Seignelay, 52, 81
Marsden, Rev Samuel, 2, 3, 196, 202, 213
Martin, Capt Thomas, 146, 147
Masonic jewels, 271, 278
McHugh, E, 130, 131
Middleton, Sir Charles, 272, 275
Mindanao, 98
Nagle, Jacob, 89, 98–101, 120–125, 130, 132, 138–139, 212, 226, 242
Naval Chronicle, 11, 16, 32, 34, 47, 51, 56, 72, 92, 259, 263, 267
Nelson, Horatio, 59, 88, 280
Nepean, Sir Evan, 170, 171, 267
Neptune, HMS, 52, 58, 61
New Britain, 95
New Caledonia, 93, 94, 125
New Ireland, 95
New South Wales Corps, viii, 3, 10, 92, 166,–169, 174–198, 200, 202, 207–209, 211–215, 224, 238, 269, 275
Newcastle, 10, 221, 258, 271, 284
Norfolk, 13, 26, 28, 30, 45, 53
Norfolk Island, viii, xi, 3, 19, 47, 89, 91, 93, 123–126, 129, 134, 137, 140, 153, 176, 193, 204–205, 213, 229, 233–238, 241–243, 247–248, 268
Paine, Daniel, 169, 196
Paisley silk, 23
Palliser, Sir Hugh, 66, 71, 74, 246
Palmer, Thomas Fyshe, 203–204, 240
Pandora, HMS, 106, 158, 161
Parkinson, Sydney, 230, 231
Parramatta, 19, 185, 187, 193, 213, 215, 218, 221
Paterson, Capt William, 168, 173, 175, 183–185, 189, 201, 206, 214, 219, 270
Patronage, ix, xi, 29, 33, 39, 48, 50, 58–61, 70–74, 78, 171, 269, 282, 284
Percival, Hon Capt T, 32, 34, 63
Perry, Dr Tom, 247
Phillip, Arthur, ix, 2, 3, 7, 10, 11, 36, 37, 44, 47, 78–84, 89, 91, 93, 104, 105, 109, 113, 114, 132, 136–137, 153, 155, 159, 164, 167–179, 182, 185–189, 193, 198, 205–206, 209, 215–216, 219, 223, 229, 232–234, 237, 243–249, 251, 265, 266–267, 274, 276

Pitt, William, the Elder, 61, 78, 171, 173, 235, 275, 278
Pittwater, 19
Plymouth, 142, 146, 173
Porpoise, HMS, 107
Port Jackson, 3, 87, 91, 94, 102, 109, 110, 111, 112, 113, 114, 116, 123, 134, 137, 151, 160, 172, 176, 180, 229, 233, 234, 238, 240, 242, 247, 248, 249, 263, 309
Portland, Duke of, 53, 169, 171, 177, 179, 180, 194, 197–208, 210, 212, 214, 221, 225, 266–268, 270, 275, 282
Portsmouth, 44, 73, 79, 80, 102, 134, 173, 249, 271
Princess Amelia, HMS, 52, 63
Public Record Office, Kew, 9, 88, 279
Raper, George, 227, 248, 250, 255, 320
Reliance, HMS, 104, 105, 145, 172, 173, 220, 222
Rienits, Rex, 154, 274
Ritchie, John, 7, 166
Rochefort, 61
Roddam, Vice Admiral, 134, 136
Rodney, Admiral Sir George, 60, 77

Ross, Major Robert, 47, 93, 112, 140, 237, 238, 239, 241, 242, 243, 245
Royal Anne, HMS, 52, 63
Royal Australian Historical Society, 4, 14, 92, 252
Royal George, HMS, 52, 63
Royal William, HMS, 139
Salvador de Mundo, HMS, 146
Sandwich, Lord, 60, 73–75
Scotland, 11, 13, 22, 24, 32, 37, 40, 41, 43, 203
scurvy, 55, 83, 84, 85, 86, 103, 260
Shortland, Lt John, 222, 229
Sirius, HMS, viii, ix, x, xi, 3, 10, 14, 19, 39, 47, 51, 52, 75, 79–89, 91, 94, 98, 103, 104, 105, 109–117, 120, 122–140, 145, 149, 151, 152, 154, 170, 226–229, 232–239, 243, 245, 248–250, 261–262, 309–310
smallpox, 151, 152, 153, 154, 155, 156, 157, 158, 159, 160, 162, 163, 164, 165
Smith, Adam, 42
Smith, Capt Detmer, 90, 91, 93, 97–101, 105, 125
Smyth, Arthur Bowes, 87, 111–113, 242
South East Cape, 116, 117
South West Cape, 249, 251

Southwell, Daniel, 19, 47, 90, 95–102, 110, 113, 118, 119, 123, 130–131, 212, 230
Spitfire, HMS, 52, 81
Spithead, 51, 70, 75, 104, 139, 170–174
St John's Church, 31, 36–37, 277
Stuart, Hon Keith, 24, 75–77, 220, 240
Suckling, Capt Maurice, 59
Sulawesi, 157, 163, 164
Supply, HMS, x, 36, 80, 82, 89, 109–110, 123–128, 130–133, 136, 138, 153, 172, 232–233, 238–242, 309, 310
Sydney Cove, 1, 19, 47, 107, 110, 113–114, 151, 216, 229, 235, 247–248, 252
Tasmania, 94, 115, 116, 118, 120, 123, 130, 222, 246, 249, 251, 261, 263, 284
Tench, Watkin, 88, 91, 110, 123, 154–162, 227, 229, 243–244
Torbay, 76, 104, 142–149, 170, 173

Tweed, HMS, 32, 52, 63, 64
Union, HMS, 22, 41, 52, 75
Venerable, HMS, xi, 14, 19, 39, 55, 56, 104, 105, 126, 141–149, 270, 271
Victory, HMS, 52, 60, 79, 80, 81
Waaksamheyd, 15, 82, 89, 92, 93, 95, 98, 99, 101, 125, 134, 145, 149, 228, 235–236, 248–250, 255
Walsingham, Commodore The Hon Boyle, 76–77
warrant officers, 63
Waterhouse, Henry, 104, 110, 139–140
Watson, Frederick, 5, 6, 11
Wentworth, William Charles, 3, 154, 168, 189, 210, 222
White, John, 35, 36, 87, 88, 89, 92, 111–112, 115, 154, 170, 204, 229, 243, 246, 251, 274, 276
Worgan, George, 36, 87, 110, 154

www.ingramcontent.com/pod-product-compliance
Lightning Source LLC
Chambersburg PA
CBHW040305170426
43194CB00022B/2898